Rise & Resurrection of the American Programmer

RISE & RESURRECTION OF THE AMERICAN PROGRAMMER

EDWARD YOURDON

To join a Prentice Hall PTR Internet mailing list, point to
http://www.prenhall.com/mail_lists/

YOURDON PRESS
PRENTICE HALL BUILDING
UPPER SADDLE RIVER, NEW JERSEY 07458

Library of Congress Cataloging-in-Publication Data

Yourdon, Edward.
    Rise and resurrection of the American programmer / Edward Yourdon.
    p.   cm.–(Yourdon Press computing series)
    Includes bibliographical references and index.
    ISBN 0-13-956160-9 (alk. paper)
    1. Electronic digital computers–United States–Programming.
I. Title. II. Series.
QA76.6.Y6682 1997   97-31107
005.1–dc21   CIP

Acquisitions editor: *Paul W. Becker*
Editorial assistant: *Maureen Diana*
Editorial/production supervision: *Jane Bonnell*
Interior design: *Gail Cocker-Bogusz*
Composition: *Patti Guerrieri, Lisa Iarkowski, and Craig Little*
Cover design director: *Jerry Votta*
Cover design: *Anthony Gemmellaro*
Cover/interior illustration: *"Earth on a Pedestal" by John Jude Palencar
    (courtesy of Stock Illustration Source, Inc.)*
Manufacturing manager: *Alexis R. Heydt*
Marketing manager: *Dan Rush*

©1998 by Prentice Hall PTR
Prentice-Hall, Inc.
A Simon & Schuster Company
Upper Saddle River, New Jersey 07458

Prentice Hall books are widely used by corporations and government agencies for
training, marketing, and resale.
The publisher offers discounts on this book when ordered in bulk quantities.
For more information, contact Corporate Sales Department, Phone: 800-382-3419;
FAX: 201- 236-7141; email: corpsales@prenhall.com
Or write: Prentice Hall PTR, Corporate Sales Dept., One Lake Street,
Upper Saddle River, NJ 07458.

Printed in the United States of America
10 9 8 7 6 5 4 3 2

ISBN 0-13-956160-9

Prentice-Hall International (UK) Limited, *London*
Prentice-Hall of Australia Pty. Limited, *Sydney*
Prentice-Hall Canada Inc., *Toronto*
Prentice-Hall Hispanoamericana, S.A., *Mexico*
Prentice-Hall of India Private Limited, *New Delhi*
Prentice-Hall of Japan, Inc., *Tokyo*
Simon & Schuster Asia Pte. Ltd., *Singapore*
Editora Prentice-Hall do Brasil, Ltda., *Rio de Janeiro*

CONTENTS

Part One
DECLINE & FALL, REEXAMINED

Part Two
REPAVING COWPATHS

Part Three
THE BRAVE NEW WORLD

PREFACE

The American programmer is dead,
long live the American programmer.[1]

In 1992, I wrote *Decline and Fall of the American Programmer,* a gloomy assessment of the competitive posture of the American software industry in the global marketplace. The book has been translated into

---

[1]Throughout this book, I use the term "programmer" in the generic sense, not just as a description of junior-level people who write computer programs without understanding the broader context of their environment. "Software person" or "IT professional" might be a more accurate term, but it's a lot clumsier. My comments are aimed at software engineers, database designers, telecommunications specialists, quality assurance and testing professionals, software project managers, systems analysts, chief information officers, and everyone else involved in the software and/or systems side of the computer industry.

half a dozen languages, thus providing (I assume) a source of joy and optimism for programmers around the world who hope they can emulate the success of Microsoft, Borland, and Lotus. Meanwhile, it has been used as a textbook in numerous American college courses, and has been distributed by MIS managers to their overworked and browbeaten application developers, thus (presumably) providing a source of gloom and doom to programmers in this country. I've received hundreds of letters, faxes, and e-mail messages from software people who have told me that it has changed their life or ruined their life—or that they completely disagree with me and wonder what planet I live on. Some have told me they can see the handwriting on the wall, and that they fully expect their software organization to collapse in the next few years, leaving them stranded with unmarketable skills in COBOL or MVS assembly language. Others have told me that software just isn't fun any more, and that they've abandoned their profession to begin a new career in some other field.

But all of that was four years ago, and things do change—especially in our field. We've gone through another two generations of hardware technology, and we've witnessed the explosion of Internet, multimedia, and other technologies that were on the horizon in 1992 but not yet in widespread use. Meanwhile, I've continued traveling around the world—typically to some 15 countries a year—to see what our international competitors are up to. Some of the trends that worried me four years ago have become even more pronounced now, but I've been pleasantly surprised to see that in other areas the U.S. software industry has demonstrated a substantial competitive advantage.

Hence this book. While my mood four years ago was one of pessimism, I'm now cautiously optimistic about the future of the American programmer. In many ways, I think my original premise was right: The traditional application developer faces increasing competition from people around the world who are cheaper, faster, and better. And I think my premise is just as relevant for the developers today who are using Visual Basic^{TM}, Delphi^{TM}, and Smalltalk as it is for the old-fashioned mainframe developers who toil laboriously with COBOL and character-based text editors. Some good things and bad things have happened along the way, slightly changing the picture I painted four years ago—but the overall conclusion that I drew is, in my opinion, largely correct.

But in many ways, it's irrelevant: *That* American programmer is indeed dead, or at least in grave peril. But there's a new generation of American programmers, doing exciting new things—which, to a significant extent, our competitors haven't begun doing yet. For those whose COBOL jobs have disappeared and whose Visual Basic projects are now being outsourced to Bangalore, this is exciting news: You *can* still find an exciting career in the software field without having your salary reduced to $3,000 per year. We are, in my opinion, witnessing the rise and resurrection of the American programmer.

Naturally, a statement like this will evoke a chorus of arguments—just as my gloomy prognostication in *Decline and Fall of the American Programmer* did four years ago. Some will agree with my assessment, some will disagree, and perhaps others will argue that it's irrelevant. Indeed, even if I'm right, there's no guarantee that the situation will persist: As I noted above, things do change rather rapidly in our field. Whatever competitive advantage we may now have could vanish rather quickly, for the treasure we now hold is simply an intellectual asset, and it can flourish almost as quickly in any other part of the world. But, as I'll discuss later in this book, there is more to it than that: The success of our software industry is also due to the overall social, economic, and intellectual culture of the North American community, as well as the success of a few key industries which *do* require large investments.

Before discussing my optimistic assessment of the present and future software industry, I want to step back to review the past. After all, not everyone has read *Decline and Fall of the American Programmer*; while it succeeded beyond my original expectations, I'm nevertheless humbled by the realization that ten times as many people bought *DOS for Dummies* during the same period. After a summary of the premise of *Decline and Fall*, I'll provide a quick update: What has changed in the competitive situation for traditional application development? As noted above, some things have gotten better, and some things have gotten worse—but the net result is about the same as it was before.

But after this quick review and update, I'll turn to the more exciting prospects for the future. What are the new technologies, the new industries, and the applications we should be pursuing during these final few years of the 20th century? If you're a COBOL programmer today, or even if you've recently made a transition to newer technologies like VisualAge™ and Delphi, what should you be looking forward to?

The discussion that follows is not intended to be a deep technical treatise. The technology is out there, and where appropriate, I'll provide references to the appropriate books, journals, and World Wide Web pages; but as we all know, the technology changes daily, and any references that I make to specific products or vendors are likely to be obsolete by the time this book is published.[2] What's important, I think, is an orientation and sense of perspective. If my perspective four years ago encouraged you to drop out of a dead-end software career, I hope my perspective this time will encourage you to seek new adventures and, in the spirit of *Star Trek*, boldly go where none have gone before.

---

[2] I maintain a Web site of my own, which contains an up-to-date list of recommended technical books, as well as links to other Web pages associated with current technology in the field. At the time this book went to press, my Web site was located at http://www.yourdon.com—but if it's not there, for some reason, when you receive this book, contact the publisher or track me down via Yahoo or Lycos or one of the other Web search engines.

Trademark Acknowledgments

1-2-3, Ami Pro, Freelance Graphics, Lotus, Lotus Notes, and SmarText are registered trademarks and cc:Mail and SmartIcons are trademarks of Lotus Development Corporation.

America Online is a registered service mark of America Online, Inc.

American Airlines is a registered trademark of American Airlines, Inc.

AppleTalk, HyperCard, Mac, Macintosh, and Newton are registered trademarks and MacOS is a trademark of Apple Computer, Inc.

AT&T is a registered trademark of AT&T, Inc.

Body Vision and Case Maker are trademarks of Learn Technologies Interactive.

Claris is a trademark of Claris Corporation.

Composer-3 is a trademark of Texas Instruments Incorporated.

CompuServe is a registered trademark of CompuServe, Inc.

Computer Associates is a registered trademark of Computer Associates International, Inc.

Delphi is a trademark and Quattro is a registered trademark of Borland International, Inc.

DHL is a trademark of DHL Systems, Inc.

Ethernet is a trademark of Xerox Corporation.

Extend is a trademark of Imagine That! Inc.

FedEx is a registered trademark of Federal Express Corporation.

Hewlett-Packard and HP are registered trademarks of Hewlett-Packard Company. HP-UX is Hewlett-Packard's implementation of the UNIX operating system.

HotJava, Java, and Solaris are trademarks of Sun Microsystems, Inc. Products bearing SPARC trademarks are based upon an architecture developed by Sun Microsystems, Inc.

IBM and OS/2 are registered trademarks and DB2 and VisualAge are trademarks of International Business Machines Corporation.

Intel and Pentium are registered trademarks of Intel Corporation.

iThink is a trademark of High Performance Systems.

Linda is a registered trademark of Scientific Computing Associates.

Magic Link is a trademark of Sony Electronics, Inc.

Maytag is a registered trademark of Maytag Corporation.

Microsoft, Microsoft Excel, Microsoft Windows, Microsoft Word for Windows, MS-DOS, PowerPoint, Visual Basic, Visual C++, Windows, Windows 95 and Windows NT are trademarks and registered trademarks of Microsoft Corporation.

Motif, Open Software Foundation, and OSF/Motif are registered trademarks of Open Software Foundation, Inc.

Motorola is a registered trademark of Motorola, Inc.

Netscape Navigator is a trademark of Netscape Communications Corporation.

NetWare is a registered trademark of Novell, Inc.

OMW is a registered trademark of IntelliCorp Inc.

Oracle Forms is a trademark of Oracle Corporation.

PageMaker is a trademark of Adobe Systems Incorporated.

Panasonic is a registered trademark of Matsushita Electric Industrial Co., Ltd.

PowerBuilder and Sybase are registered trademarks of Sybase, Inc.

Prodigy is a registered trademark of Prodigy Services Company.

Quark is a trademark of Quark, Inc.

Quicken is a trademark of Intuit, Inc.

Rational is a trademark of Rational Software Corporation.

SPARCstation is a trademark of SPARC International Inc., licensed exclusively to Sun Microsystems, Inc.

Synchronicity is a trademark of Easel Corporation.

SyQuest is a registered trademark of SyQuest Technology, Inc.

TeamWork is a registered trademark of Cadre Technologies Inc.

The Sharper Image is a registered trademark of Sharper Image Corporation.

Together is a trademark of Object Intl., Inc.

UNIX is a registered trademark in the United States and other countries licensed exclusively through X/Open Company Ltd. X/Open is a trademark of X/Open Company Ltd.

Visual Wave is a trademark of ParcPlace-Digitalk.

WordPerfect is a registered trademark of WordPerfect Corporation.

X Window System is a trademark of X Consortium, Inc.

Other product names mentioned herein are the trademarks or registered trademarks of their respective owners.

Part One

DECLINE & FALL REEXAMINED

THE ORIGINAL PREMISE

A powerful idea communicates some of its strength to him who challenges it.

Marcel Proust, Remembrance of Things Past, vol. 3, *"Within a Budding Grove,"* pt. 1, *"Madame Swann at Home"* (1918; tr. by Scott Monkrieff, 1924).

The premise of *Decline and Fall of the American Programmer* was simple and blunt: The American programmer, I argued, was about to go the way of the dodo bird because of three major factors:

- Software professionals are far less expensive in many parts of the world than they are in North America.
- Software professionals in many parts of the world are substantially more productive than the average software person in North America.
- Software professionals in many parts of the world can develop software with much higher levels of quality than the average software produced in North America.

Before I discuss these issues in detail, let me remind you why all of this is relevant. Software is a huge global business, generating an estimated $120 billion in annual revenues, and it's been growing at double-digit rates for the past 30 years. Equally important, approximately 50 percent of the global software market is located in the United States. For a startup software company in Uruguay, the U.S. is the pot of gold at the end of the rainbow: It might sell a few copies of its software to the local companies in Managua, but what it *really* wants to do is sell millions of copies to the companies in New York, Chicago, and Los Angeles. On the other hand, if 50 percent of the market is *in* the U.S., then clearly the other 50 percent is somewhere else; thus, for the U.S. software producers, the international market is becoming more and more interesting. If the startup software company in Uruguay can't sell millions of copies of its software in North America, it can probably eke out a reasonable living in its own domestic market—and it can generate fees and commissions by serving as a distributor for the North American companies who don't have the resources or the expertise to invade the Uruguayan market.

If we were talking about oil or automobiles or steel or a number of other traditional industries, all of this would involve competition among mammoth companies; and the stakes would be enormous, because of the capital investment required to drill an oil well or launch a new auto manufacturing facility. But software, as we all know, can be developed by one person with a clone PC costing a thousand dollars or less. Whether you're a "shrink-wrap" software-products developer or a "body-shop" consulting firm, it takes very little capital to get started; indeed, the largest cost is the labor involved, which is why the issue of salaries is so important.

Salaries in North America typically range from $25,000 per year for junior technicians to well over $200,000 per year for senior veterans with specialized experience in "hot" areas of technology. Employers typically have to add another 50–100 percent to this figure for insurance and employee benefits, as well as office space, administrative support, and other overhead costs—so the "loaded" cost of a software person is typically in the range of $50–200,000 per year; assuming 2,000 working hours per year, that works out to an average of $25–100 per hour. Salaries in Western Europe, Japan, Singapore, and various other "advanced" parts of the world are approximately the same; they may be 10 to 20 percent higher or lower depending on the fluctuations of exchange rates or the vagaries of the local market, but they're in the same ballpark.

By contrast, salaries in Eastern Europe, South America, Africa, and most of Asia are *substantially* less—typically 5 to 10 times lower than the figures quoted above. These figures can be distorted somewhat if the salaries are paid by a multinational firm trying to maintain parity with its workers in Europe and North America; and they can be distorted significantly if a programmer from a low-wage country is sent to North America on a six-month software project; not only will the programmer's employer (typically a consulting firm based in the low-wage country) add its own substantial overhead for administrative costs and profits, but the customer will inevitably end up paying the cost of transportation and local housing. Nevertheless, the basic economic reality that we have to be aware of is that a competent, university-educated software professional in India, Argentina, or Egypt, with a few years of experience in C and UNIX®, may be earning a base salary of $3,000–4,000.

Competitive pressures in the software industry are based partly on salaries but also depend on productivity and quality. During my travels in the late 80s and early 90s, which led to my gloomy prognostications in *Decline and Fall of the American Programmer*, I saw programming shops in Manila, Delhi, and Tokyo that reported programming productivity 5 to 10 times higher than what I found in traditional mainframe COBOL shops in the U.S. Of course, many mainframe COBOL shops have disappeared because of the *domestic* competition from higher-productivity 4GL shops, which I'll discuss below. But the original warning that I issued was still an important one: Somewhere in the world, there is probably a software organization doing the same job that yours is doing, delivering the same kind of products and services, but they're operating at a level of productivity as much as ten times higher.

Productivity has a number of important consequences.[1] In the simple case, it means that the same amount of software can be developed in the same amount of time by a proportionately smaller number of people; indeed, it may be a *dis*proportionately smaller number, because fewer technical workers also means fewer supervisors, fewer administrative support people, fewer meetings, etc. In any case, higher productivity translates almost immediately to lower costs— and for the organizations going through reengineering revolutions and downsizing exercises, this is a welcome message. Since IT is often one of the largest cost centers and since it's regarded by many organizations as an "overhead" cost (as opposed to a revenue producer or even a revenue supporter), telling CEOs that their 2,000-person IT staff could be reduced to 1,000 people (or perhaps even *zero* people, if the whole operation was outsourced) is welcome news indeed.

Another aspect of productivity involves *cycle time*: If the productivity of your software people is dramatically higher, then the same number of people can deliver the same amount of software in much less time—e.g., a few days instead of a few months, or a few months instead of seven years. It was already evident in the early 90s, when I first wrote *Decline and Fall of the American Programmer*, that this could be an important competitive issue; as I'll emphasize below, cycle time pressures have become even more extreme in the past few years.

Finally, there is the issue of quality: Primarily because of a series of visits to Japanese software organizations, I warned my U.S. compatriots that we could find ourselves outmaneuvered by competitors who produced software with 10 to 100 fewer defects per function point, or per line of code. As with productivity, software quality has a number of indirect consequences. For example, a higher-quality program, with better documentation and better-organized logic, will almost certainly be easier to maintain and modify; thus, we would expect that the cycle time for maintenance activities would also be dramatically impacted.

What concerned me most about these issues was the compounding effect: A competitor whose labor costs are ten times lower than ours, and whose workers are ten times more productive, and whose products have ten times fewer defects, is—at least in a simplistic sense—offering the marketplace something that's a thousand times

---

[1] Productivity also has to be discussed within the context of the size of the system and the demands of the industry within which the system is built. Metrics gurus like Capers Jones continually remind us that on large projects, an enormous percentage of the project resources are devoted to meetings, travel expenses, paperwork, and other noncoding activities; on small projects, "pure" software-development activities predominate. For a variety of reasons, many of the application development projects within in-house IT organizations could be regarded as "programming in the small," where tools such as 4GLs make it possible for small teams of 3 to 5 people to accomplish what used to require 30 to 50 COBOL programmers.

better than ours. Of course, the situation is never quite so simple, but on the other hand, the comparisons could be even more extreme: What if the competitor has a level of productivity a hundred times higher and a level of quality a thousand times higher? I'm not so worried about differences of 10 to 20 percent, because those can be overcome (or explained away) through marketing and non-software-producing issues such as service and support; and in any case, a 10 percent shortfall in productivity or quality can easily be overcome by incremental improvements, including the time-honored tradition of unpaid overtime. But if we're facing competition that's a hundred times, or a thousand times, more effective than ours, we really are in serious trouble. Dodo birds may have had a far easier time than the beleaguered American programmer.

1.1 AN UPDATE OF THE ORIGINAL PREMISE

So much for the original premise. What has happened to confirm it or invalidate it in the past five years? And for that matter, was the argument ever valid in the first place? There has been enough debate about all of this on various Internet forums to fill several books, but it's worth summarizing some of the key issues below.

It's important to acknowledge that many serious, thoughtful software professionals never did believe my gloom-and-doom scenario; they didn't think it was right then, and they probably don't think it's relevant today. The majority of objections I've heard over the past five years have been experiential, e.g., the manager who tells me earnestly, "A friend of mine told me that he contracted one of his projects to a company in India, and while they were very inexpensive and worked very hard, they didn't succeed because of X, Y, and Z." While these experiences are certainly valid, the conclusion drawn from them may not be—for the problems associated with X, Y, and Z may have been tactical problems, not strategic failures. The first few projects undertaken by an ambitious outsourcing vendor—whether in India, Mexico, or Hungary—could run into problems because the vendor sends the wrong people, or because his people get homesick and quit, or because the U.S. State Department turned the visa application process into a bureaucratic quagmire, or a dozen other reasons.

But there's one reason for failures, one problem that *could* turn out to be strategic, and it's one that I may have underestimated: differences in cultures. Different cultures have different forms of communication, both verbal and nonverbal; they have different priorities and expectations; they have dramatically different approaches to negotiations, discussions, and resolution of disagreements; and they make different assumptions in a wide range of software project-related issues, including user requirements, testing, documentation, and so on.

To the extent that these issues can be discussed explicitly (either orally, by e-mail, or by some other written communication), the growing acceptance of English as the *de facto* standard for human communication in the computer industry makes it more and more practical for software projects to be carried out in many parts of the world. True, it's still a problem for some software professionals in Russia and China to communicate with a North American end user, and I've found that while software professionals in many parts of the world can read and write English competently, conversational English is still clumsy and difficult.[2] But the real problem involves the nonverbal communications that amplify or qualify the verbal and written communications; facial gestures, body language, and a variety of social amenities can have a dramatic impact on the success of the project.

Obviously, none of this has anything to do with the technical nature of computer programs; one can easily imagine software engineers from dramatically different cultures being placed in isolated offices, where they turn out perfect C++ programs. Assuming that (a) the user requirements have been clearly communicated and are rela-

---

[2] On the other hand, whatever problems exist in this area pale in comparison to our inability to communicate in French, Spanish, German, Portuguese, Japanese, and a dozen other languages; the user manuals and error messages of the "international" versions of many of our most popular software packages are so butchered and clumsy that they're the laughing-stock of the local marketplace. That's one reason why U.S. software companies have a difficult time competing in many foreign marketplaces and why the local software producers can often succeed with indigenous products. It also helps explain why foreign software distributors are so important to the success of U.S. software firms; they can help with the translation of user manuals, and they can provide on-site support and service in a fashion that the hotline help desk in Silicon Valley could never match.

tively stable, and (b) the software process has been rigorously and formally defined and is well understood by all concerned, and (c) testing and quality assurance can be carried out in a quantifiable fashion, based on a detailed, formal, rigorous description of user requirements...then the communication problems described above may not be so serious. And it's important to note that some software projects *do* fit these requirements—e.g., some scientific and engineering applications, and many systems programming projects such as compilers and operating systems, as well as straightforward "conversion" projects to translate an application from one hardware/software environment to another.

But the majority of software projects, as we all know, don't meet the criteria described above. The users have only a vague, fuzzy idea of their requirements, and the environment is so volatile that the requirements change every day. Meanwhile, the IT organization has a software process that borders on anarchy carried out by "cowboy" programmers, so it's almost impossible to interface with an offshore software shop that needs precise "entry" points and "exit" points to each stage in the development life cycle. And since the requirements are vague and unstable, acceptance and quality assurance is often a matter of negotiation after the fact, rather than predetermined criteria before the project starts. No wonder that communication and cultural issues become so important.

And there's one aspect of modern-day software projects that exacerbates the communication problem: Whether it's known as RAD or prototyping or iterative software development, it means that there is *constant* interaction between the end user and the software developers (and everyone else in the organization too!). It's difficult enough managing this kind of interactive development when the users are located right next door to the software developers; it's *much* more difficult when the developers are on the other side of the world. Obviously, the required interaction has become much more practicable with the widespread availability of e-mail, Lotus® Notes®, and the Internet; and exotic videoconferencing technology can be combined with mundane fax technology to assist in the communication process. But there are still the nonverbal communication difficulties, combined with the more subtle cultural barriers—and these can be exacerbated considerably by geographical distance. So, effective offshore programming is undoubtedly more difficult than I originally suggested, and even though modern telecommunications technology is making things easier, the human problems remain.

But all of this turns out to be irrelevant, from the perspective of corporate business activity in the past five years. If you ask the typical COBOL programmer in Chicago or New York if he's worried about being put out of a job by competitive pressures, he will almost certainly agree. *But he's not worried about competition from programmers in India.* Instead, he's worried that his company is getting rid of its mainframe and that it plans to downsize the entire IT department to a skeleton crew. The hundred-person COBOL projects are being replaced by five-person Visual Basic projects, and the software is being developed in a client-server environment that renders our COBOL programmer's expertise in MVS, JCL, CICS, and IMS utterly irrelevant. The application development projects might be out-sourced, but it's more likely that the work will be done by a few new-hires from college whose salary is only half that of the COBOL veteran. In the extreme case, the applications are being developed by the end user, so that no programmers are needed at all.

True, this represents an extreme scenario; there *are* still COBOL programmers making a decent living in the U.S. (particularly on the Year-2000 projects that have been launched during the second half of the decade), and there are still mainframes doing useful work in a more cost-effective fashion than would be possible on PCs and work-stations. There are still large development projects, and there are still a few thousand-person IT empires out there in middle America. But when you read about massive layoffs at IBM and DEC a few years ago and when you continue to read about downsizing projects going on in *Fortune* 500 IT departments across the country, you can be reasonably sure that those jobs are *not* moving, en masse, to a low-wage software producer overseas.[3]

But *some* of the jobs *have* moved, and while it may only be a small blip on the radar screen, it's important to be aware of it. When I

---

[3] Indeed, some of the layoffs didn't involve software people at all, but administrative support people and middle layers of management. The layoffs at DEC and IBM also involved hardware designers, as well as marketing people and various other categories. Nevertheless, a lot of programmers have disappeared—I've visited organizations that used to have 100 software people developing and maintaining software for mainframe systems, and then returned two years later to find that the staff had been reduced to a dozen younger and less expensive people supporting the same business applications with an entirely different set of tools and technologies.

visited India in 1989, for example, its nascent software industry generated $30 million in annual export revenues, of which approximately 88 percent consisted of "body-shop" programming services carried out at the customer's site. When I returned in 1994, annual software exports had grown to $325 million, of which only 56 percent came from offshore body-shop programming.[4] A tenfold growth is nothing to sneeze at, especially since India expects its industry to continue growing at a compounded 50 percent annual rate for the rest of this decade. On the other hand, it will be several more years before the U.S. software industry takes notice of numbers like this; after all, Microsoft reported 1995 revenues of $5.94 billion, and it's just one of the many players in the U.S. market.

What about the three competitive factors that I discussed above— i.e., salaries, productivity, and quality? To some extent, the cost issue has stabilized in the U.S. because we've enjoyed a low inflation rate for the past few years. But a much larger factor, as noted above, has been the replacement of expensive, middle-aged COBOL programmers with cheap, young C++ programmers. Combined with substantial downsizing and corporate reengineering, it's evident that senior IT managers are finding a number of ways to reduce their costs.[5]

Meanwhile, things have changed somewhat in the international marketplace. Because of the collapse of the former Soviet Union, there are now more programmers available from Eastern Bloc countries than there were in the late 80s and early 90s. Russian, Hungarian, Polish, and East German programmers are now being aggressively recruited by Western European software firms, and a steady trickle of emigrants is flowing into the U.S. A few of the more enterprising U.S. software firms have opened offices in Moscow and

---

[4] See "Software in India," *Guerrilla Programmer,* September 1994 (Arlington, MA: Cutter Information Corp.) for a more detailed report on my 1994 visit to India.

[5] One of the consequences of this phenomenon—in the software industry and in many other white-collar professions—is a widespread belief that the "social contract" between employer and employee has vanished. At IBM, long regarded as one of the most paternalistic and benevolent of companies in the U.S., the massive layoffs have not only diminished the loyalty of the remaining workers but have also sent a message to the rest of the software industry: "You are expendable and if your skills are obsolete and your cost is too high, you're likely to be laid off." To the COBOL programmer who worries that his company's next project may be outsourced to a firm with up-to-date skills in Java and Visual Basic, the notion of offshore outsourcing just adds fuel to the fire.

have set up software departments in other Eastern European countries, but the language barrier remains a more serious obstacle for American software firms than for the Western Europeans.

On the other side of the world, the People's Republic of China (PRC) has begun expanding its software activities. In preparation for its 1997 repatriation of Hong Kong, PRC programmers have been given visas to work in Hong Kong, where their low salaries and their UNIX expertise makes them a valuable commodity. When I visited Hong Kong in 1994 and 1995, the average salary of a PRC UNIX programmer was approximately $180 per month, or $2,000 per year.

However, I don't expect this tenfold salary differential to last—not in China, nor in India, Malaysia, the Philippines, nor any of the low-wage countries. Indeed, the situation is already changing in India, where the growth of the software industry and the demand for experienced software professionals is pushing the annual turnover rate in high-tech centers like Bangalore to 30 to 50 percent per year. In response to this turnover and in an attempt to buy loyalty, Indian software firms are raising salaries quickly and dramatically and offering bonuses and other forms of compensation—just as American software firms did in the growth period of the 70s. Also, many Indian software companies have proportionately higher overhead costs than their counterparts; in addition to "normal" benefits like insurance, they sometimes provide housing for their software professionals, and they often pay a premium for workstations and the telecommunications infrastructure that makes it possible to communicate with the rest of the world.

This doesn't mean that Indian software salaries will achieve parity with North American salaries in the next 12 to 18 months, but the tenfold salary differential is rapidly disappearing. To see how close the "fully loaded" salaries (including overhead) really were in 1995, take a look at Figure 1.1. It suggests that the average ratio of Indian salaries to U.S. salaries for all categories of software professionals is approximately 3:1; equally interesting is the difference between U.S. and Canadian salaries![6]

What about the issue of productivity? Obviously, it's still important—if anything, it's become even more important in the mid-90s than it was in the early 90s when I first wrote *Decline and Fall of the American Programmer*. We now recognize that software productivity is the result of a large number of factors—of which people, processes,

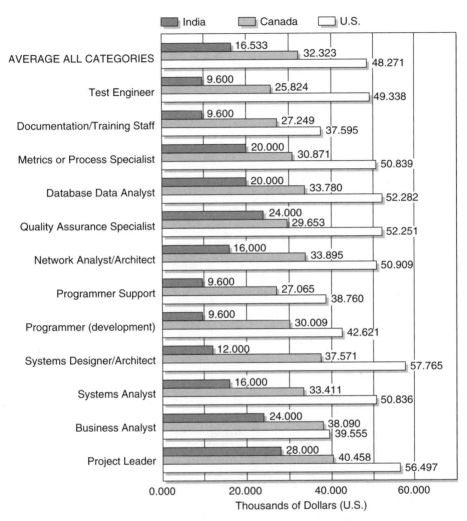

FIGURE 1.1 1995 SALARY COMPARISON FOR U.S., CANADIAN, AND INDIAN SOFTWARE PROFESSIONALS

---

[6] These data shown in Figure 1.1 were gathered as part of a worldwide software productivity benchmarking project for the Canadian government in which I participated as a co-principal investor in 1995. For more information, contact the principal investigator of the project, Dr. Howard Rubin, at Rubin Systems Inc., 5 Winterbottom Lane, Pound Ridge, NY 10576 (phone: 914-764-4931, fax: 914-764-0536, e-mail: 71031.377@compuserve.com)

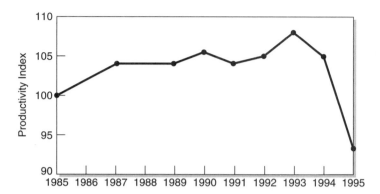

FIGURE 1.2 U.S. SOFTWARE DEVELOPMENT PRODUCTIVITY TRENDS

and tools are perhaps the most important—and it should be obvious that none of those factors are unique to the U.S. or any other region in the world.

Two interesting things have happened in the past few years. First, it appears that software productivity in the U.S. may be declining. And second, the *range* of productivity between various companies around the world has increased dramatically. The productivity decline, shown in Figure 1.2, may be a short-term anomaly associated with the transition from mainframe legacy systems to client-server GUI applications, or perhaps it's the result of the 1994 baseball strike or some other subtle factors. However, it does suggest that the U.S. software industry may face even greater competitive pressures in the next few years if offshore producers can demonstrate that they can deliver the same applications faster and cheaper.

However, the performance of the "average" software development organization, and whether it compares favorably with the average software development organization in Bombay or Budapest, may be less and less relevant as we reach the end of the century. What really matters is whether you're better than *any* of the competitors to which your customer has access (whether it's a captive in-house end user or an external customer). The implicit premise in *Decline and Fall of the American Programmer* was that all U.S. software organizations were more or less the same when it came to salaries, productivity, and quality—and that we faced a competitive risk from overseas software producers who were uniformly cheaper, faster, and better.

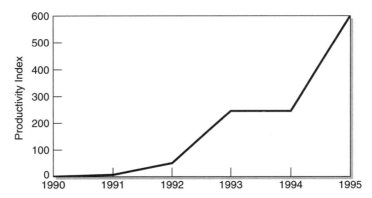

FIGURE 1.3 RANGE OF OBSERVED PRODUCTIVITY AT ENTERPRISE LEVEL

But while software producers in the developing nations and the Pacific Rim countries may be uniformly inexpensive, their productivity and quality is not uniform; as many software professionals have been reminding me for the past few years, there are sloppy, unproductive programmers in Calcutta and Cairo, just as there are in Chicago and Cleveland. The question is whether your competitors—wherever they may be located—are just a few percentage points more productive or whether they are orders of magnitude more productive. Many software customers and consumers—especially the captive in-house end users—are reluctant to change suppliers and the nature of software that they use, in order to reduce their costs or speed up their cycle time by 5 percent. But 50 percent is more interesting, and 500 percent makes the argument for change compelling indeed. And as Figure 1.3 illustrates, the difference between high-productivity shops and low-productivity shops has increased from 4:1 to 600:1 in the past decade.

But if the productivity situation has gotten worse, the quality situation has improved. As Figure 1.4 illustrates, the quality of U.S. software—measured in terms of postrelease defects—has improved substantially in the past 10 years. It's interesting to note that much of the improvement occurred in the second half of the 1990s, when CASE tools, structured methods, software inspections, and various other disciplines were being introduced; during the period immediately before and after the publication of my *Decline and Fall of the American Programmer*, software quality remained at about the same level—but since 1994, it has begun showing further improvements.

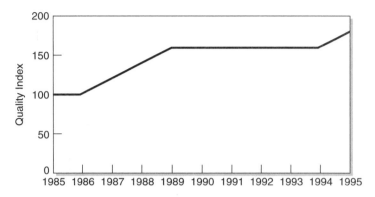

FIGURE 1.4 U.S. SOFTWARE QUALITY TRENDS

But just as the range of productivity observations has increased dramatically in the past few years, so has the range of quality: The difference between the best and worst was 10:1 at the beginning of the decade but has now risen to 100:1, as illustrated in Figure 1.5.

As with productivity, there are exemplary, high-quality software shops in every country in the world. In the U.S., organizations like Motorola and Hewlett-Packard have long enjoyed a reputation for producing software that was as nearly zero-defect as possible; a few organizations in England, Germany, and other parts of Western Europe enjoy a similar well-deserved reputation. But when I looked for similar examples in the developing nations of Africa, Latin America, and Asia, all I could find were reports of spectacular software quality in Japan—hardly a "developing" nation, and a nation whose

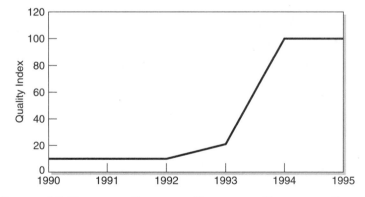

FIGURE 1.5 RANGE OF OBSERVED QUALITY AT ENTERPRISE LEVEL

competition in the software field has turned out to be far less than originally anticipated.

Once again, all of this may be changing. In late 1993, a report on the software industry in India [2] made a stunning announcement:

> ...The communications company [Motorola], which has sites across the globe, has obtained the highest rating for its team [in Bangalore, India] under criteria established by the Software Engineering Institute....Indeed, no other Motorola plant anywhere has managed to obtain an equivalent rating, and around the world only a handful of organizations have attained this standard.

In simple language, the Motorola group in Bangalore had achieved a level-5 assessment on the Software Engineering Institute's process maturity scale. When I went to India in mid-1994 to visit the Motorola installation, I found that there were many other Indian organizations that were intent on acquiring ISO-9000 certification for their software work, which is roughly equivalent to level 3 on the SEI scale; having achieved ISO-9000 certification, many of these organizations plan to switch over to the SEI scale and begin marching up the ladder to level 4 and level 5. My conclusion: While there have been good and bad software organizations in every corner of the world all along, many of the ambitious software organizations in countries like India are eager to obtain international recognition for their high-quality work so they can compete more effectively.

Meanwhile, there has been a shift in an entirely different direction in the United States: While many of our pundits, textbooks, and large-scale software development shops continue to work toward higher levels of quality measured in terms of low defect levels (the basis for the chart in Figure 1.4), other software organizations—especially the shrink-wrapped software-package producers in Silicon Valley—have begun emphasizing an approach to quality known as "good-enough" software. Consciously or unconsciously, many application development groups have been pushed into this paradigm, too—for what their customers really want is not zero-defect software, but software that's good enough, cheap enough, functional enough, and available soon enough. This doesn't mean that we want the software for our nuclear reactors to be riddled with bugs, but it does mean that we're willing to tolerate word processors, desktop PC operating systems, and rapidly developed business applications that have a considerable number of bugs and glitches, as long as none of them are "show-stoppers." Indeed, this new outlook on software quality is so important that I've devoted a separate chapter to it later in this book; because it's so compatible with the so-called "cowboy" culture of American software professionals, I believe that it's part of the "rise and resurrection" of the U.S. software industry that we'll be enjoying through the rest of this decade.

1.2 WHAT DO SOFTWARE CUSTOMERS REALLY WANT?

The discussion above reflects a common tendency among software professionals: We often think that we know better than the customer or end user what the software should really do, and we often make the mistake of determining strategies and setting policies as if we had unilateral control of our own destinies. Of course, this is becoming more and more passé as users take control of their own destiny and begin telling *us* what they want and what it is we should be focusing on.

As part of the worldwide productivity benchmarking study illustrated in Figures 1.1 through 1.5 above, we asked survey participants to prioritize some 30 factors in selecting an outsourcing software vendor from a low-wage country. Obviously, such a choice is only one of many alternatives available to end users today, but the survey results nevertheless provided some fascinating results, as illustrated in Figure 1.6. Among other things, the survey indicated that virtually all of the 30 factors are significant—i.e., only one item had a rating of less than "neutral" or "indifferent." The rating of "moderate" importance for most of the factors speaks for itself; however, we felt it was useful to provide some commentary on the seven *most* important factors and the seven *least* important factors.

1.2.1 High-Importance Factors

On a scale of one to five, where five indicated "strong agreement" that the related factor was important, all seven of the items discussed below had a mean score of 4.67 or above. It's also interesting to note that these factors were also the lowest in terms of variance—i.e., there was a very strong consensus among the survey respondents about the importance

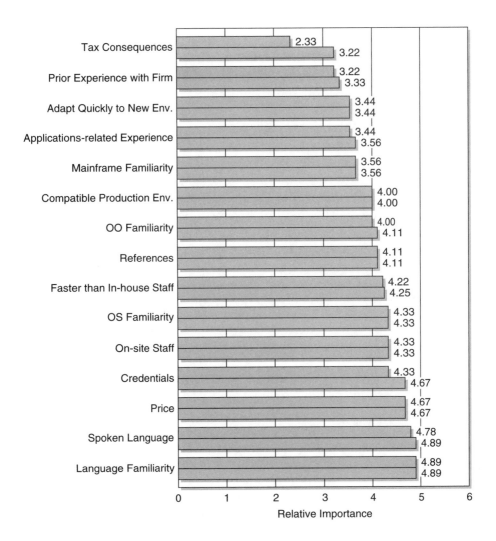

FIGURE 1.6 LOW-WAGE OUTSOURCING FACTORS

of the factors, as compared with the issue of familiarity with mainframe computers, which had a very high variance in its score.

1. Language familiarity

Customers are typically looking for specific language skills. To be an acceptable supplier, it's not sufficient to simply say "Our people are very smart and have a Ph.D. in computer science"; customers are looking for specific experience in COBOL or C++ or some other language. In many cases today, the language familiarity involves new, popular 4GL and rapid prototyping languages—e.g., Visual Basic, PowerBuilder®, Oracle Forms™, etc. In other cases, it may represent a language being used to implement object-oriented applications, such as Smalltalk or C++. In any case, it's likely to be a relatively new language (as compared to COBOL, FORTRAN, or PL/I) where there is a shortage of readily available people in the customer's indigenous marketplace.

Most interestingly, the high score achieved by this item strongly implies that the customer has already determined the language to be used on the project. This may be because the language is a company standard or because the project has already gone through the analysis/design phases. If the latter case is true, it suggests that companies are not looking for low-wage software suppliers to take over complete project responsibility—but merely to fill in on the final stages of development of a project, when language-specific programming skills are needed.

2. Telecommunication connections

This factor is obvious—since the software work under consideration was intended to be carried out in the low-wage country, efficient telecommunication connection to the customer's computer system would be essential. It's interesting to note that this is also an area of emphasis and priority for some of the low-wage countries themselves, especially if the government is trying to promote or subsidize the growth of the indigenous software industry. India is a good example of a country whose government has invested considerably in satellite links and telecommunications infrastructures in order to make its software industry more competitive.

3. Spoken language

At first glance, this would seem obvious: The customer wants to hire a software firm that speaks the same native language; within the North American marketplace, this typically means English. As such, countries like India have an advantage, whereas countries like China and Korea (as well as much of Eastern Europe) have a disadvantage. Nevertheless, it's interesting to see that the factor is rated so highly—it strongly implies that the customer expects that the low-wage software company will bring its personnel to work on-site at the customer's location. Otherwise, one could imagine a situation where a small number of liaison personnel carried on communications with the customer, while the remainder of the software staff stayed home, using its own native language skills to write the software.

4. Large staff

Companies looking for low-wage software services are apparently involved in large projects, which require large numbers of people; it's only when such large numbers are involved that it's worth going through the overhead and nuisance associated with establishing an offshore software project. After all, if the customer had a project that only involved three people for six months, it would probably be much easier to find indigenous staff members within the local marketplace.

There is also an assumption of credibility associated with size, just as there is in most industries: Regardless of whether it's accurate, the size of an organization implies something about stability, respectability, and so on. This is especially important, of course, if the software company is located far away: One wants the reassurance of knowing that the company is large and reputable—and one does not want to deal with "three guys in a garage" located on the other side of the world.

5. Price

The importance of price is obvious: One of the primary reasons that companies typically look to low-wage countries in the first place is the prospect of saving money. However, the fact that it was not judged among the top three items is interesting. Price is obviously important, but it's not the only factor—and it's not even the most important factor.

6. Rapid start

Many organizations today are developing systems that have ambitious schedules and nonnegotiable deadlines—e.g., the customer says, "We have a project that would normally take two years, but we have to finish it in six months, and it must be finished by January 1, 1997." Scenarios like this obviously put a premium on the software supplier's ability to form a project team almost overnight. This would not be a difficult issue if we were talking about small projects—but as noted in item 4, the survey responses strongly imply that customers are working on big projects, where it can't be taken for granted that the requisite skills can be assembled quickly. This may be another reason that customers are looking for software companies with a large staff, in order to have more confidence that it will have the personnel resources to assemble a project team on a rapid basis.

7. Credentials

This factor received the same importance rating as price and the ability to begin working on a project quickly. As noted earlier, price is important—but so, obviously, are the vendor's credentials as a reputable, ethical, dependable organization. While this is obviously a factor in any customer-supplier relationship, it's compounded when the customer is dealing with a supplier located far away, and where there may be some concern that the supplier is from a "primitive" country that is not up to date with the latest technology. Thus, it's very important, according to the survey respondents, for the software supplier to be able to show substantial credentials that it has worked on other, similar projects with other, similar customers.

Note that a related factor typically associated with "credentials"—the number of years that the software supplier has been in business—received only a slightly lower importance rating.

1.2.2 Least Important Factors

The factors that were rated least important also tended to have a high variance—i.e., opinions differed quite a lot more than with the factors discussed above, and there was much less of a consensus. The seven least important factors are discussed below.

1. Location convenient to customer's preference for establishing an offshore software factory of its own

When conducting this survey, we were curious to know whether companies were going through the exercise of working with an offshore software supplier in a low-wage country as a precursor to setting up their own software factory in the same country; this might be a rational strategy for "testing the water" before making a major, long-term commitment with a factory of its own. However, the bottom-level rating for this factor strongly implies that most companies have no such long-term plans of this kind—they simply want to deal with a low-wage, offshore software supplier for its own intrinsic benefits.

2. Tax consequences

This factor explored the concern that companies might have about the tax consequences that might be associated with having software done offshore—either in terms of tax preferences from the supplier's home country or possible tax penalties from the customer's home country.

The factor received a mean score of 3.22, indicating that respondents felt marginally more than neutral about the factor, i.e., it was not something they felt they could ignore altogether but also something they didn't feel strong about. One could infer from this that tax consequences are a "nuisance factor" that companies feel they must pay attention to, but which they don't regard as a significant benefit to be pursued.

3. ISO 9000 credentials

This factor might be more important to European customers than to customers in North America, simply because the ISO 9000 standard is more popular in Europe; however, the SEI factor (see item number 7 below) was rated only marginally more important. Given the relative importance of a supplier's credentials (discussed above), it's fairly evident that customers don't want to deal with a "fly-by-night," low-quality software supplier. On the other hand, there doesn't seem to be much expectation that the supplier will be emphasizing its ISO 9000 credentials.

An interesting aspect of this factor is that several Indian software suppliers are placing a major emphasis on achieving ISO 9000 certification—in order to make it easier to persuade customers that they are not only cheap, but high quality.

4. Prior experience with the customer's organization

One way of establishing credentials and reducing risk is to ask whether the software supplier has done any other projects for the customer's organization. It's interesting that this factor received a relatively low rating—but it also had the third-highest variance of all factors. One possible interpretation of this result is that many organizations are looking for their first relationship with a low-wage, offshore producer—so there is no prior experience.

5. Network familiarity

This was one of several technical factors that were surveyed—along with questions about the supplier's familiarity with specific DBMS packages, object-oriented technologies, and so forth. As noted earlier, the issue of language familiarity had the highest rating, and several other technology-related factors had moderate-to-low high ratings. However, note that it was a factor with a fairly high variance: it is important to some customers, but not to others.

The relatively low rating for network technology skills seems to contradict the somewhat higher importance attached to client-server technology skills.

6. Ability to adapt quickly to new and unfamiliar technology

The fact that this item received a relatively low rating probably indicates that customers perceive that they are primarily using "standard" technologies, with which they assume most suppliers would already be familiar. However, the ability to adapt readily and quickly to new situations is important in at least two situations: (1) the customer is using leading-edge technology, which no one in the industry is likely to have seen before, and (2) the customer is migrating legacy applications from an ancient technology platform, which everyone in the current generation of software professionals is unfamiliar with.

7. High rating on the SEI process maturity evaluation

As noted earlier, this survey question is somewhat similar to the item about ISO-9000 certification. Note that it had a marginally higher level of importance, presumably because of a higher percentage of survey responses.

The survey response here is intriguing, because the SEI assessment is used within the U.S. Department of Defense to assess the "predictability" of a software organization—i.e., the likelihood that it will actually be able to deliver a software project on time and within its budget. One would have assumed this would be important to customers, especially since "credentials" and "years of experience" received a fairly high rating. On the other hand, the use of SEI assessments is itself not yet widespread, especially within the private sector. So the low rating may simply reflect the relatively low level of awareness of the SEI model, and/or the reality that most organizations haven't even assessed themselves and are thus not yet ready to apply the assessment to any other organization.

There may also be an assumption that software producers in low-wage countries would be unlikely to have achieved an ISO-9000 certification or an SEI assessment. But as noted above, several Indian software organizations have achieved an ISO-9000 certification, and of those companies so certified, several are now beginning to prepare for an SEI assessment to demonstrate even higher levels of competence and quality. In this context, it's interesting to note that Motorola's software division in Bangalore has achieved a level-5 SEI assessment (the highest possible rating)—which no other Motorola software organization has achieved anywhere in the world and which only a handful of software organizations from any company have achieved.

1.3 CONCLUSION

The idea of "good-enough" software will strike many conventional software professionals and managers as heresy; and some of the other ideas that I'll be discussing in Part 3 of this book might also be considered too "far out" to provide a rational basis for optimism about the U.S. software industry. What if you're still building conventional applications with conventional technology, and you're worried about competition from either domestic or international software producers who might have higher levels of productivity and quality?

To address that competitive threat, I suggested a number of "silver bullets" in *Decline and Fall of the American Programmer*. This was in response to a warning from Fred Brooks, author of *The Mythical Man-Month*, who warned us several years ago that

> ...as we look to the horizon of a decade hence, we see no silver bullet. There is no single development, in either technology or in management technique, that by itself promises even one order-

of-magnitude improvement in productivity, in reliability, in simplicity. [1]

This reality continues to haunt us today, and many well-intentioned IT managers continue to invest vast sums of money in the hope that the newest miracle from Silicon Valley will somehow make it possible to generate infinite amounts of bug-free software in zero time and at zero cost. But while this utopia may not be possible, I suggested in my *Decline and Fall* book that there were nearly a dozen "potential" silver bullets whose collective impact on software development could be significant indeed. Those silver bullets were as follows:

1. Better programming languages
2. Better people
3. Automated tools
4. Joint Application Development (JAD)
5. Rapid Application Development (RAD)
6. Prototyping
7. Structured techniques
8. Information engineering
9. Object-oriented technology
10. Software reuse
11. Software reengineering

Ironically, the first item on the list was one that I chose not to discuss any further; but that was because in 1991, when I was doing the writing for *Decline and Fall*, "better programming language" typically meant nothing more than a new, improved version of an existing third-generation procedural language. True, Smalltalk and C++ were available at that point, but the real development in programming languages in the past few years has been associated with the "visual" paradigm—e.g., Visual Basic, Delphi, PowerBuilder, and a dozen other variants. Perhaps I should have been more prescient about the coming impact of those languages in *Decline and Fall*; in any case, the Visual Basic genre of languages has now been around long enough that it's almost passé, and I've devoted a chapter to the next generation of programming languages in Part 3 of this book.

Most of the other silver bullets on my original list remain relevant, and some are now so familiar and/or mundane—e.g., structured techniques, JAD, RAD, and prototyping—that I won't belabor them by discussing them in this book. But some silver bullets do bear a second look; in the next several chapters, I'll summarize what I regard as the new developments, opportunities, and/or problems in the area of peopleware, process improvement, CASE, object technology, reuse, and metrics. Indeed, if you *are* still in the business of developing payroll systems or airline reservation systems or any of the hundreds of conventional types of software applications we've been building for the past 30 years, you really should be taking full advantage of these technologies—for your competitors around the world are rapidly becoming aware of them and are putting them to good use.

And there are some additional strategies and techniques that you should be aware of, too, even if you're still building conventional applications. You might not want to put "good-enough" software in this category, but you certainly should be familiar with the concepts of system dynamics models of software processes, as well as "best practices" and "personal software practices." I'll discuss these ideas in Part 2 of this book, along with a discussion of "service systems" that represent an evolution from the payroll/order-entry kinds of "core" systems to the kind of software development work that I think we'll be focusing on in the latter half of this decade. Read on!

REFERENCES

1. Brooks, Fred. "No Silver Bullet." *IEEE Computer*, April 1987.
2. Gargan, Edward A. "India is among the leaders in software for computers." *New York Times*, December 29, 1993.

PEOPLEWARE

2

If the people are happy, united, wealthy, and powerful, we presume the rest. We conclude that to be good from whence good is derived.

Edmund Burke, Reflections on the Revolution in France *(1790).*

2.1 THE BASIC CONCEPT

It's an old idea: Good people develop good software. While tools and methodologies are important, and while rational managers and a decent working environment are important, too, the starting point for a highly productive software organization is good people. Indeed, really talented people can overcome primitive tools and can work without any formal methodology whatsoever; they can survive squalid office cubicles and tyrannical managers; with today's powerful laptop computers and Internet technology, they can hide in a closet, shut out the distractions of their immediate environment, and turn out software that will make you gasp with amazement.

All of this was true when I wrote *Decline and Fall*, as it had been when the first programming project began; it continues to be true today, and there is every reason to believe it will continue to be true for the foreseeable future. Obviously, the continuing improvements in tools and processes make it possible for us to be less dependent on prima donna geniuses; but one could also argue that the growing sophistication and complexity of modern-day software engineering tools and processes increases the need for talented, educated, and well-motivated software professionals.

Given the timeless importance of peopleware in a software organization, what has changed since the publication of *Decline and Fall of the American Programmer*? The simple answer is: not much. Indeed, the most surprising thing for me in the past five years, as I've traveled around the world preaching the importance of recruiting, hiring, training, rewarding, and motivating good people is that so many organizations *don't* concentrate on the essential aspects of good peopleware practice. But that's understandable: Even though hardware and software technologies change at lightning speed in our field, management and organizational cultures change very slowly.

2.2 BREAKING THE SOCIAL CONTRACT

Actually, there has been one dramatic change for the worse in the culture of many organizations during the first half of the 1990s: The endless rounds of downsizing, reengineering, and layoffs have essentially destroyed the "social contract" that bound worker and employer together in an atmosphere of trust and respect. This has been true for a wide range of white-collar knowledge workers, of course, and it has been substantially more common in North American organizations than in European organizations because our culture (including the absence of government regulations) *does* allow relatively abrupt dismissal of employees. One could argue that the elimination of several layers of white-collar middle managers in corporate America has been a good thing for the overall competitiveness of our industries, and one could make the same Darwinian argument in favor of wholesale sacking of COBOL programmers and their replacement with younger, cheaper C++ programmers. But the peopleware impact has been staggering: Just ask the thousands of hardworking, competent people at IBM and DEC (not to mention several hundred other IT organizations) who have been laid off in the past five years.

The negative aspects of this cultural change are obvious: Large companies have demonstrated repeatedly during the past decade that they cannot or will not make long-term commitments to their employees. And employees have responded by withdrawing their loyalty, as well as their commitment and dedication to the well-being of the company they work for. My colleague Rob Thomsett, one of Australia's most esteemed management consultants, argues that this trend is particularly relevant with the "Generation-X" software people that are entering the work force today. Thomsett argues that many large IT organizations are populated by "virtual" employees; people whose bodies are still present, but whose heads and hearts have tuned out.

Obviously, there are exceptions to this gloomy picture; and there are apologists who argue that it was inevitable and unavoidable. But whether it's good or bad, and whether it has been avoided in a few rare cases, it's fair to say that, by and large, the social contract between a software professional and the IT organization has been broken, probably forever. As a young college graduate, I was offered a job by IBM in 1965; if I had accepted it, my supervisor and I would have assumed implicitly that I was making a lifetime commitment. This is no longer true at IBM, and for all practical purposes, it's no longer true at *any* large company.

In small companies, though, such an assumption was *never* valid. After all, an implicit part of the social contract between employer and employee in a small organization is the common understanding of risk: The company might go bankrupt at any moment. But there was a social contract nonetheless, and it was usually honored more diligently than in the larger organizations even in good economic times. The reasons for this are fairly obvious, and the only thing that has changed in the past five years is that things have generally gotten worse in large organizations and better in smaller organizations. This has been particularly true for IT organizations, and the net result is that many software professionals have found that they have a far brighter future in small IT shops than in large IT shops.

In a subtle way, I believe that this trend is contributing to the overall rise and resurrection of the American programmer—because it has led to a steady shift of software people away from the large organizations and into the smaller companies. Some software veterans in the large companies have become so burned out and frustrated that they've left the field altogether; while there are some personal tragedies associated with this, it may be good for the industry as a whole, since it provides room for the next generation of enthusiastic young software people who bring with them a more up-to-date set of skills. By the way, ask yourself a question about those young hotshots, the ones who are just graduating from college this year with a degree in computer science or software engineering—or perhaps, with a degree in one of a dozen other business disciplines that make use of computing in innovative new ways. The question is: How many of them want to go to work for large, boring IT shops anyway, especially if it becomes obvious that the first five years of their career will be spend maintaining programs written in archaic programming languages by people old enough to be their parents? If you're a veteran with 20 years of experience under your belt, imagine what you would do if you could start all over again today. Would you go to work for the MIS department of XYZ Mega-Bank, where you're one of 2,000 anonymous COBOL programmers—or would you go to work for a 10-person software startup building interactive multimedia virtual-reality applications to be deployed on the Internet? Would you even think twice about such a choice?

This perspective may seem unnecessarily critical of large software organizations. In theory, large IT organizations have the potential for higher levels of software productivity, because they have the resources to make long-term investments in better tools and processes; but in practice, there has been only limited evidence of this positive effect. Indeed, Paul Strassmann, one of the preeminent gurus in the area of the business value of computing, argued recently that:

> I have studied over 50 industrial sectors and in each case found that the following generalizations apply:
>
> - The level of spending for information technology is very similar. It varies with the size of organizations.
>
> - The technologies used in each industry are almost indistinguishably identical. As a matter of fact, many industries not

only use the identical hardware and software suppliers, but also adopt similar telecommunications solutions; yet

- The profit performance of each company is totally unrelated to the amounts of information technology it employs.

There is absolutely no correlation between information technology budget and profitability.... The only plausible explanation for any differences is the manner in which any enterprise has taken a unique approach to combining its various elements of people, skill, motivation, and technology to deliver a result that differs from what competitors do with the identical resources. [22]

As a generalization, one could argue that software professionals in a small IT organization are better motivated and rewarded more equitably (including bonuses, stock options, etc.) than comparable software people in a large organization. As a result, they're likely to work with more energy and enthusiasm, and they're likely to volunteer for the late nights and weekends that software projects seem to entail. By contrast, the result of the broken social contract in many large IT shops is projects staffed by listless, disillusioned, frustrated, bitter IT professionals who figure they might as well go home at 5:00, because additional effort won't be rewarded or recognized. If they're pressured by their manager to work overtime (because the project and the entire organization is understaffed) they may do so grudgingly—but in Thomsett's terms, they'll be virtual employees looking for their first opportunity to escape.

There's an even more important aspect of this situation, in terms of the long-term optimism that I feel about the U.S. software industry. Regardless of the level of productivity and the overall morale of the programmers, it has typically been true that large IT organizations are working on *boring* projects. The most boring of all has been the continuing maintenance of legacy applications written in COBOL or RPG in the 1960s[1]; but even the new development projects are often intrinsically boring. Who on earth wants to work on yet another order-entry application or inventory control system? Yes, such projects—both the legacy maintenance projects and the development of new "core" applications—have to be done, and the enterprise can typically make a good case for it. But so what? It's been done before, and projects like these can be done anywhere. The technology involved is a commodity, and the pricing of commodity services and products in a global marketplace is precisely the reason for the gloom I expressed in *Decline and Fall of the American Programmer*. Even with the new tools and technologies that have excited our industry, such as Delphi and object-oriented technology, most IT organizations are simply paving over cowpaths with applications like these.

But the small software shops are doing new things, creating new applications, inventing new markets. They have to, or they won't succeed; it's possible to eke out a living as a three-person consultancy firm writing Visual Basic programs, but if you really want to make a fortune, you've got to be involved in inventing or developing the "killer app." Ten years ago, it was Lotus 1-2-3®; today it's Netscape Navigator™ and Java™; five years from now, it will be something we can't even imagine today. It won't come from IBM, and it probably won't come from Microsoft. It will come from three obsessed programmers in a garage, living off pizza and beer while they code furiously for weeks on end to build a better software mousetrap.

All of this will sound rather depressing to the employer or an employee accustomed to "business as usual," circa 1982. For the senior IT manager who must still find a way of maintaining those ancient legacy system, and whose users are still demanding run-of-the-mill order-entry applications, my advice is to start thinking of *all* of this work as a commodity. If you can produce it more effectively in-house, fine; if not, outsource it to someplace across the street, across the country, or across the world. As you do this, you'd better be prepared for the departure of the best and the brightest from your IT staff; and you'd better watch out that you don't end up with thoroughly incompetent zombies who can't find employment anywhere else. Commodity software, like commodities of any kind, is going to be developed by competent, trained factory workers in an automated

---

[1] There is one aspect of the ancient legacy system that's likely to involve a large percentage of our tired old COBOL programmer during the final few years of this decade: conversion efforts required to make the applications "Year-2000 compliant." The Year-2000 phenomenon is shaping up to be the single largest project our industry has ever undertaken—estimates range from 50 cents to one dollar for every line of legacy code, and most Fortune 500 companies have application portfolios of 50–100 million lines of code. For the mainframe programmers who get sucked into this kind of conversion effort, my advice is very simple: Make sure you have enough money in the bank to survive after January 1, 2000 because at that point, your skills will really be obsolete. This might be a good time to quit, become a consultant, charge consulting fees equivalent to twice your salary, and put half of it in the bank.

environment...and the inescapable truth is that those factory workers have no social contract, and they care as little about your project and your company as you do about them.

But for the software professional who still *enjoys* the process of developing software, there is a very simple and exciting message associated with these changes: *You are in charge of your own destiny.* Even four years ago, in *Decline and Fall*, I advised programmers to vote with their feet; I repeat the advice again now. If you think your management doesn't know what it's doing or that your organization turns out low-quality software crap that embarrasses you, then leave. If you think your company will chain you to your desk and sentence you to a lifetime of COBOL maintenance, it's *your* responsibility to find something better. After all, if your company continues to make strategic mistakes and eventually goes bankrupt (or if the IT department is reengineered out of existence by bloodthirsty users intent on finally getting revenge after being screwed for 20 years), no one is going to apologize to you when they throw you out and send you to the unemployment line with unmarketable skills.

One aspect of this strategy is particularly important: training and professional development. In 1994 and 1995 I published a newsletter called *Guerrilla Programmer* (whose mission was implied by its title), and I constantly received e-mail from readers who said, "My employer won't send me to any training classes; I know my mainframe COBOL career is doomed, but they won't train me in C++ or any new technologies." My response: *Do it yourself.* The personal time and the out-of-pocket expenses required for this ongoing professional development is part of the cost of being in the software business. Your employer may have decided, as part of its breaking of the social contract, that it won't subsidize that cost any longer; but if someone doesn't pay for it, you will indeed be put out of business by faster, cheaper, smarter programmers in some other part of the world.

If your employer still has some vestiges of the social contract, then you might be able to negotiate a reasonable compromise in the area of professional development. For example, you might agree that the *time* required for training will come from your weekends, holidays, and vacation time; but the *money* (for seminar fees, textbooks, college courses, etc.) will come from your employer. Or vice versa: you pay for the training, but the employer gives you time off from work. If money is an issue, perhaps you can negotiate a "package deal" that allows you to substitute training monies for other benefits (e.g., dental care) that you don't need.

Here's a more innovative approach to the training activity, which I've seen in a couple of IT organizations that are trying to reengineer themselves in a meaningful way: *Fire the training department!* Give the money and the decisions directly to the software professionals: At the beginning of each year, software professionals each should be given their own personal training budgets and told to make their own decisions about when, where, and how to spend it. Some will decide that they'll buy a library of books, others will pursue a Master's degree, still others will decide to attend OOPSLA and Comdex. Such an approach is obviously radical, and it may not work in your organization for a variety of reasons. But if you suggest this idea to your boss and you're turned down flat, you should take it into account when you begin to ponder the relevance of the social contract between you and your employer.

2.3 OTHER CHANGES IN PEOPLEWARE

For those who feel that the demise of the social contract between software professionals and their employers is irrelevant or that they must continue muddling through their current systems development project regardless of the state of the social contract, most of the fundamentals of "peopleware" that I described in *Decline and Fall of the American Programmer* haven't changed. If you and/or your IT managers have never heard of this concept, the best starting point is *Peopleware* by Tom DeMarco and Tim Lister. The other references at the end of this chapter are also good background reading.

The changes and improvements that I've observed in the peopleware area since I wrote *Decline and Fall* include the following:

- The "audition" process for selecting new staff members has caught on in some parts of our industry.
- The factors that influence the likelihood of people leaving an IT organization have been studied in detail in the form of a model that could be explored with system dynamics.
- One of the obvious factors—salary and other forms of remuneration—continues to change with the times.

- Companies are taking another look at the issue of training for beginners, and this is being combined with the notion of mentoring.
- Performance reviews are being enlarged to include so-called "360" reviews.
- The concept of software *teams* has been refined considerably.
- The notion of providing a pleasant working environment has gained credence in many of the software-products companies.
- An organized approach for improving the peopleware situation has been proposed by the Software Engineering Institute, with their "peopleware maturity model."

Each of these ideas is discussed briefly below.

2.3.1 Changes to the "Audition" Process

In addition to the traditional procedures for selecting candidates for a software organization—e.g., interviews and checking references—I suggested the idea of "auditions" in *Decline and Fall*. Asking candidates to give an oral presentation on some technical topic worked spectacularly in my consulting firm in the 70s and 80s, but most audiences to whom I explained the concept sat silently, with fishy-eyed stares, and showed no interest in trying it.

But it's caught on in a big way in many software organizations around the world where software is the essence of what the enterprise does. In what I've come to describe as the Silicon Valley audition, the candidate is given a technical problem to solve—in contrast to the auditions I carried out in my consulting firm, where the candidate could give a presentation on the topic of his choice and could spend as much time as he wanted to prepare the presentation before arriving at our office. The Silicon Valley candidates typically have *not* seen the problem before it is handed to them (though, like the College Board exams, the grapevine provides a rich source of rumors about what the problems are likely to be at certain companies, such as Microsoft); they are asked to begin solving the problem with little or no preparation, typically by writing code on a blackboard or on a laptop computer. The interviewer, who is typically the manager to whom the candidate would report if hired, then reviews the proposed solution, looks for common types of errors, and asks the candidate to explain (a) why he made the mistakes, and (b) what he would do to correct them.

If you're hiring technical people who will actually write computer programs, there are some obvious advantages to this approach. As one Microsoft manager said to me, "If you want to be a bricklayer, you have to show us how you lay bricks. You can't just talk about it." And since the same problem is used for numerous auditions, the manager becomes more and more proficient at spotting logic errors and other flaws in the solutions proposed by the candidates.

The downside of this audition variation is that it typically provides little or no opportunity for the candidate to *think* about the problem and to plan a well-organized solution. A reasonable compromise might be to give the candidate an hour to study the problem before launching into his coding activities, but the overall thrust of this audition approach is likely to be one of hiring people who are fast on their feet, but not necessarily thoughtful, well-organized people. Also, since the manager typically conducts the audition alone, it runs the risk of eliminating the "social" aspects of the audition I described in *Decline and Fall*: The people who are likely to be working side-by-side with the candidate on a day-to-day basis can play an important role by commenting on the nontechnical aspects of the candidate's personality and background.

2.3.2 Studying the Reasons for Employee Departure

For some reason, nobody likes to talk about the people who quit. They may be regarded as martyrs or incompetent nuisances, but once they're out the door, the history books are rewritten, a la *1984*, and life goes on. This can be a tragedy, though, since it's often the best people who leave first; they're often the ones who are most frustrated by the way their talents are being squandered, and they usually have lots of other opportunities to pursue in other companies. And it's all the more important now, because our IT organizations are gravitating towards smaller, leaner groups where small, tight-knit teams use today's powerful tools to build applications for their customers. Losing one person in a hundred-member team may not matter very much, unless that person is the chief designer and the only one with a brain in his head, but it's likely to be *much* more serious if you lose one person in a three-person team.

How strange it is, then, that we have little idea of the reasons why software professionals leave their current jobs—and in some cases, why they leave their profession altogether to take up a different career. For the industry as a whole, it hasn't been a pressing concern during the first half of the 90s, for we've been going through an enormous transformation that involves an overall shrinking of the work force in many large IT organizations. If you're trying to shrink a 500-person organization down to a leaner, more productive 100-person organization, you probably don't care very much why people are leaving—even though the result of these downsizing operations is typically that the *best* 200 people quit when they see what's going on, while the *worst* 200 people are terminated, which leaves behind 100 people of merely average talents who somehow have to cope with the workload previously carried out by 500.

For those parts of the software industry that are growing—the shrink-wrapped software producers, the multimedia software companies, the software companies producing wonderful new stuff for the Internet, etc.—the loss of key software talent can be the same kind of disaster it was for the IT organizations in banks and insurance companies a decade or two ago. Fortunately, we now have some models of the factors that influence employee departures; Figure 2.1 shows a model developed by Magid Igbaria and Jeffrey Greenhaus [12].

Companies that are *really* concerned about the possible departures of their best people have incorporated the kind of models shown in Figure 2.1 into a *system dynamics model* that can be used to simulate the feedback effects of various scenarios, using modeling tools like the ones discussed in Chapter 4. Suppose, for example, that your IT organization introduces a completely new set of software development tools and methodologies, mandates that the new environment *must* be used on all projects, but neglects to provide any training. The immediate, short-term effect is pretty predictable: Productivity will go down, not up. This phenomenon, combined with the general reaction to management's heavy-handed edict, is likely to cause morale to plummet in the organization. When morale goes down, turnover goes up. And when turnover goes up, the first people to march out the door are the smartest, most highly motivated, highest-producing software people. Their departure drives

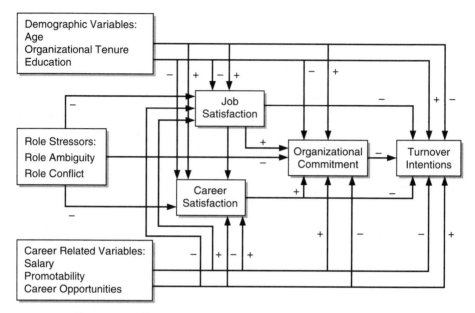

FIGURE 2.1 FACTORS INFLUENCING EMPLOYEE TURNOVER

productivity down further, which drives morale down further...which pushes up turnover, which pushes out more talented people. It's a scenario being acted out in dozens of IT organizations daily, but most IT managers don't worry about it and don't have any idea that they might be able to study the phenomenon in an organized fashion.

2.3.3 Compensation for Software Professionals

Software professionals have long enjoyed above-average salaries, compared to most other white-collar knowledge workers; as the salaries in Figure 1.1 (Chapter 1) indicate, none of us are in any danger of starving to death. But there have always been questions about whether we're being paid what we're really worth and whether our remuneration has any relationship to our level of productivity. If I can produce ten times as much software as another person in my software group—and if all other aspects of our behavior and performance are essentially the same—shouldn't I be making ten times as much money? And if the software that I produce makes millions of dollars for my company, shouldn't I be able to share in the bonanza?

As with the comments earlier in this chapter, the significant change in the past five years has been one of lowered expectations. Not only is the average software professional vaguely aware that there are people on the other side of the world who can do the same job for 5 to 10 times less money, but there are people coming out of college every year in the U.S. who seem to have more up-to-date, marketable skills at salary levels 50 percent below that of the veteran with ten years of mainframe COBOL experience. In circumstances like this, asking for a 50 percent bonus at the end of the year is not a politically wise move.

In software producing firms, though, free-enterprise capitalism is alive and well—just as it always has been. In some of the more prosperous Silicon Valley firms, lead software developers with a track record and a reputation are being paid like baseball stars; and the notion of providing stock options, profit-sharing participation, and performance bonuses is so obvious that it's almost taken for granted. Indeed, one of the startup software companies I've been associated with for the past couple of years has paid some of its key people *entirely* in "sweat equity"—i.e., a salary of zero dollars, combined with stock options that turned out to be quite lucrative when the company was acquired.

But what about the more traditional companies and the government agencies that can barely manage to cough up an annual cost-of-living increase for their people? Not only do the IT departments in these companies have to deal with cheaper outsourcing firms and cheaper college graduates, but they have to cope with the increasing attitude on the part of the end-user departments that IT is an "overhead" that should be subject to cost-containment measures. And in addition, the end-users feel (with some justification) that some of the development work that has traditionally been carried out by very expensive software professionals can now be carried out by their own people. Again, this combination of circumstances makes it difficult for the IT department to justify the kind of salary increases and performance bonuses that would normally provide the kind of motivation that enables software developers to cope with the long hours of overtime and the stress of high-pressure projects.

If money isn't available, there *are* some innovative ways of rewarding software professionals, and I've begun seeing more efforts in this area during the past few years; indeed, modest financial bonuses may not be all that necessary anyway, since much of it disappears for taxes and the remaining amount makes little impact on an already-comfortable life style. But instead of a 10 percent bonus, what if your company offered you 10 percent more time off? That would be exciting, for the additional time is tax-free. What if your company allowed you to attend a conference or a training course as a bonus? What if you were allowed to spend three months working on "Project X," which looks official and respectable on all of the organization charts, but turns out to be a three-month sabbatical for pure research on whatever aspect of software technology you're most interested in?

Obviously, some managers will react to this by saying, "Bah, humbug! They're lucky to have a job at all! When they finish this project, I'll have them assigned to another project the next morning!" That kind of attitude, which implies that the software developers are expendable resources that can be disposed of when fully depleted, is precisely the kind of attitude that will make the best software professionals update their résumé, seek greener pastures, and eventually march out the door.

2.3.4 Training and Mentoring

As noted earlier, training continues to be a major area of concern for employer and employee alike in the software field. In the worst case, software professionals are receiving little or no investment in ongoing professional development—which will eventually lead to obsolescence, to which the worst companies respond by sacking the unfortunate software veteran and replacing him with a younger, cheaper, more up-to-date person. In the more creative organizations, employer and employee look for ways to jointly invest in the ongoing professional development; and in any case, the software professional is beginning to realize that he must take personal responsibility for his professional development.

Two interesting things have occurred since I wrote *Decline and Fall of the American Programmer*. First, some organizations have realized that training doesn't have to involve formal, off-site attendance at seminars, conferences, or training courses. A particularly effective approach known as a "study group" has been popularized during the past few years by consultants such as Rich

Cohen (70007.6607@compuserve.com) and Rick Zahniser (70313.1325@compuserve.com). It consists of an informal gathering of interested software professionals on a regular basis—e.g., Friday afternoons at 5:00, or Mondays at lunch time—to carry out in-depth discussions of professional topics of interest. The topics may not be directly related to any of the projects currently under way, but they're typically concerned with major, long-term professional areas of interest such as client-server development tools, object-oriented methodologies, etc. Quite often, the group will use a textbook to help focus their discussion; thus, the group might decide that everyone will read Grady Booch's latest book on object-oriented design and that one chapter will be discussed in each week's meeting.

The nice thing about this approach is that it doesn't cost any money and doesn't involve any overhead. Enlightened managers will see the value of this kind of activity and will donate some company resources to help it along—e.g., encouraging the meeting to begin at 4 P.M. on Friday, rather than 5 P.M., and providing a modest supply of beer and pizza to loosen everyone's tongue. But even in the most reactionary, hostile management environment, the software professionals can carry out the study groups on their own; if necessary, they can retire to the nearest pub after official workhours and carry on the discussions by themselves.

The second training issue that I've seen discussed a lot in the past few years involves entry-level people. As noted earlier, the software engineers that we hire from our best universities today already have a wealth of technical training in languages, environments, methodologies, etc.; many of them have been programming since they were in high school, and they are often more up-to-date on current technologies than the veterans in the IT organizations they're about to join. So why train them at all?

Many of the smaller software-consulting and software-producing firms have concluded that there is little or nothing to be gained from such training—and if they're a young, startup company, they can't afford it anyway. A manager at Microsoft told me, during a 1994 visit, that newly hired programmers spend their first morning on the job filling out insurance forms in the personnel office and are assigned to their first project right after lunch; they're expected to write code, or do something useful, by the time they go home at the end of the first day. For software managers in many large Fortune 500

IT organizations and government agencies, this sounds ridiculous; but for the software companies in Silicon Valley and other high-tech areas around the world, it makes perfectly good sense.

As a contrast to the entry-level training procedure at Microsoft, consider the approach in the Motorola software department in Bangalore that achieved such renown for its SEI level-5 assessment. Newcomers to this group, who are usually recruited from the best graduates of the top computer science institutes in India, are given 42 days of training before being assigned to a project. Obviously, nobody needs to teach these new hires the technical details of UNIX and C++ and structured analysis; they've learned that already. But what they don't know is Motorola's software process; and for a level-5 software organization, the process is formal, detailed, and all-important.

For the organizations that have no formal process, there is a practical alternative to the 42 days of entry-level training: mentoring. The newly hired programmer at Microsoft, for example, quickly learns that every line of code that he writes will be read by a personal mentor (who may turn out to be the project leader or lead designer on his project team). And the new person is expected to read every line of code written by his mentor, a process that continues until the master/mentor and the apprentice mutually agree that it's no longer needed. An approach like this is sometimes found in more traditional IT organizations, but it's usually informal, ad hoc, and sporadic in nature.

2.3.5 Performance Reviews

Performance reviews continue to be the basis for employee evaluations, which lead to promotions, salary increases, and rewards of various kinds. The significant development in this area has been the introduction of so-called "360" reviews, which involve assessments of the software professional's performance by his peers, customers, managers, and everyone else in the 360-degree circle around him.

Obviously, this is an idea that's not restricted to software people; what's intriguing is the growing realization that software people no longer work entirely alone and that their value (and the assessment of their performance) depends on how well they interact with a wide variety of people in the environment around them.

Though this concept is simple and natural, I fear that it may turn out to be another of the management fads that sweeps through large organizations and then fades away. If it becomes part of the overall culture in an organization, it would certainly benefit software people to participate in the process; but if it fades away from the rest of the organization, it won't survive in the IT department either.

2.3.6 Refinements in the Concept of Teams

Another crucial aspect of peopleware involves teams; it had been a critical factor in the success of software projects for many years before I discussed it in *Decline and Fall of the American Programmer* in 1992, and it continues to be a critical factor today. Unfortunately, most of the IT organizations that I visit still don't do a good job in this area, and management's team-related actions seem destined to cause "teamicide" by the end of a project. If you're not familiar with the term, and if the collective wisdom about teams in your organization is "throw a bunch of people together and call them a team," then you should begin by carefully reading Tom DeMarco and Tim Lister's classic work, *Peopleware*.

But you should also be aware of some of the things that have evolved in the past few years. Perhaps the most important is the realization that there are many different types of teams—each one reflecting the culture of the organization and/or the organizational culture in which the team operates. Larry Constantine's work on teams, summarized in his recent book, *Constantine on Peopleware*, provides some important insights for organizations who think all teams are alike: There are "open" teams and "closed" teams and "synchronous" teams, each with its own style and personality and modus operandi. None of these categories is generically right or wrong; nor is any one of them better or worse in all situations. But if the project circumstances or the organizational culture creates a team with an "open" or "closed" or "synchronous" style, it's important to know what kind of people will function easily within that style; and it's important to know which kinds of internal procedures and external stimuli are likely to be most effective and which ones are likely to be distracting and destructive.

From an operational perspective, consultant Robert Binder has demonstrated that different types of teams are appropriate for common categories of IT projects. As illustrated in Figure 2.2, the "tactical" team might be more appropriate for the maintenance of an

Broad Objective	Degree of Teamwork	Dominant Theme	Process Focus	Member Selection Criteria
Problem-solving	Situational	Trust, working relationship *get the process right*	Issues	Intelligence, sensitivity
Creative	Spontaneous	Autonomy from rules, bureaucracy *get the people right*	Possibilities and alternatives	Independent thinkers, self-starters
Tactical	High, systematic	Clear and comprehensive planning *get the plan right*	Directions, well-defined operational standards, role clarity	Loyal, responsive, conforming

FIGURE 2.2 TEAM STYLES (FROM ROBERT BINDER)

ongoing legacy system; the "problem-solving" team might be appropriate for choosing a new software package or developing a traditional business application; and a "creative" team would probably be best suited to finding an innovative way of providing IT support for a business reengineering effort.

Of course, the idea of teams is not restricted to software development and IT organizations; from the early experiments in automobile factories in 1960s, interest in teams has spread through the entire spectrum of white-collar knowledge workers. A number of interesting new books have been written on the subject, some of which are listed in the references at the end of this chapter. And techniques like the Briggs-Meyers test, which I recommended in *Decline and Fall* as a good mechanism for finding team members with compatible personalities, has now shown up on the World Wide Web; you can find it at http://sunsite.unc.edu/jembin/mb.pl

2.3.7 Decent Working Conditions

There's a world of difference between the office environment one typically sees in the IT organization of a bank, insurance company, or government agency and that of the office environment in a software-product company where the software developers are the key intellectual asset of the enterprise. Things haven't changed much in this area: The companies that regard IT as an overhead nuisance tend to put their software developers in cramped cubicles, located in sterile office floors where views of the outside world are nearly impossible. The Silicon Valley companies may also have cubicles, but there's a *much* higher chance that their software professionals will have private offices with a door that closes; they'll have access to a company kitchen, or a refrigerator well stocked with soda and juice; and when they look outside their office window, they're more likely to see trees, mountains, or some visible evidence that Nature still exists.

Does all of this matter? It's a matter of opinion, and the opinions bear only a small resemblance to rational thought. No matter how many studies are published showing the relationship between software productivity and quiet, private working conditions, management in many IT organizations doesn't want to hear it. Part of this is because office space represents an illiquid capital investment; cubicles are preferred by cost-conscious managers, because they can cram more of them in the same physical space and because they can rearrange them every time there's a reorganization in the company. I don't expect this situation to change in the foreseeable future: Those who believe private offices are important will continue to provide them, and those that don't won't.

However, there has been one interesting development in the discussion of working conditions and office environment for the professional software staff: It has become more and more important to work in an environment that is fully networked. A software project team whose members work without at least being connected to one another via a LAN would be considered prehistoric today; there's simply no excuse for forcing project teams to use a "sneaker-net" mode of file transfers and communication.

Similarly, most software professionals assume that their workstation or PC will be connected to the rest of the organization via networks, so they'll have access to the mainframe computing resources and the ability to communicate across the entire organization via e-mail. But there is a more ambitious form of networking that, ironically, many software developers do not have today: the Internet. For reasons that are partly technological, but largely political (e.g., paranoid fear of intrusions and break-ins by external hackers), several organizations do not allow their software developers full access to the Internet and the World Wide Web.

Even as this book is being written, such a state of affairs is, in my strong opinion, intolerable; and I suspect that by the time the book is published, it will be so laughable that it will have disappeared except in the most Luddite of software organizations.[2] The Internet represents a vast, worldwide resource of information, assistance, tools, utilities, feedback, and gossip for professional software developers. The manager who refuses to provide access to this resource to his software professionals might as well put a paper bag over their heads and demand that they code in the dark.

But access to the Internet for supporting traditional software development projects is just the beginning. It's important, but as I'll discuss in Part 3 of this book, it's just the tip of the iceberg. The Internet represents a whole new world of technology and opportunities and markets for everyone, and it's a new world that I believe the U.S. will take the lead in exploiting. If your company is adamantly refusing to let you access the Internet today to support your conventional projects today, then it's probably going to drag its feet when it comes to the new world tomorrow. My advice is to leave now, before it's too late.

2.3.8 The SEI Peopleware Maturity Model

For the organizations that aren't quite sure how good a job they're doing in the peopleware area and for the organizations that need an organized, prioritized approach for improving, the Software Engineering Institute now provides a "peopleware capability maturity model," which it refers to as the P-CMM. Some of the early ideas behind this model had been published when I first wrote *Decline and Fall*, but a much more fully developed book-sized document is now available from the SEI. You can also find it on the World Wide Web at http://www.sei.cmu.edu/technology/p-cmm.html

---

[2]In a survey of Internet usage by IT organizations that I conducted in the spring of 1997 (*Riding the Internet Tiger*, published by Cutter Information Corp., Arlington, MA), I found that approximately 32% of IT organizations provide Internet tools to less than half of their developers; only 35% of the organizations provide access to *all* of their developers.

The P-CMM focuses on key process areas associated with five basic categories:

- *Managing the staff*, which includes recruiting, selection, and planning of hiring.
- *Managing performance*, which includes performance reviews as well as more sophisticated approaches to anticipating and guiding employee behavior on a day-to-day basis. One of these was discussed in *Decline and Fall* under the heading of "performance management," in which the personal consequences of a management decision are studied, in order to distinguish between the "positive, immediate, certain" personal consequences and those that are uncertain or, in the worst case, "negative, immediate, and certain."
- *Developing staff members*, which includes training, mentoring, and coaching.
- *Motivating the staff*, which includes compensation practices and team-based practices.
- Organizing and empowering the staff, which involves aspects of the work environments (such as the issue of office space discussed above), creation of participatory culture, and team-building.

Assuming that most organizations are currently at level 1 on the SEI P-CMM scale (which the lead author of the P-CMM model, Bill Curtis, once described as the "herded" level, in which management treats its software professionals as a herd of cattle, or replaceable commodities), there needs to be an organized plan for progressing through higher stages of peopleware practices. Before embarking on advanced, esoteric team-building practices, for example, the SEI recommends instilling basic disciplines into the current ad hoc processes—much the way it recommends instilling discipline in basic software processes before moving into exotic new object-oriented methodologies.

2.4 STRATEGIC IMPLICATIONS

In a nutshell, the fundamentals of peopleware haven't changed in the past five years; this isn't surprising, since people are still people. The changes and improvements described above are interesting and important, but they won't help in an organization that remains convinced that all software development problems are purely technical in nature and that peopleware is "sissy stuff" best left for the psychologists to argue about. If you believe this, then I thank you for having the patience and endurance to read this far; I'm sure I haven't changed your opinion.

But if you're essentially neutral about the idea of peopleware, you might be muttering to yourself at this point, "Yeah, fine, but what does this have to do with the original *Decline and Fall* theme that we're going to face greater competitive pressure from people who are cheaper, faster, and better than us?" Simple: One important element of the equation for higher levels of productivity and quality is having highly skilled people who are well managed and highly motivated. There's no reason to believe that any country, anywhere in the world, has a monopoly on good peopleware practices; the traditions and cultures in each country provide some advantages and disadvantages when it comes to recruiting, selecting, training, rewarding, and motivating the professional staff, but the simple truth is that *any* software organization can do a good job in this area. On the other hand, it is probably a fair generalization to suggest that the larger IT organizations around the world tend to do a worse job in peopleware, because they're saddled with politics and bureaucracy and because they find it harder to focus on the individual strengths and weaknesses of each member of their professional staff.

In any case, the best software organizations that I've seen really *are* aware of this, and are making concerted efforts to improve what they do well, and to rectify the weaknesses they see in their current policies and procedures. Regardless of whether you intend to continue developing conventional software, or whether you intend to become part of the "brave new world" of software development that I discuss in Part 3, you need to be aware of the impact of peopleware on your company's effectiveness and competitiveness.

REFERENCES

1. Cohen, Rich, and Warren Keuffel. "Pull Together." *Software Magazine*, August 1991.

2. Constantine, Larry. *Constantine on Peopleware.* (Englewood Cliffs, NJ: Prentice Hall, 1995) ISBN: 0-13-331976-8.

3. Couger, J. Daniel, and Robert A. Zawacki. *Motivating and Managing Computer Personnel.* (New York: John Wiley & Sons, 1980) ISBN: 0-471084-85-9.

4. Curtis, B., H. Krasner, and N. Iscoe. "A Field Study of the Software Design Process for Large Systems." *Communications of the ACM,* November 1988, pp. 1268–1287.

5. Curtis, B., W.E. Hefley, and S. Miller. *People Capability Maturity Model,* Draft version 0.3. (Pittsburgh, PA: Software Engineering Institute, April 1995).

6. DeMarco, Tom, and Timothy Lister. *Peopleware.* (New York: Dorset House, 1987) ISBN: 0-932633-05-6.

7. DeMarco, Tom, and Timothy Lister. "Programmer Productivity and the Effects of the Workplace." *Proceedings of the 8th ICSE.* (Washington, DC: IEEE Press, 1985).

8. Gardner, John. *Excellences.* (New York: W.W. Norton, 1987).

9. Hackman, J. Richard (ed.). *Groups That Work (and Those That Don't): Creating Conditions for Effective Teamwork.* (San Francisco, CA: Jossey-Bass, 1990) ISBN: 1-555421-87-3.

10. Herzberg, Frederick. "One More Time: How Do You Motivate Employees?" *Harvard Business Review,* September–October 1987.

11. Humphrey, Watts. *Managing for Innovation: Leading Technical People.* (New York: McGraw-Hill, 1987) ISBN: 0-135503-02-07.

12. Igbaria, Magid, and Jeffrey H. Greenhaus. "Determinants of MIS Employees' Turnover Intentions." *Communications of the ACM,* February 1992.

13. Katzenbach, J.R., and D.K. Smith. *The Wisdom of Teams.* (Boston, MA: Harvard University Press, 1993) ISBN: 0-8754843067-0.

14. Kawasaki, Guy. *The Macintosh Way: The Art of Guerrilla Management.* (Glenview, IL: Scott Foreman and Company, 1989) ISBN: 0-06-097338-2.

15. Klubnik, J.P. *Rewarding and Recognizing Employees.* (Chicago, IL: Irwin Publishers, 1995).

16. Kroeger, Otto, and Janet M. Thuesen. *Type Talk: The 16 Personalities That Determine How We Live, Love, and Work.* (New York: Bantam Doubleday, 1988) ISBN: 0-440-50704-9.

17. Mohrman, Susan A., Susan G. Cohen, and Allan M. Mohrman, Jr. *Designing Team-Based Organizations.* (San Francisco, CA: Jossey-Bass, 1995).

18. Page-Jones, Meilir. "The Seven Stages of Expertise in Software Engineering." *American Programmer,* July–August 1990.

19. Schulmeyer, G. Gordon. *Zero Defect Software.* (New York: McGraw-Hill, 1990) ISBN: 0-07-055663-6.

20. Senge, Peter. *The Fifth Discipline: The Art and Practice of the Learning Organization.* (New York: Doubleday, 1990) ISBN: 0-385260-94-6.

21. Sheppard, S.B., B. Curtis, P. Milliman, and T. Love. "Modern Coding Practices and Programmer Performance." *IEEE Computer,* December 1979.

22. Strassmann, Paul. "Internet: A Way for Outsourcing Infomercenaries?" *American Programmer,* August 1995.

23. Thomsett, Rob. "Effective Project Teams: A Dilemma, a Model, a Solution." *American Programmer,* July–August 1990.

24. Uris, Auren. *88 Mistakes Interviewers Make and How to Avoid Them.* (New York: American Management Association, 1988).

25. Valett, J.D., and F.E. McGarry. "A Summary of Software Measurement Experiences in the Software Engineering Laboratory." *Journal of Systems and Software,* Vol. 9, no. 2, 1989, pp. 137–148.

26. Webber, Susan. "Performance Management: A New Approach to Software Engineering Management." *American Programmer,* July–August 1990.

27. Weinberg, Gerald. *The Psychology of Computer Programming.* (New York: Van Nostrand Reinhold, 1971) ISBN: 0-442-29264-3.

28. Weinberg, Gerald M. *Understanding the Professional Programmer.* (New York: Dorset House, 1988). ISBN: 0-932633-09-9.

29. West, Mike. "Empowerment: Five Meditations on the Soul of Software Development." *American Programmer,* July–August 1990.

30. Whitaker, Ken. *Managing Software Maniacs.* (New York: John Wiley & Sons, 1994) ISBN: 0-471-00997-0.

THE OTHER SILVER BULLETS

...as we look to the horizon of a decade hence, we see no silver bullet. There is no single development, in either technology or in management technique, that by itself promises even one order-of-magnitude improvement in productivity, in reliability, in simplicity.

Fred Brooks, "No Silver Bullet," IEEE Computer, April 1987.

As I pointed out in Chapter 1, there are a number of silver bullets that can have an aggregate impact on software productivity and quality. Of these, peopleware is arguably the most important, and it deserved a chapter of its own. But the other ones are important, too, and in this chapter I'll summarize some of the recent developments in such areas as process improvement, object technology, reuse, and software metrics.

3.1 SOFTWARE PROCESS IMPROVEMENT

Unless you've been hibernating in a cave for the past five years, the SEI process maturity model illustrated in Figure 3.1 should be firmly

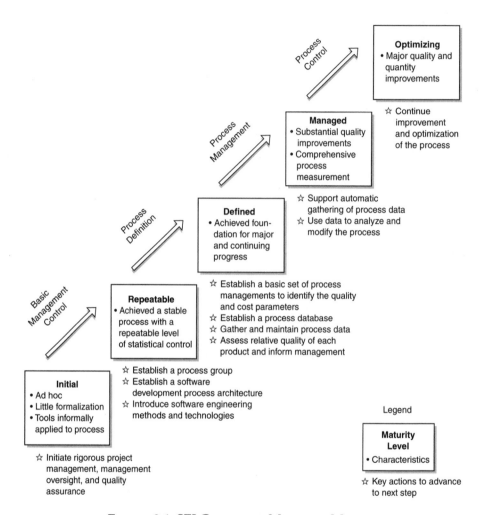

FIGURE 3.1 SEI CAPABILITY MATURITY MODEL

tattooed on your forehead. Indeed, the only thing I find surprising is that there are still so many people who have *not* heard of the SEI's Capability Maturity Model—typically abbreviated as CMM and often referred to as the "process maturity model." In presentations to audiences around the world, I still find that 50 percent of the software professionals and managers in the audience haven't heard a thing about it, and many others have only a passing familiarity.

Meanwhile, many software organizations in Europe, Asia, and other parts of the non-U.S. galaxy have focused their effort instead on the ISO-9000 certification for software quality. There continues to be substantial debate about the relevance and merits of ISO-9000, which was *not* developed originally for software processes but which has been adapted and revised over the past few years. Members of the ISO-9000 community and the Software Engineering Institute have been working on a joint model, in a project called SPICE, which may produce tangible results within the next few years.[1] And various other initiatives are under way, such as the European BOOTSTRAP project, to create process maturity models along the lines of the SEI-CMM, but with variations and extensions that reflect local needs and preferences.

Though my discussion in this book does reflect an American bias, I'm not religiously wedded to the SEI model; any reasonable variation is fine with me. I do have one major concern about the ISO-9000 approach, as it is typically used in software organizations: It's a "binary" certification, compared to the five-level evolutionary paradigm of the SEI-CMM. With ISO-9000, you're either certified or you're not certified—and if you're not, it may be difficult to organize and prioritize your efforts to improve. ISO-9000 certification is approximately equal to level 3 on the SEI scale; as of late 1994, about 90 percent of U.S. IT organizations were *below* level 3, which means they would not be able to acquire ISO-9000 certification easily; but with the SEI-CMM, they would know which key process areas to focus on in order to move up to level 2, and from there to level 3.

I discussed the SEI model in some detail in *Decline and Fall*, and I won't repeat the basics again here; besides, if you really do want to read about it for the first time, there are now a number of excellent references, as indicated at the end of this chapter. And that is one of the most significant developments of the past five years: whereas we had only one book by Watts Humphrey and a few papers from the SEI to guide us, now there is a wealth of published material, as well

---

[1]However, after listening to a presentation on the status of the SPICE project at the Fifth International Software Quality Conference in Austin, Texas, in October 1995, I now believe that it could be another three or four years before the "real world" actually sees the results published by the various standards bodies involved in this effort. By then, it will be irrelevant.

TABLE 3.1 Productivity and Quality Improvements Associated
with SEI-Style Process Maturity Efforts
(from James Herbsleb et al. [4])

Category	Range	Median	No. of Data Points
Years of effort	1–9	3.5	24
Process improvement cost: $/person	$490–$2,004	$1,375	5
Productivity gain/year	9%–67%	35%	4
Early defect detection gain/year	6%–25%	22%	3
Time to market gain/year	15%–23%	19%	2
Post-release defect reduction/year	10%–94%	39%	5
Savings/cost ratio	4.0–8.8	5.0	5

as a rich storehouse of up-to-date information provided by the Software Engineering Institute on the Internet.[2]

Among this published information are the reported experiences of numerous firms who have invested considerable time and money to carry out process assessments and then to invest in the effort to improve their maturity level from the "initial" stage to the "repeatable," "defined," and beyond. Though we don't yet have enough data to constitute a statistically unimpeachable sample, there is also some limited data that confirms the benefits of process improvements in terms of productivity and quality; one such set of data, provided by James Herbsleb and his colleagues at the SEI, is shown in Table 3.1. Though a serious SEI process improvement campaign should indeed be justified on a case-by-case basis, the cost-benefit ratio shown in Table 3.1 strongly implies that there is a good business case for most companies to follow the SEI process improvement approach.

But it's apparent, after five years of passionate debate and discussion—especially on several of the Internet/Usenet discussion groups—that not everyone believes this to be the case.[3] In addition to

---

[2]The best place to start is at the SEI's home page on the World Wide Web, at http://www.sei.cmu The Capability Maturity Model (CMM) can be found at http://www.sei.cmu/technology/cmm.html, and the peopleware maturity model can be found at http://www.sei.cmu/technology/p-cmm.html

the iconoclastic contrarians, some very thoughtful and serious software engineers, such as James Bach [1], have argued that the SEI process maturity model has a number of limitations and weaknesses and that it may actually be dangerous in some circumstances.

Many of the limitations and weaknesses in the original CMM model have long been evident, and the SEI has worked diligently over the past few years to produce a revised model. Version 1.1 of the CMM was released in 1994, and a new book has recently been published to describe the latest version. While Humphrey's 1989 opus is still an excellent foundation, you should really be using Mark Paulk et al. [8] as a guideline if you're serious about implementing an SEI-style process maturity initiative.

Certainly one of the major limitations in the original CMM was its lack of emphasis on peopleware. But as we discussed in Chapter 2, the SEI has also been working in this area, and the emerging peopleware maturity model dovetails with the familiar five levels of the process maturity model. This makes sense: It's hard to support advanced peopleware practices if you have primitive software processes; and it's hard to encourage and support advanced software processes if your peopleware practices are left over from the Dark Ages. Thus, if you're at level 1 on both the peopleware scale and the process maturity scale, it makes sense to develop a plan that will see both areas improve in a parallel fashion.

But what else might be wrong with the SEI-CMM? Why might some actually believe that it's dangerous? As I pointed out in *Decline and Fall*, it includes little or nothing about creativity and innovation, which are the basis for my optimism about the software industry in Part 3 of this book. Indeed, the CMM doesn't indicate whether an organization has the right process; it simply indicates whether the IT organization has some kind of process that's well-defined, repeatable, measured, and in a constant state of evolutionary improvement. But this says nothing about the overall needs of the enterprise: In theory, one could imagine a level-5 SEI organization with a near-perfect development process but which still fails to meet the needs of

---

[3]In a survey of IT organizations that I conducted in the spring of 1997, approximately 85% of the organizations indicated that they had not conducted an SEI assessment; the most commonly cited reason was the lack of credible proof of the benefit of such an assessment.

the organization. The SEI defenders would probably argue that part of the process improvement associated with level 5 (which, alas, *very* few organizations have reached) would be one of improving the alignment of activities and outputs of the IT organizations with those unfulfilled business needs. Still, that might not be sufficient to force the organization to make a quantum-leap change from, say, a waterfall-based software process with third-generation programming language to an iterative, prototyping-based process with a fourth-generation, visually-oriented language like PowerBuilder or Delphi.

But there's a more fundamental characteristic of the SEI model that is being questioned by the members of the software community often referred to as the "cowboy culture," which is so prevalent in Silicon Valley. Does it make sense, they ask, to focus so much of our effort on formalizing and institutionalizing a software process in an industry where all of the rules change so quickly and so radically? SEI critics like James Bach [1] argue that we live in a "mad world," where the hardware technology changes dramatically every six months; where the software tools and environments that we use change almost as frequently; where the government regulations and external business conditions change daily; and where competitors appear and disappear at a moment's notice and make loud claims about competitive products that may or may not appear a month before *your* product is introduced. In such a world, he argues, what we really need are highly skilled, flexible, empowered software professionals (surrounded by equally skilled, flexible, empowered managers, marketing specialists, and other members of the business enterprise) who can respond to this ongoing chaos in a creative, proactive fashion.

Unfortunately, the debates taking place on the Internet give one the impression that the SEI defenders and the SEI critics are at opposite ends of the spectrum and that they advocate mutually exclusive philosophies about the best way to develop software. True, the SEI model has been largely influenced by the needs of the U.S. Defense Department, which desperately needs to improve its track record for developing large, complex systems; and it's also true that the SEI-CMM is based on a classical quality-control paradigm of defining and standardizing a process, then measuring it to reduce variance, and then applying incremental improvements. But while Silicon Valley might argue that it lives in a world of chaos, it's also beginning to live in a world of "big numbers": When any of the major software producers, such as Microsoft, Lotus, or Computer Associates, ships a new product, they're shipping millions of lines of code to a potential marketplace of millions of customers. And while the company may be making grandiose claims about the improvements in its new Version N+1 product, it's likely to be little more (from the perspective of a neutral observer) than an evolutionary improvement over Version N. Hence, testing and quality assurance and process standardization and predictable software projects are becoming just as important for many of the Silicon Valley companies as for the venerable Defense Department.

But that doesn't eliminate the argument about chaos—and the important thing to realize, of course, is that chaos is just as much a factor for the Defense Department as it is for the newest startup company in Silicon Valley. The software-product industry does indeed seem chaotic, but many business people today will tell you that *their* industry is chaotic, too, whether it's banking or telecommunications or airlines or insurance or beer distribution. To the extent that IT department supports the overall business (which, of course, is a subject in itself) and to the extent that the business environment is chaotic, then it follows that IT and its software projects have to not only tolerate chaos, but take advantage of it in a proactive fashion. And, yes, there *is* a danger that a well-intentioned SEI process improvement initiative can degenerate into a bureaucratic regime of following procedures that were developed five years ago and won't be updated until the turn of the century.

Fortunately, there's no need to take an extreme position in this argument, and thoughtful software managers can usually find a way to take advantage of the benefits of SEI-style process improvement while retaining the flexibility needed to operate creatively in a mad, chaotic world. As suggested earlier, Silicon Valley has become painfully aware of the consequences of shipping buggy, low-quality software products to a mass marketplace; consequently, many of these companies have gradually instituted *very* formal processes for testing, quality assurance, and configuration management of their product releases. But they retain a great deal of flexibility at the front end of the software process, where product requirements and features are discussed, debated, and constantly changed in an innovative environment. Meanwhile, innovation has become more and more essential in the development of traditional business applications in Fortune 500 companies, and many IT departments have replaced the waterfall software process with a prototyping approach to avoid being locked in to a software application that no longer meets the user's needs when it's delivered.

There are two other aspects of the SEI model which I'll discuss in detail in Part 2 of this book. As noted earlier, the SEI model carries the influence of the U.S. Defense Department, and it has been used most aggressively by defense contractors, aerospace firms, and other organizations building very large, complex systems. And it's precisely for that reason that many of the smaller software shops (where the really exciting software work is going on!) are predisposed against the SEI-CMM: They don't want the bureaucracy and the overhead, and they don't feel that it applies to projects involving three people for three months. But as we'll see in Chapter 5, the chief architect of the original SEI-CMM, Watts Humphrey, anticipated this problem several years ago and has recently published a *personal* software process, or PSP. Intended for small projects and even single-person programming tasks, this new model may bring the best concepts of the SEI-CMM down to the level where it makes practical sense for *every* software development project.

The other aspect of the SEI model that we'll discuss in Part 2 involves the concept of "best practices." My concern here is not so much what those practices *are*—e.g., a "best practice" might involve the use of inspections throughout the software development process—but rather with the manner in which those practices are identified and then introduced into the organization. As we'll discuss in Chapter 6, the SEI-CMM is typically introduced in a "top-down" fashion; it's considered vital to get the support and commitment of senior IT management, which then promulgates and enforces the various practices associated with the SEI-CMM. But Humphrey's PSP, as well as the best-practices initiatives in many of the smaller software organizations, are typically introduced and evangelized in a "bottom-up" fashion, with or without the awareness and endorsement of higher levels of management. Indeed, this may be the only practical way to make things work in a large organization, as well, since senior management doesn't have a clue about best practices and since the software professionals are predisposed to disbelieve everything management tells them...but I'm getting ahead of myself: Take a look at Chapter 6 for more details.

3.2 OBJECT TECHNOLOGY

Peopleware and software processes may well be "silver bullets" for improving productivity and quality, but they're certainly not technology-related improvements. For many people, the most important technological silver bullet of the 1990s has been object technology[4]; I discussed it *Decline and Fall*, and it's interesting to see what has happened to the technology since then.

Objects were already well understood when I wrote about them in *Decline and Fall*; indeed, Peter Coad and I had already written two books on object-oriented analysis and design, dozens of books on object-oriented programming had been published, and languages like C++ and Smalltalk had been in existence for a decade. But when I wrote *Decline and Fall* in the summer of 1991, only about 3 to 4 percent of the software development projects around the world were using object technology; by late 1993 that figure had tripled, and as this tome is being written in the summer of 1995, the "market share" of object technology on software projects has probably reached the 15 to 20 percent level.

A survey of attendees at a 1994 Object World conference suggests that the trend will continue. Notwithstanding the likelihood that attendees at such a conference were already somewhat predisposed in favor of objects, their plans for the 1994 to 1996 period were quite interesting, as shown in Figure 3.2. Nearly a third of the survey respondents indicate that they planned to devote *none* of their application development budget to object technology in 1994; but by 1996, that category of hard-core resisters is expected to drop to about 5 percent. At the other end of the spectrum, about 5 percent of the respondents indicated they were devoting *all* of their application development budget to object-oriented tools and techniques, and that category is expected to nearly double by 1996. Between the two extremes of object fanatics and object resisters, Figure 3.2 shows a steady shift in favor of objects over a two-year period.

Nobody has a crystal ball when it comes to forecasting trends like these, and many of the surveys are tainted by a predisposed sample (like the one shown in Figure 3.2) or by vendors who have their own agenda. Nevertheless, it's hard to avoid the conclusion that the object-oriented tsunami has begun; sooner or later, it will be a pervasive technology that affects all of our programming languages, tools,

---

[4]Though it's definitely important, I do not think object technology is the most important thing that has happened in this decade. Far more important, in my opinion, is the technology of networking—and, specifically, the Internet. I'll discuss this in more detail in Part 3.

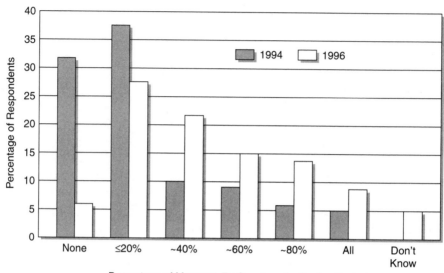

FIGURE 3.2 INCREASING USAGE OF OBJECT TECHNOLOGY
(FROM "CORPORATE IS CONSIDERS OBJECT PLANS,"
COMPUTERWORLD, JANUARY 24, 1994)

databases, and methodologies. Software guru Grady Booch argued in a recent article (*IEEE Software*, November 1994) that object technology has moved past the "early-adopter" stage of implementation and is now a "mainstream" technology. It's reasonable to assume that object technology will be used by approximately 40 percent of application development projects by 1996, 60 percent in 1998, and 80 percent by the turn of the century. If you're not on the OO bandwagon now, you'd better start thinking about it pretty seriously in the next year or two or you'll be left behind forever.

However, even though popular usage of object technology is increasing, it appears that the risk of OO-related project failures is increasing, too. As Chris Pickering's technology survey in Table 3.2 illustrates, a very small percentage of application development projects used object technology in 1991, but those projects were remarkably successful—indeed, even more successful than those that used structured methods or fourth-generation languages. By mid-1996, as illustrated in Table 3.3, the popular usage of OO technology had increased by a factor of three, but the success rate had plummeted to the point where it was the *least* successful of the technologies included in Pickering's survey.[5] And in its May 1994 issue, *Byte* magazine published a cover story suggesting that object-oriented had "failed." [33]

What's going on here? Is this the end of objects? No, but it suggests that the honeymoon is over; there may indeed be a backlash phenomenon for a couple years as IT organizations begin to realize that yet another preordained silver bullet doesn't have magical powers after all. As we moved from 1991 to 1993, we began to see object technology used on larger projects by larger groups of people, many of whom hadn't been trained at all, and some of whom weren't sure that they wanted to use objects in the first place. With small projects carried out by highly motivated zealots, success is a lot easier to achieve. With larger projects, technical issues begin to be overshadowed by politics and bureaucracy, and the overall success is determined much more by management decisions than clever C++ code. This doesn't mean that OO has failed, but merely that it's grown up; now it has to take its place with all of the other technologies listed in Tables 3.2 and 3.3, where it suffers the risk of misuse and mismanagement.

One interesting consequence of this increased risk has been a gradual awareness of the importance of object-oriented design, analysis, and business reengineering—instead of regarding OO as nothing more than a coding discipline and a decision to implement an application in Smalltalk. Participants in many of my OO analysis/design workshops have told a similar story; one systems analyst in a Dallas workshop in early 1995 told me:

---

[5]Meanwhile, notice what happened to structured methods between 1991 and 1996, as illustrated by Tables 3.2 and 3.3. The popular usage of the technology declined incrementally, as did the success rate. In 1991, it was somewhat difficult to make a business case for abandoning structured methods in favor of object technology; after all, as Table 3.2 suggests, the probability of success only increases by 1.5 percent. On the other hand, if you knew in advance, in 1991, that you needed to develop a distributed, client-server application with a GUI front end and you needed to take advantage of reusable class libraries, etc., then you may have had *a priori* knowledge that you were going to be part of the 9.8 percent minority in Table 3.2 for whom structured methods would fail; and in that case, adopting object technology would have made sense. One other thing: Notice what the most successful technology was in 1996 in terms of "effective penetration"—relational databases, followed by fourth-generation languages. We finally figured out how to succeed with Oracle and Sybase® and DB2™!

TABLE 3.2 Technology Usage in 1991
(from *Survey of Advanced Technology—1991*, by Chris Pickering)

Technology	Percentage of Projects Using Technology	Percentage that Succeeded	Effective Penetration
OO/OOPS	3.8	91.7	3.5
Structured methods	71.4	90.2	64.4
4GLs	20.6	86.6	17.8
RDBMSs	39.3	84.2	33.1
Model-based systems	23.1	80.7	18.6
End-user computing	25.0	75.0	18.8
Packages with models	9.4	73.1	6.9
Imaging	4.4	70.0	3.1
PC/WS-based development	27.5	67.8	18.7
EIS	6.9	63.1	4.4
CASE	28.8	59.7	17.2
AI/expert systems	3.9	55.3	2.2

Our company decided to build a small client-server application last year, and since we didn't know anything about the technology, we brought in a consulting firm to do the job. The consulting firm used Visual Basic, and they finished the job in record speed and then disappeared. Management and the end users were dazzled by the speed of the project and the elegance of the GUI interface, and they insisted that the next project also be done in this fashion. This one is going to be ten times larger and will impact the whole company, and management wants us to do it ourselves without any outside consultants. Meanwhile, we've had a chance to look at the Visual Basic code left behind by the consultants, and it's *awful*. It's absolutely unmaintainable, because there was no coherent design; so it's obvious to us that we need to invest some serious time and effort in a front-end, object-oriented analysis and design before we begin cranking out code.

TABLE 3.3   Technology Usage in 1996
(from *Survey of Advanced Technology—1996*, by Chris Pickering)

Technology	Percentage of Projects Using Technology	Percentage that Succeeded	Effective Penetration
Packages with models	17.0	96.0	16.3
Model-based systems	15.0	93.0	14.0
RDBMS 64.0	92.0	58.9	
PC/WS-based development	53.0	91.0	48.2
AI/Expert systems	8.0	90.0	7.2
4GLs 32.0	88.0	28.2	
Client-server	40.0	88.0	35.2
Internet 6.0	87.0	5.2	
Structured methods	82.0	87.0	71.3
Imaging 10.0	86.0	8.6	
CASE 34.0	85.0	28.9	
Data warehouse	20.0	84.0	16.8
End-user computing	31.0	83.0	25.7
EIS 14.0	79.0	11.1	
OO/OOPS	12.0	74.0	8.9

This is a healthy realization, and it may explain the increasing popularity of OO methodologies. Most of the "first-generation" OO analysis/design methodologies that appeared in the late 80s and early 90s have now evolved into second-generation methodologies that take advantage of the "use-case" concept popularized by Ivar Jacobson [23][6]; many of the OO methodology vendors also emphasize the use of objects as the basis for business reengineering *before* the traditional analysis/design phases of an application development project. I've listed a selection of recently published OO books in the references at the end of this chapter; most of these have little or nothing to do with OO programming but may prove useful if you're trying to apply object technology.

Along with improved OO methodologies, there has been a steady increase in the availability of CASE tools to support object-oriented analysis and design. In addition to the "traditional" CASE vendors like Cadre and INTERSOLV and Popkin, a number of smaller vendors such as Protosoft have begun offering low-cost, sophisticated tools for modeling the requirements and design of an object-oriented application and then generating a working system. The vendors and the products change so rapidly that there's no point listing them all in a book like this; you can find them easily in trade magazines[7] and industry conferences. But there are two features that I suggest you look for in an OO CASE tool, in addition to the obvious support for OO methodologies:

• *Animation* of the model. Analysis/design methodologies have typically used graphical models (e.g., structure charts, entity-relationship diagrams, and now various flavors of object diagrams) to describe user requirements and systems designs; unfortunately, these models are abstract and often not very meaningful to a nontechnical end user. Most of the popular diagramming techniques predate CASE tools, and when they were simply drawings on a piece of paper, they were, of necessity, *static* in nature: They didn't move or change as the end user looked at them. Unfortunately, the first few generations of CASE tools perpetuated the static nature of the diagrams; however, some of the very new OO CASE tools animate the models, so that the user can actually *see* objects passing messages to one another. The same thing could have been done with structured analysis CASE tools, but the object paradigm cries out for it: The very essence of the models created by OO methodologies is an asynchronous network of collaborating objects that communicate with one another to respond to an external event. Two of the OO tool vendors

---

[6]Structured analysis aficionados will recognize a strong relationship between Jacobson's use-case concept and the "event-partitioning" approach first popularized by Steve McMenamin and John Palmer in *Essential Systems Analysis* (Prentice Hall, 1984). Whether you use the term "use-case," or "event," or "scenario," the basic point is that modern OO methodologies focus on external events in the business environment to help determine what objects are required in the system being developed. Tracing those events, as they enter the system and cause "threads" of messages to be sent through collaborating objects, turns out to be an excellent way of explaining an otherwise abstract and incomprehensible system model to the business user.

[7]One source of information is the November 1995 issue of my newsletter, *Application Development Strategies* (Arlington, MA: Cutter Information Corp.), which focused on the products of six different OO CASE vendors.

who support animation are Intellicorp (with its OMW modeling tool) and ObjectTime.

- *Bidirectional synchronization* between the analysis/design model and the code. The idea here is simple: After creating high-level, graphical models of the analysis and design phases of a software project, the application developer obviously has to produce code. In the primitive case, he writes the code manually—which means that it's difficult to determine whether the code really does implement the requirements, *all* the requirements, and nothing but the requirements. With sophisticated CASE tools, the code is generated automatically; but at that point, whether the code was generated manually or automatically, things begin to get out of control. This is because most programmers, during the final stages of testing and debugging, prefer to make their modifications directly to the code; thus, the code and the design model, even if originally synchronized via automated code generation, will begin to drift apart. The newest CASE tools cope with this by allowing the programmer to change *either* the code "model" (i.e., the source code) *or* the high-level models, and then automatically reflect those changes in the other model. Such a feature could have been implemented in the earlier generation of CASE tools supporting the pre-OO methodologies; but it's something that I began seeing with OO CASE tools from Vmark (with its Synchronicity™ product) and Object International (with its Together™/C++ product) in 1994. Since then, more traditional vendors, such as Rational and Aonix, have begun referring to this concept as "round-trip engineering," and have incorporated the capability into their product.

As suggested above, I believe that the most important object-oriented activity in the next five years will be its achievement of "mainstream" status. This is already beginning to occur: Nearly every tool, language, method, and software product now claims to be object-oriented. But we still have a vast inventory of legacy software that needs to be converted, as well as a vast army of "legacy people" who need to convert their skills and expertise from older, procedural paradigms to the object-oriented approach. This is now happening in a steady fashion, helped along by the gradual retirement of older-generation programmers and the influx of new-generation, OO-trained people.

One aspect of "mainstream" objects is the consolidation of a Tower of Babel of OO methodologies. When *Decline and Fall* was first published, there were nearly a dozen "brand-name" methodologies, many involving a pair of consultant names (e.g., Martin-Odell, Shlaer-Mellor, Coad-Yourdon). But in 1994, one of the key methodologists, Dr. James Rumbaugh, joined the firm of Rational Software Corporation, the home of OO guru Grady Booch. And in the fall of 1995, Rational announced the acquisition of Objectory AB, the home of OO guru Ivar Jacobson. At the fall 1995 OOPSLA conference, Booch and Rumbaugh presented a draft version of their "unified" OO analysis/design methodology; in January 1997, Rational formally submitted its "unified modeling language" (UML) as a proposed standard to the Object Management Group. The net result of all this is quite simple: Rational has become the Microsoft of OO methodologies, and IT organizations (as well as CASE vendors!) can stop worrying about which brand-name methodology will prevail. A few of the other methodologies will fight over the remaining 20 percent of the market, but for most object-oriented application developers, it will be a Booch-Rumbaugh-Jacobson world for the remainder of this decade.

As the object paradigm becomes firmly entrenched, the notion of *distributed objects* will become more and more important. If we were all still using dumb terminals attached to massive mainframes, this might not be true; but since the entire computing field is moving rapidly toward networked, client-server architectures, we are beginning to find that *everything* is distributed. Up until now, we've tended to focus on distributing data and programs; but since objects represent the encapsulation of data *and* programs, successful use of the object paradigm requires distribution, too. Accomplishing this will require most organizations to concentrate on the various competing technologies for implementing distributed objects—OLE, SOM, CORBA, etc.—which are far too detailed to discuss in this book.

An exciting new development in the object-oriented field, which is pursued now mostly by the academic and research community but which will enter the mainstream after the basic OO concepts have been assimilated in the next few years, is that of *patterns*. Again, it's not a new idea altogether: I discussed it briefly in *Decline and Fall* and paid homage (as many other have) to architect Christopher Alexander's work from the late 70s [9, 10, 11]. OO methodologists have grabbed the concepts with enthusiasm and have argued that many common software applications (and business models) can be described in terms of "patterns" of objects and class hierarchies that can then be modified to meet specific circumstances. The recently published work of Coad et al. [14] and Pree [29] is a good example of both the practical and the academic perspectives on object-oriented patterns. My advice in this area: If you want to be ahead of the rest of the pack, spend a little less time memorizing the syntax of C++ and Smalltalk and investigate the concept of patterns; it's likely to become a far more powerful form of reuse than what most people practice today.

Of course, reuse is one of the most common justifications for adopting object technology in the first place. But whether it's "patterns" or "class libraries," or "components," object technology is just one technology for implementing what turns out to be largely a management-oriented paradigm. As such, I'll discuss reuse separately below.

3.3 SOFTWARE REUSE

We've known for a long time that reuse can have a dramatic impact on productivity and quality—this, too, was already old news when I wrote about it in *Decline and Fall*—but many IT organizations have concluded that new forms of technology such as OO are required to really make it work. While technology can play an important role in reuse initiatives, the major problem remains the same as it was five years ago: management and cultural resistance. When I asked one programmer at Microsoft about reuse in 1994, his off-the-record answer was fascinating: "Every programmer here," he told me, "firmly believes that he or she is the *only* competent programmer in the place; everyone else is an idiot. Why would you want to reuse code written by idiots?"[8]

After some half-hearted and unsuccessful efforts at implementing reuse initiatives, some organizations have begun a second

---

[8]Whatever your opinion on the matter might be, I want to go on record to say that I don't believe Microsoft is populated by idiot programmers. Also, reuse is practiced to some extent at Microsoft, and when I visited the company in 1994, I could see that the practice was spreading. But it's not because of an edict from Bill Gates: The reuse initiative at Microsoft is a good example of the bottom-up "best practices" approach that I'll discuss in Chapter 6.

attempt by refocusing on the management issues. How do you measure reuse? How do you manage it—e.g., from a project management perspective, a configuration management perspective, and an enterprise-level capital-investment perspective? How do you encourage and motivate members of the IT organization to emphasize reuse—and what's an appropriate mechanism to reward them when they do so? Without answers to these questions, the best object-oriented technology in the world will do little more than facilitate "passive" reuse, which typically hovers at the 15 to 20 percent level in most IT organizations today. There haven't been any radical new management theories about any of this since I discussed it in *Decline and Fall*, but we're beginning to see more and more useful, practical discussions about how to accomplish it; the September 1994 issue of *IEEE Software*, for example, was devoted to the topic of "systematic reuse," as was the August 1993 issue of *American Programmer*, as well as the December 1994 and February 1997 issues of *Application Development Strategies*.

If there has been one exciting development in the field of reuse in the past five years, it's been the growth of a cottage industry of third-party component developers. Many of these small companies and independent consultants are providing class libraries for C++ and Smalltalk, but an even larger number—estimated at over 600 companies by my colleague J. D. Hildebrand—are supporting Visual Basic, which isn't even a full-fledged object-oriented language. For the marketplace, though, such academic concerns are irrelevant: There are hungry consumers who want GUI widgets and VBX controls, many of which can be acquired for $50 or even downloaded as shareware from the Internet.

Why is this approach succeeding? Partly it's because the community of object-oriented enthusiasts are prone to favor reuse anyway, and partly it's because those who surf the Internet love to download and plagiarize anything they can get their hands on. But as mentioned above, Visual Basic hardly qualifies as the ideal language for OO bigots; and many of the commercial transactions involving components have not had anything to do with the Internet. The *real* reason, in my opinion, for the growth in reuse, is simply the business pressure for more rapid development. The people who build client-server GUI applications—whether in Visual Basic, C++, Smalltalk, or assembly language—are typically *very* sensitive to this pressure, and they know that even though it would be more fun to write all the code themselves, it's far more important to have a prototype available to show the user tomorrow morning. Indeed, many of this new breed of application developers don't consider themselves professional programmers (e.g., they'll give you a puzzled look if you ask them where they got their computer science degree), and unlike professional programmers, they may not even get any pleasure from writing their own code. If they could find components to build an entire application, they would do so without a second thought.

So, for small pockets of the software development community, reuse is a fact of life, and it works quite well. But at this level of activity, it's usually ad hoc and personalized, and it doesn't represent any organized effort on the part of the IT organization to develop, maintain, and capitalize on the intellectual asset represented by those reusable components. That's why the formal enterprise-level reuse initiatives remain so important and why they can continue to have such a major impact on productivity and quality. When you see passive-reuse organizations with a 10 percent level of reuse and compare them to aggressive-reuse organizations with 50, 60, or even 80 percent levels of reuse, it's not difficult to see why their overall productivity levels are so different.

3.4 SOFTWARE METRICS

I recommended metrics as a silver bullet in *Decline and Fall of the American Programmer*, and I still do. But it's obvious that most IT organizations haven't done much about the concept: The number of organizations at level 4 or level 5 on the SEI scale (where metrics have been formally incorporated into the software process) hovers around one or two percent. Even the more optimistic assessments, such as Chris Pickering's 1993 technology survey [49], indicate that only about 25 percent of IT organizations have any kind of formal metrics program. Metrics guru Howard Rubin provided the following assessment in his 1993 "black hole" survey of 10,000 MIS professionals:

- Only 1 in 5 companies is measuring anything about the size of their IT asset base—i.e., the portfolio of systems and projects in the organization.
- Only 1 in 30 knows how much its asset base is changing.
- Only 1 in 100 has comprehensive quality data available.

All of these numbers suggest that metrics still aren't being taken seriously in most IT organizations. Does it matter? Another of the country's top metrics gurus, Capers Jones, argues that:

> If your company has no measurement program in place, it will probably be subject to the law of inertia and drift along on its current path until something happens. If what happens is a takeover, bankruptcy, or a loss of market share, then that is just the way things turn out. [47]

If metrics are so important, why aren't people doing more of them? Presumably the most important reason is that IT managers feel it's not crucial or that whatever ad hoc measures they have in place are sufficient. If this seems like an unreasonable assessment, keep in mind that the vast majority of small "Mom-and-Pop" businesses operate with little or no "metrics" about their business other than the macro-level measurements required to file their tax returns every year and the micro-level measurements required to see if they have enough money in the cash register to meet the payroll every week. And the reality is that most software organizations still do business with the same level of sophistication as the owner of the local newspaper shop.

Even the organizations that do recognize the importance of metrics often flounder when they begin, for it's not immediately apparent what they should be measuring. Unlike the owner of the local newspaper shop, who could use a standard chart of accounts for measuring his business and who could find numerous books suggesting what metrics are important to monitor the financial health of a small business, software organizations have no agreed-upon standards in this area. Capers Jones proposed one such chart of accounts in *Applied Software Measurement* [46], and the consulting firms that specialize in metrics practices usually begin their engagements by concentrating on this question.

It's important to realize that technical metrics such as function points or McCabe's cyclomatic complexity metric may have only limited value in a metrics initiative. The key, as Howard Rubin argues, is to identify the key stakeholders and shareholders in a metrics initiative and determine what metrics *they* need to see whether the IT organization is meeting its objectives. Especially for senior management, it's usually crucial to express software metrics in business terms, so that a relationship can be seen between the software activities and such business metrics as revenue, profit, return-on-investment, and so on. Very, very few organizations do a good job in this area, though Paul Strassmann [52] has provided a very thorough foundation for making such business-oriented measurements of the value of IT.

Assuming that the IT organization knows what it needs to measure, the other major problem with metrics initiatives has been the "social" factor. As Bill Hetzel points out in *Making Software Measurement Work* [45]:

> Practitioners' attitudes tend to range from barely neutral to outright antagonistic. It is rare to find the practitioner who really thinks of measurement as a useful and indispensable tool for good software work. Most feel that they get back very little from the measurement activity, and if management would only leave them alone they could get their work done just fine....
>
> The psychological dislike and distrust our practitioners have about measurement is a significant challenge facing us...This must change in the next decade if measurement is to come close to fulfilling its potential.

This has placed a new emphasis on diplomacy and etiquette. As Hewlett-Packard's Bob Grady argued in a recent paper [44] (and which he discusses at greater length in a recent book [43]):

> ...software development is still a very people dependent and creative activity. We do not have automated processes to develop software yet, so people must collect, interpret, and own metrics data.
>
> There is a sensitivity at all organizational levels that we must recognize and accommodate if we expect our data to be useful. Perhaps we need to acknowledge these sensitivities by developing a formal code of behavior, some "rules of etiquette."

The advice should be heeded well by those IT organizations that are just now commencing their first serious metrics initiative. There are appropriate rules of etiquette for technical-level software professionals (e.g., "Don't brag about your metrics, or someone will find a political excuse to find some bad metrics about your work") and management-level people (e.g., "Don't *ever* use metrics to punish people, or they'll stop feeding you metrics data").

As problems like these are overcome and as the drive for SEI-style process improvement continues during the next few years, it's

likely that we'll gradually see more and more companies implementing a reasonably sophisticated set of metrics. Note, by the way, that
this involves an evolution beyond *product*-related metrics, such as the
number of lines of code (or function points) that were developed, and
the defect density per function point, and so on. Instead, the emphasis will shift—as it must, for organizations to reach level 4—to metrics about the *process* that is used to develop the software product.

And as they do this, IT organizations will begin to notice an
interesting phenomenon: What's *really* interesting about the software
process is not the behavior of the individual process activities (such
as analysis, design, coding, and testing) themselves, but rather the
interactions between them. For example, if a defect occurs during the
analysis phase of the process, what are the chances that it will be
detected and corrected *during* the analysis of the process? What percentage of the analysis errors will "leak" downstream to the design
phase or the coding phase? If the analysis error is discovered during
the coding phase, then we'll have to "cycle" back to the analysis
phase to redo the activity correctly; and it's possible that sufficient
time will have passed that it will be difficult to find the analyst and
the end user who did the work in the first place. Even worse, there's
always a chance that the second attempt will be faulty, too, and even
more cycles may be required until the original activity is eventually
done correctly and reaches the very end of the process.

Obviously, a well-tuned metrics initiative will provide lots of
interesting data about all of this. But the point of the parable above is
that there are *time delays* and *feedback loops* between various elements
of the software process (and virtually any other nontrivial process,
too, such as those encountered in a business reengineering project).
These are the key elements of *system dynamics*, which we discuss in
Chapter 4. I mention it here simply to emphasize the point that metrics and system dynamics go hand in hand: If you're planning on
implementing a metrics initiative and you really want to compete
with the best-in-class software organizations around the world,
you're going to need to learn how to build and calibrate a system
dynamics model of your process.[9]

---

[9]When I visited the SEI level-5 Motorola group in Bangalore, India, in July
1994, I presented a summary of the system dynamics version of a software process
model that I'll discuss in Chapter 4. I don't know if they've implemented it yet, but
they clearly understood its significance.

3.5 SUMMARY AND CONCLUSIONS

Each of the topics in this chapter deserves a full book or more. As you'll see from the references at the end of the chapter, several have already been written; but in large part, the fundamentals haven't changed in the past five years. We've gone through five generations of PC hardware technology, we've made an enormous transformation from mainframe-based technology to distributed, client-server, GUI-based systems, and we've made a much-heralded move from Windows 3.1 to Windows 95, but the basic methods, techniques, and strategies that we use for doing all of this are much the same as they were in 1991.

A surprisingly large number of IT organizations and individual software professionals still haven't assimilated those fundamental "best practices." I include individual software professionals in this critique, because, as I discussed in the previous chapter, the breaking of the long-term social contract between employer and employee means that every individual is responsible for his or her own destiny; and that destiny will very much depend on mastery of the such things as process improvement, object-orientation, reuse, and metrics.

My publisher would be delighted, of course, if you decided to buy a copy of *Decline and Fall of the American Programmer* as a basis for learning about the key software practices and techniques for survival in the software industry. But one of the implicit lessons of *this* chapter is that the best IT organizations and the best individuals have already moved on. While the fundamentals haven't changed, the details have. There's a wealth of new information in the references below, and you're going to have to assimilate all of that, too, if you want to keep up with the leaders.

Throughout this chapter, I've also mentioned some new concepts, techniques, and technologies, above and beyond the ones originally discussed in *Decline and Fall*. These include visual programming languages, system dynamics, best-practices initiatives, and personal software processes. These form the basis of the second part of this book...read on!

REFERENCES

Software Process Improvement References

1. Bach, James. "The Immaturity of the CMM." *American Programmer*, September 1994.

2. Curtis, Bill. "A Mature View of the CMM." *American Programmer*, September 1994.

3. Daskalantonakis, Michael K. "Achieving Higher SEI Levels." *IEEE Software*, July 1994, pp. 17–24.

4. Herbsleb, James, David Zubrow, Jane Siegel, James Rozum, and Anita Carleton. "Software Process Improvement: State of the Payoff." *American Programmer*, September 1994.

5. Humphrey, Watts. *Managing the Software Process.* (Reading, MA: Addison-Wesley, 1989).

6. Humphrey, Watts. *A Discipline for Software Engineering.* (Reading, MA: Addison-Wesley, December 1994).

7. Humphrey, Watts. *Introduction to the Personal Software Process.* (Reading, MA: Addison-Wesley, 1997).

8. Paulk, Mark, Charles Weber, Bill Curtis, Mary Beth Chrissis, et al. *The Capability Maturity Model: Guidelines for Improving the Software Process.* (Reading, MA: Addison Wesley, 1995).

Object Technology References

9. Alexander, Christopher, Sara Ishikawa, and Murray Silverstein, with Max Jacobson, Ingrid Fiksdahl-King, and Shlomo Angel. *The Oregon Experiment.* (New York: Oxford University Press, 1975).

10. Alexander, Christopher. *A Pattern Language.* (New York: Oxford University Press, 1977).

11. Alexander, Christopher. *The Timeless Way of Building.* (New York: Oxford University Press, 1979).

12. Booch, Grady. *Object-Oriented Design.* (Menlo Park, CA: Benjamin-Cummings, 1994) ISBN: 0-8053-0091-0.

13. Carmichael, Andy (editor). *Object Development Methods*. (New York: SIGS Books, 1994).

14. Coad, Peter, David North, and Mark Mayfield. *Object Models: Strategies, Patterns, & Applications*. (Englewood Cliffs, NJ: Prentice Hall/Yourdon Press, 1995) ISBN: 0-13-108614-6.

15. Coad, Peter, and Jill Nicola. *Object-Oriented Programming*. (Englewood Cliffs, NJ: Prentice Hall, 1993).

16. Coleman, Derek, Patrick Arnold, Stephanie Bodoff, Chris Dollin, Helena Gilchrist, Fiona Hayes, and Paul Jeremaes. *Object-Oriented Development: The Fusion Method*. (Englewood Cliffs, NJ: Prentice Hall, 1993).

17. Connell, John, and Linda Shafer. *Object-Oriented Rapid Prototyping*. (Englewood Cliffs, NJ: Prentice Hall, 1994).

18. Embley, David W., Barry D. Kurtz, and Scott N. Woodfield. *Object-Oriented Systems Analysis*. (Englewood Cliffs, NJ: Prentice Hall, 1992) ISBN: 0-13-629973-3.

19. Firesmith, Donald G. *Object-Oriented Requirements Analysis and Logical Design*. (Reading, MA: Addison-Wesley, 1993) ISBN: 0-471-57807-X.

20. Goldberg, Adele, and Kenneth S. Rubin. *Succeeding with Objects: Decision Frameworks for Project Management*. (Reading, MA: Addison-Wesley, 1995) ISBN: 0-201-62878-3.

21. Graham, Ian. *Object-Oriented Methods*, 2nd ed. (Reading, MA: Addison-Wesley, 1993).

22. Henderson-Sellers, Brian, and Julian Edwards. *BOOKTWO: The Working Object*. (Englewood Cliffs, NJ: Prentice Hall, 1994).

23. Jacobson, Ivar, et al. *Object-Oriented Software Engineering*. (Reading, MA: Addison-Wesley, 1992) ISBN: 0-201-54435-0.

24. Jacobson, Ivar. *The Object Advantage: Business Process Reengineering with Object Technology*. (Reading, MA: Addison-Wesley, 1994) ISBN: 0-201-42289-1.

25. Lewis, Ted. *Object-Oriented Application Frameworks*. (Greenwich, CT: Manning Publications Co., 1995) ISBN: 0-13-213984-7.

26. Martin, James, and James Odell. *Object-Oriented Analysis and Design*. (Englewood Cliffs, NJ: Prentice Hall, 1992) ISBN: 0-13-630245-9.

27. Martin, James. *Principles of Object-Oriented Analysis and Design.* (Englewood Cliffs, NJ: Prentice Hall, 1993) ISBN: 0-13-720871-5.

28. Meyer, Bertrand. *Object Success: A Manager's Guide to Object Orientation, Its Impact on the Corporation and Its Use for Reengineering the Software Process.* (Englewood Cliffs, NJ: Prentice Hall, 1995) ISBN: 0-13-192833-3.

29. Pree, Wolfgang. *Design Patterns for Object-Oriented Software Development.* (New York: ACM Press, and Reading, MA: Addison-Wesley, 1995) ISBN: 0-201-42294-8.

30. Selic, Bran, Garth Gullekson, and Paul T. Ward. *Real-Time Object-Oriented Modeling.* (New York: John Wiley & Sons, 1994) ISBN: 0-471-59917-4.

31. Taylor, David. *Object-Oriented Technology: A Manager's Guide.* (Reading, MA: Addison-Wesley, 1991).

32. Taylor, David. *Business Engineering with Object Technology.* (New York: John Wiley & Sons, Inc., 1995) ISBN: 0-471-04521-7.

33. Udell, John. "Object Orientation Has Failed." *Byte,* May 1994.

34. Wilkie, George. *Object-Oriented Software Engineering: The Professional Developer's Guide.* (Reading, MA: Addison-Wesley, 1994).

35. Wirfs-Brock, Rebecca, B. Wilkerson, and L. Wiener. *Designing Object-Oriented Software.* (Englewood Cliffs, NJ: Prentice Hall, 1990) ISBN: 0-13-629825-7.

36. Yourdon, Edward. *Object-Oriented Systems Development: An Integrated Approach.* (Englewood Cliffs, NJ: Prentice Hall, 1994).

37. Yourdon, Edward, and Carl Argila. *Case Studies in Object-Oriented Analysis and Design.* (Upper Saddle River, NJ: Prentice Hall, 1996).

38. Yourdon, Edward, Katharine Whitehead, James Thomann, Karin Oppel, and Peter Nevermann. *Mainstream Objects.* (Upper Saddle River, NJ: Prentice Hall, 1995).

Reuse References

39a. Bassett, Paul G. *Framing Software Reuse: Lessons from the Real World.* (Upper Saddle River, NJ: Prentice Hall, 1996).

39b. Betz, Mark. "Enterprise Object Frameworks: Foundations of Reuse." *American Programmer,* November 1995.

39c. Cox, Brad. "'No Silver Bullet' Reconsidered." *American Programmer*, November 1995.

39d. Pfleeger, Shari Lawrence. "Reuse Measurement and Evaluation." *American Programmer*, November 1995.

40. Frakes, William. "Software Reuse As Industrial Experiment." *American Programmer*, September 1993.

41. Lim, Wayne C. "Effects of Reuse on Quality, Productivity, and Economics." *IEEE Software*, September 1994.

42. McClure, Carma. "Reuse: Re-engineering the Software Process." *Managing System Development*, September 1994.

Metrics References

43. Grady, Robert. *Practical Software Metrics for Project Management and Process Improvement*. (Englewood Cliffs, NJ: Prentice Hall, 1993).

44. Grady, Robert. "Software Metrics Etiquette." *American Programmer*, February 1993.

45. Hetzel, Bill. *Making Software Measurement Work*. (QED Publishing Group, 1993).

46. Jones, Capers. *Applied Software Measurement*, 2nd ed. (New York: McGraw-Hill, 1997).

47. Jones, Capers. "Software Measurement: Why, What, When, and Who." *American Programmer*, February 1993.

48. Jones, Capers. *Assessment and Control of Software Risks*. (Englewood Cliffs, NJ: Prentice Hall, 1994).

49. Pickering, Chris. *Survey of Advanced Technology—1993*. Systems Development Inc., Overland Park, Kansas, December 1993.

50. Rubin, Howard. *The Software Engineer's Benchmark Handbook*. (Phoenix, AZ: Applied Computer Research, 1992).

51. Snyder, Terry, and Ken Shumate. "Kaizen Project Management." *American Programmer*, December 1992.

52. Strassmann, Paul. *The Business Value of Computing*. (New Canaan, CT: The Information Economics Press, 1990).

Part Two

REPAVING
COWPATHS

4

SYSTEM DYNAMICS

...to the dismay of executives and customers, technological innovation in the engineering of software has not been matched by a corresponding maturity in the capability to manage the production of software. There continue to be too many project failures...

Recently, it has become more and more evident that in software, product innovation is no longer the primary bottleneck. The bottleneck is project management innovation.

Tarek Abdel-Hamid, "Organizational Learning: The Key to Software Project Innovation," American Programmer, June 1991.

As Tarek Abdel-Hamid argues, perhaps what we need to be really successful in software development is innovative project management, rather than innovative programming languages, software tools, and methodologies. That message is getting a more receptive audience these days, simply because so many IT organizations are finding, the hard way, that the silver-bullet technologies usually don't produce the required miracles.

I discussed this from a different perspective in Chapter 2: Our software development problems are not so much *technical* as they are managerial, social, cultural, and people-oriented. And as we saw in Chapter 2, there are a number of peopleware-oriented approaches that can improve things considerably: recruiting and hiring better people, training and motivating them more effectively, organizing them into productive teams, etc. But the problem is that all of this works within an organizational context—and the organizational "system for building systems" is so complex that we often don't understand how it works. Indeed, quite often it *doesn't* work; the whole IT organization is paralyzed because of the subtle and unexpected consequences of management decisions and policies.

This has occurred despite the noble efforts of many IT organizations to formalize and improve their software processes along the lines of the SEI capability maturity model. As we'll see in this chapter, many of these improvement efforts fail because they fail to take into account the *dynamics* of the process (especially the time delays and the feedback loops) and because they ignore the "soft" processes that play a major role in the real-world behavior of software projects. Hence, there has been a great deal of interest in the past few years in the concept of modeling and simulating the dynamics of such processes.

Indeed, this is a concept that can be applied to a wide spectrum of processes; not only is it relevant for business process reengineering (BPR) projects, but it's even been applied to projects as ambitious as President Clinton's ill-fated proposal for reengineering the U.S. national health-care system. It's also an idea that has been around for a long time; much of the work carried out in the U.S. in this area can be traced back to the pioneering efforts of Jay Forrester [10] at MIT in the early 1960s. But much has changed since then; we now have desktop computers that facilitate instantaneous, interactive model simulation, rather than batch systems with one-week turnaround; we have visual modeling languages, rather than FORTRAN-like languages like DYNAMO, which were difficult for end-users to grasp; and we've applied the general concepts of system dynamics to somewhat smaller, more specific problems than the "global model" project that Professor Forrester and his colleagues at the Club of Rome undertook in the 1960s.

One example of a smaller, more specific problem area is that of software processes. Beginning with the pioneering effort of Tarek Abdel-Hamid [5] at MIT, researchers and process-improvement mavens have been experimenting with the use of system dynamics to achieve a deeper understanding of how the software process *really works* in an organization, in order to have a better chance of improving it. My intention in this chapter is to provide enough of an over-view of these efforts to get you interested. To be a world-class IT organization in the latter half of this decade, I believe that you'll have to start building such models of your own software processes, and the references at the end of this chapter will help you do that.

In the context of this book, system dynamics models for soft-ware processes do not represent a "secret" technology where the U.S. can necessarily claim to be years ahead of its competitors. The salient ideas have been widely published, as indicated by the references at the end of this chapter. I've had a chance to present many of the ideas in this chapter to audiences on five continents, and software develop-ers in many countries have been quite interested in them. Neverthe-less, my experience has been that most of the interesting system-dynamics modeling tools have been developed in the U.S., and most of the ambitious modeling initiatives have been undertaken in the U.S., too. I regard it as a technology like Visual Basic in 1992: widely available in the U.S. first, but likely to spread elsewhere in the next few years.

4.1 MODELS OF SOFTWARE PROCESSES

In the preceding paragraphs, I used the term "model" and "model-ing" eight times, but they probably caused little or no confusion for the average software-oriented reader. Aside from our informal understanding of the term, most of us interpret the word "model" in the context of discussions about software management and software methodologies, in terms of graphical abstractions of software—e.g., data flow diagrams, structure charts, and entity-relationship dia-grams. And in the context of software "processes" and business reengineering, it's quite common to see models in the form of "work-flow" diagrams or flowcharts.

But that's not how most real-world software managers organize their day-to-day activities. When was the last time a project manager said to everyone on his or her team, "Okay, team, let's gather around the conference table to look at our work-flow models to see what we should be doing today?" Indeed, managers *do* use such models to plan and discuss overall strategy, but they use a variety of alternative forms of models to cope with problems and to make the day-to-day operational decisions of running a project. Of these alternative forms, the two most important to discuss are *mental models* and *spreadsheet models*.

4.1.1 Mental Models

A mental model is just what the term implies: a model that one carries around in one's head for dealing with a problem or situation. Such a model may be based on experience or intuition, or on folklore and myth; it may be influenced by politics and a wide spectrum of human emotions. But the key characteristic of a mental model is that it hasn't been written down; and in many cases, it hasn't been articulated in any form and simply represents the "private practice" of software managers as they go about their jobs.

The "official" portions of an organization's software process typically *have* been written down (whether anyone reads them, understands them, or has any intention of following them is an entirely different matter!). Thus, the official model of the software process might say, "First we determine the requirements of our software product, and until those requirements have been accepted by the testing department, detailed design and coding are not allowed to begin—because we want the testing department to be developing testing procedures in parallel with the implementation work, and they can't do that if they don't know what requirements they're supposed to test for." All of this involves some issues that are important and perhaps controversial; and one can imagine constructive discussions taking place where the activities described above are modeled in terms of data flow diagrams or some other mechanism.

But what about the *mental* model that pops up in a manager's head when his programmers arrive in his office one morning, halfway through the project, and glumly announce, "Surprise! We have no idea how this happened, but when we woke up this morning, we figured out that we're six months behind schedule!"? The immediate mental model used by the inexperienced project manager concludes with the action plan: "Hire more people right away!" Why? Because the mental model says something like this: "We need to have more work done within a fixed amount of time, because we can't delay the project deadline. More people will do more work; therefore, the way to get all the required work done is to hire more people."

Of course, many veteran project managers have an entirely different model. They quote, both from their textbook reading of Fred Brooks' *The Mythical Man-Month,* and from their own personal experience, Brooks' Law: *Adding more people to a late software project just makes it later.* Same situation; different mental model. And so the reaction of many project managers is based on another mental model: *We have an infinite amount of unpaid overtime available.* If the project is behind schedule, ask the team to go on a "death march" and begin working heavy overtime.

And in case you think there are only two, here's a third mental model that has been attributed to Charles Wang, the CEO of Computer Associates: If you're behind schedule halfway through the project, cut the project team in half. Darwinian principles will ensure that only the fittest will survive the cut, and those survivors will hunker down and start coding furiously; they won't have any time to attend meetings, write memos, or other time-wasting activities. If you're still behind schedule six months later, cut the project team in half again.

And if you think that one is controversial, here's another mental model from a tough-as-nails project manager who has overseen a number of high-pressure development projects for Wall Street financial services firms. It goes like this: *All* projects are behind schedule— it's just a question of when you discover that fact and how the project team will respond to the discovery. So you might as well plan for it: Create an *extreme* "artificial" crisis in the early days of the project and observe what happens. Predictably, some people will quit because they can't stand the pressure; some will ignore the crisis and continue to work 9-to-5 schedules; some will respond to the pressure in a variety of neurotic or antisocial ways (nervous breakdowns, breaking into tears, bringing a gun into the office, etc.). And some—who often turn out to be the quiet, unassuming members of the project team— will rise up and become heroes, taking charge of the situation and dealing with the crisis.

The Wall Street manager likens the process to a shakedown cruise of a battleship. The artificial crisis allows him to "calibrate" the project team, so he knows how it will respond when the *real* crisis occurs, which it inevitably will. Having accomplished the calibration, he declares the crisis "solved," relaxes the pressure, and continues with the project.

The point here isn't whether you agree or disagree with *any* of these mental models for dealing with a deadline crisis; the real point is that there are probably a dozen variations of these mental models in your own organization and you've never discussed them with your colleagues or fellow project managers. Obviously, all of these models can be discussed in a normal conversation; but you can imagine how heated the debates will become when discussing the "artificial crisis" model, or even the time-honored "death march" model. Instinctively, we all know that the actions suggested by these models have consequences; our instinctive reaction is to shout, "Yeah, but if you do X then Y will happen...and in turn, that will make Z happen..." How can we communicate our ideas about these issues without degenerating into shouting matches? As we'll see later in this chapter, there are now some very powerful *visual* modeling techniques that make rational discussions of these mental models much easier.

There is also an issue of "organizational learning" involved here. Let's assume, for the purposes of discussion, that all of the mental models illustrated above are actually being used within your IT organization. It's reasonable to imagine that some of the mental models work very well and that others are a disaster. It's also quite possible that a crude, primitive mental model has been refined over the years by (successful) veteran project managers, to the point where it's now fairly subtle and sophisticated. How do we pass on this knowledge to fledgling project managers who are about to undertake their first "real" project?[1] Wouldn't it be nice to have a mechanism for discussing and illustrating the key mental models, so that experience could be passed on? How else are we *really* going to accomplish "process improvement" in an IT organization?

There's something else to notice about the examples used above: They would almost never be incorporated in the "official" software process model of the organization, for they deal primarily with "social" issues. As Tarek Abdel-Hamid [1] points out:

> Many studies have indicated that managers often deal with the problems they encounter in terms of mental models that do not

---

[1] As my colleague Tim Lister likes to say, the training we provide for new project managers usually consists of two words: "Good luck!"

necessarily include all the elements or aspects of the problematic situation.

Technically trained managers, in particular, tend to underestimate the influences of their internal social systems. The result is often dysfunctional behavior.

While the "official" components of a software process model—e.g., the choice of a waterfall model versus a prototyping or iterative model—are obviously important, the "soft" issues are just as important. Indeed, they're often *more* important precisely because we don't talk about them. So, if we're going to improve our software processes, we need to have a mechanism for discussing and illustrating, and learning about the "soft" components of the overall software process model.

4.1.2 Spreadsheet Models

What else do project managers use for guiding their projects, besides the "mental models" formed by experience, intuition, or superstition? Obviously, many managers use the PERT charts or Gantt charts provided by today's convenient PC-based project management packages. Indeed, if you walk into a project manager's office, you're likely to find several people huddled around a PERT chart showing the "critical path" for the project; such diagrams do provide a useful and important visualization of key aspects of the project.

But it's also quite common to see project managers hunched over their desk, staring intently at rows and columns of a spreadsheet; it wouldn't be too much of an exaggeration to suggest that Lotus 1-2-3 or Microsoft Excel^{TM} are the most commonly used project management tools in IT organizations. Consider, for example, the spreadsheet shown in Figure 4.1, which shows some planning figures for a hypothetical software development organization. Such a model provides useful information, and most managers would argue that they provide some degree of "insight" into the process (or project, or organization) they are studying. And as everyone knows, a number or formula can be changed in any of the spreadsheet cells, and all of the other cells will be updated appropriately.

Nevertheless, there is a fundamental problem with Figure 4.1: It's *visually static*, in the sense that it hasn't changed between the time you first looked at it a moment ago and the time you've looked at it

FISCAL QUARTER	1	2	3	4	5	6	7	8
CASE Tools ($000)	$75	$75	$75	$75	$75	$75	$75	$75
CASE Training ($000)	$50	$50	$40	$30	$20	$20	$10	$5
Flextime	Y	Y	Y	Y	Y	Y	Y	Y
Raises (%/yr)	0.05	0.05	0.05	0.05	0.05	0.05	0.05	0.05
Office space	$650	$650	$650	$650	$650	$650	$650	$650
Participation	0.7	0.7	0.7	0.7	0.7	0.7	0.7	0.7
Capital budget	$17,495	$17,495	$17,495	$17,495	$17,495	$17,495	$17,495	$17,495
Operating budget	$9,865	$9,678	$9,409	$9,056	$8,620	$8,070	$7,457	$6,769
Backlog (systems)	147	144	141	136	132	126	121	115
Rookies-headcount	45	43	41	39	37	35	34	33
Veterans-headcount	152	154	156	158	160	161	162	163
Development rate	15.19	14.58	14.14	13.72	14.31	14.91	16.01	17.15
Turnover: people quitting	3	4	5	6	5	4	4	3

FIGURE 4.1 TYPICAL SPREADSHEET MODEL FOR PROJECT PLANNING

again just now. While the columns of the spreadsheet clearly imply that the behavior of a software organization *over time* is being modeled, we don't *see* the dynamics in any visual sense. Among other things, we don't see the behavior—which might or might not turn out to be interesting—*between* the "snapshots" represented by the columns for fiscal quarter 1, 2, etc. And if we're dealing with a "pattern" that takes more than eight fiscal quarters to become apparent, we won't see it at all on the spreadsheet.[2]

There's another interesting problem with spreadsheets: Because they're often associated with financial planning activities, we tend to include only the "tangible" things that the "beancounters" in our organizations want to measure—e.g., people, money, workstations and lines of code. As a result, there's a subtle bias against measuring the "soft" factors in a project—e.g., morale, motivation, perceived quality, and accumulated knowledge about a software development methodology.

To illustrate how important this can be, imagine the behavior of a project manager as he watches his team attempt to use a new software methodology—e.g., object-oriented design and programming—on a mission-critical project with a tight deadline. The manager's fundamental question is, "Will my project team accumulate enough knowledge, *quickly enough*, about this new technology, in order to reap enough benefits from the technology to obtain enough of a pro-

---

[2] Obviously, we could add more columns to the spreadsheet, but we rapidly run out of room within the constraints of most printed sheets of paper. We could rotate the paper by 90 degrees and let the columns march down the page, but it's a clumsy solution.

ductivity improvement to finish the project earlier than would have been possible with the conventional technology we were using previously?" If it appears that the team is struggling with the new technology and failing to accumulate knowledge quickly enough, then the new technology can be abandoned before the project is doomed.

"Accumulated knowledge" is a good example of a "soft" factor; while experienced educators might have some more-or-less quantitative metrics in this area, most software project managers would argue that it's not something they can express in inches, gallons, or pounds per square inch. Consequently, many will argue that no attempt should be made to measure it at all, and they ultimately eliminate it as a "real" phenomenon in their planning. But though they may lack some acceptable quantitative metrics, they can tell you whether the project team has a "lot" or a "little" accumulated knowledge, and they can tell you whether it's increasing or decreasing. That's enough to form the basis for a rough, but useful, measurement approach. And it's important: Failing to measure it is equivalent to arguing that it doesn't exist—and yet most managers will agree that the presence or absence of accumulated knowledge *does* matter.

Precisely because such a phenomenon *is* "soft" in nature, we have to treat any associated metrics about it with some healthy caution; it's usually not appropriate to measure such things to three decimal places. But we can use the soft metrics to look for major trends and order-of-magnitude differences in behavior. A very practical question that the project manager might want to ask about the above scenario, for example, is "What would happen to my budget and my schedule if I sent my project team members to some intensive training classes, and as a result they accumulated knowledge about the object-oriented methodologies twice as quickly?"

4.1.3 Static versus Dynamic Models

In the discussion above, I referred to Figure 4.1 as a "visually static" model, but there's a far more important aspect of "static" versus "dynamic" that needs to be discussed. Virtually all of the interesting, nontrivial processes that we're likely to study will have a number of important but subtle interactions between the components of the process, and those interactions change over time. The situation above involving "accumulated knowledge" is one example: It changes on a day-to-day basis, and the manager has to continually reassess it in order to make the best possible decision.

Also important is the nature of the interactions between various components in a process. As my colleague Tom DeMarco once observed in a moment of deep metaphysical insight, "Everything is deeply intertwingled." If we change one component of a system, it's likely to have an impact somewhere else—and the interactions involve time delays and feedback loops. These interactions may have been incorporated into a spreadsheet model, such as the one shown in Figure 4.1, but they're not visible to the casual observer. The interactions are equivalent to relationships between cells in the spreadsheet, and those relationships are expressed by appropriate mathematical formulae embedded in the spreadsheet cells. If we use a spreadsheet package and "click" on a cell, then we can see the formula it contains; but if we look at the spreadsheet as a whole, none of the cell-to-cell relationships are visible.

The combination of several interacting components can cause an interesting "ripple effect" in a software organization. Consider the first two items in Figure 4.1, in which a hypothetical software development organization is investing heavily in CASE tools but spending progressively less money each quarter on associated training. If the CASE tools impose a formal, rigid methodology for which the staff has not accumulated much knowledge, it wouldn't be surprising to see the development productivity *decline* for the first few time periods; indeed, this is indicated near the bottom of Figure 4.1. But in many organizations, when there is a combination of declining productivity and frustration with inability to use new CASE tools, morale plummets. Morale, being a soft factor, wasn't included in Figure 4.1, but it certainly does exist. And when morale goes down, employee turnover goes up—more people are likely to quit.

But here's where things start to get interesting. If people in a software development organization quit, who are the first ones out the door? *The people with the highest productivity!* After all, they're the ones who can get the best job offers, and they're also the ones likely to be most frustrated by the situation in their current environment. As a result of their departure, the *average* productivity in the organization falls further, which drives down morale...which raises the turnover rate...which pushes more of the remaining highly productive people out the door...and the vicious cycle continues, until the organization is left with nothing but zombies who look like cast extras from *Night of the Living Dead*.

If this example sounds too contrived,[3] consider a more mundane example involving project estimating. When estimating a software project, almost all managers add a "safety" factor (otherwise known as a "contingency factor," or a "fudge factor," or various other colorful terms), and they often do this without considering the dynamics involved. But as Abdel-Hamid and Madnick [4] point out, a different safety factor creates a different project. If a project team learns that its manager has published an official project schedule with a safety factor of *zero*, its members immediately modify their behavior by eliminating what they consider "nonessential" work; depending on the nature of the project, this may include documentation, testing, quality assurance, attendance at weekly staff meetings, answering electronic mail, or taking time off to watch their children participate in school events. Conversely, a project schedule with an enormous safety factor leads to "Parkinson's Law": The work expands to fill the available time.

The organizations that have reached level 3, 4, or 5 on the SEI process maturity scale have begun to realize that these issues of "process dynamics" are indeed important. Even if we leave out the soft factors for the moment, the impact of feedback loops and time delays on the process can have an enormous impact on the success of the software process. To use a simple example, consider the impact of defects that are injected into the analysis phase of a classic waterfall software process, but that are not detected until the programming or testing phase. In a formal, rigorous software process, this means that we must "cycle" back to the analysis activity again to fix the defect— and then push the corrected analysis-product forward through design and coding until it reaches the testing step again. Of course, it's possible that the defect-correction activity was faulty, and our testing process may uncover yet another defect...which means that *several* cycles may be necessary before a satisfactory result can "exit" from the testing phase. All of this has a significant impact on the

---

[3] It *is* realistic, by the way—I've seen it on consulting visits in several large Fortune 500 organizations and government agencies. To make matters worse, management often exacerbates the problem by putting more and more pressure on the ever-shrinking staff, insisting that they work long hours of overtime, and so on.

overall "cycle time" of the process, which our software development organizations are striving to improve.

4.2 VISUAL MODELS

If the dynamics of a software process are important, how can we study them? As suggested above, spreadsheets are inadequate, for they don't illustrate the interdependencies and feedback loops between components of a process. Instead, visual models are usually better for illustrating the "holistic" nature of a process; such models invite discussions, comments, and "yes...but..." arguments.

The argument for visual models should not come as a shock to most software professionals, for we have long used visual modeling techniques to illustrate the technical components of the systems we build for our customers. And since a software process could be regarded as the "system for building systems," it makes good sense to use familiar modeling tools such as data flow diagrams, entity-relationship diagrams, object-oriented diagrams, etc., as the basis for modeling a software process.

There's only one problem: All of these familiar graphical notations are *visually static*. With few exceptions, the notations were invented prior to the introduction of modern CASE tools—and as a result, we're accustomed to drawing the pictures on a piece of paper or displaying them on a passive CASE display. When you display a data flow diagram on a typical CASE tool, it doesn't "move"—it doesn't show the dynamics of the underlying process for which it serves as a model. To do that would require animation, which most CASE vendors have never considered.[4]

As a result, the software organizations that are trying to achieve a deeper understanding of their software processes are turning to simulation tools that provide simple, but powerful, mechanisms for representing the dynamics of a system. One such product is iThink[TM], which uses a notation somewhat like data flow diagrams to represent

---

[4] To be fair, the CASE environment from Cayenne Software does have a simulation capability, though the vendor advertises the capability primarily as something useful for modeling the behavior of real-time systems. Interestingly, it has been the object-oriented CASE vendors that have taken the lead in supporting animation in their high-level analysis tools, as I noted in Chapter 3; the OMW® product from Intellicorp is one example of such a product.

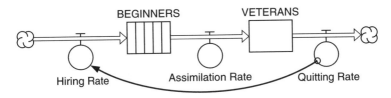

FIGURE 4.2 TYPICAL ITHINK MODEL

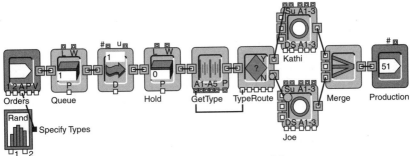

FIGURE 4.3 TYPICAL EXTEND MODEL

a system; a small example is shown in Figure 4.2. Another popular product is Extend™, which uses a somewhat more elaborate notation but also supports simulation and system dynamics; a typical Extend diagram is shown in Figure 4.3.

Obviously, these diagrams are visually static, too, when you see them in a printed book like this. But when displayed on a computer screen, the model-builder has the ability to animate the diagrams by instructing iThink or Extend to run a simulation of the process. In addition to an animation of the diagrams in Figures 4.2 and 4.3, both software packages can produce the usual array of charts and graphs to describe the behavior of key process variables over time.

4.3 SOME EXAMPLES

The syntax of iThink and Extend would fill a book of its own, and the details of building system dynamics models is also a subject unto itself. But while some of the real-world modeling projects have turned out to be enormously ambitious and complicated, it takes relatively little work to become sufficiently familiar with this kind of technology to begin building useful models of the software process. Some examples are provided below.

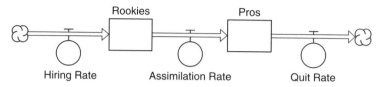

FIGURE 4.4 ABDEL-HAMID AND MADNICK'S
HUMAN RESOURCE MODEL, PART 1

4.3.1 Tarek Abdel-Hamid's Software Process Model

Perhaps the most famous example of a system dynamics model of the software development process has been created by Professor Tarek Abdel-Hamid and published in textbook form by Abdel-Hamid and Madnick [5]. It represents the project management activities in a medium-sized software development project, using conventional development tools and a classic waterfall development process. While it doesn't accurately represent many of today's projects that use rapid prototyping, visual development tools, libraries of reusable components, etc., it nevertheless provides a very important starting point for an organization that wants to better understand the interactions between different components of its software development process.

The model contains components that describe human resource management within a project, as well as software production, testing, quality assurance project control, and project planning. For a full description of the model, including its implementation in a simulation language known as DYNAMO, consult Abdel-Hamid and Madnick [5]. For the purposes of illustration, I'll describe portions of the human resource component of the model.

From the project manager's perspective, the members of the team can be categorized as beginners or veterans; Abdel-Hamid and Madnick use the term "rookies" and "pros," as shown in Figure 4.4.[5] The "dynamics" of the human resource management process involve the hiring of new people, as required, the "assimilation" of rookies into pros as they become experienced, and the eventual departure of

---

[5] It's typically useful to make such a distinction, because the rookies can be presumed to have a different productivity and a different cost (salary, benefits, etc.) than pros.

pros as they quit or die of old age. In the visual notation of iThink, the "clouds" represent the "boundary" of the model; we don't know or care where the rookies come from, nor do we care where the pros disappear to when they leave the project. Project team members "flow" through the "pipelines" represented by the double-lined arrows, and they remain for periods of time in the "reservoirs" represented by the rectangular boxes in Figure 4.4. The "bubbles" attached to the pipelines are "flow regulators," much like a spigot on a water faucet; they control the rate at which items move through the pipelines.

One of the advantages of *any* visual model is that it gives us something to talk about. For example, when considering the model in Figure 4.4, a number of things occur to us:

- We could question the basic assumption implied by Figure 4.4 that all newly hired people are rookies; why not allow for the possibility of hiring experienced "pros"? Abdel-Hamid and Madnick address this issue explicitly by arguing that *all* new members in a project team are rookies, even if they have worked in the software field for 25 years. While the newcomers to the project team may be experts in hardware and software technologies, they typically don't know the nuances of the project itself— e.g., the buzzwords and acronyms, the politics and personalities, and the details of whatever technical work took place before they arrived. However, someone with 25 years of experience will probably be assimilated into the project team much more rapidly than someone who just graduated from college last week; thus, as we'll see below, the "assimilation" regulator in Figure 4.4 is *not* a constant.

- What about the assumption that rookies don't quit? Figure 4.4 clearly implies that rookies either remain rookies forever (if they're trapped within the Rookies reservoir) or they eventually flow through the pipeline and are promoted to the status of Pros; the model clearly shows that only Pros disappear into the clouds. Obviously, this might not be a realistic assumption in some organizations, and the model might have to be adjusted to make it more realistic.

It's important to note that the second issue is one that can be discussed and debated without any consideration of the dynamics—i.e., a traditional data flow diagram, as well as the visually static

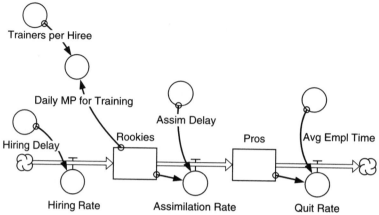

FIGURE 4.5 ABDEL-HAMID AND MADNICK'S
HUMAN RESOURCE MODEL, PART 2

representation of Figure 4.4, is adequate for ensuring that all of the decision-makers in our organization have the same "shared mental model" about how the process of software people entering and leaving the organization.

But the reality of human resource management is actually more complex than shown in Figure 4.4; one level of elaboration is shown in Figure 4.5.

This version of the model shows three "converters" that influence the behavior of the regulators on the pipelines. In a real-world environment, we could imagine that an appropriate means of describing the assimilation rate and the quitting rate might be a "normal distribution"—i.e., a certain percentage of the pros quit almost immediately after entering the Pros reservoir, and a certain percentage remain in the reservoir until they die of old age. If we're willing to accept the notion of a normal distribution, then the parameter that we'll probably want to "play with" is the "avg empl time" that represents the "mean" quitting rate.

But the "hiring delay" bubble in Figure 4.5 represents something entirely different: a time delay. Without describing how it actually works in iThink, think about the reality of what happens in most organizations when the project manager calls the Human Resource department and says, "I need two more programmers for my project." The answer is typically something like, "Okay, fine, that will take three months." Meanwhile, the project has to continue muddling along, and the project manager has to continue worrying about the

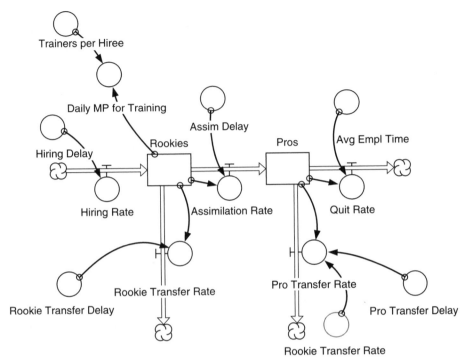

FIGURE 4.6 ABDEL-HAMID AND MADNICK'S
HUMAN RESOURCE MODEL, PART 3

chances he'll meet his deadline. One of the "system dynamics" questions that becomes relevant in such a discussion is, "How would the behavior of the entire project change if the hiring delay imposed by the Human Resource department was only one month instead of three months? What would happen if it were reduced to *zero*?"

Two bubbles in the top-left portion of Figure 4.5 describe another aspect of newly hired people: They need to be trained. When combined with other portions of the overall Abdel-Hamid/Madnick model, we begin to see one aspect of Brooks' Law, which argues that adding more people to a late software project just makes it later: The addition of new people consumes some of the resources of existing staff members, for training purposes.

Figure 4.6 shows a further elaboration of the human resource component of a software-process model: Now we take into account the possibility that staff members may be *transferred* from a project team to some other part of the organization. One might argue that from the project manager's perspective, a "transfer" is no different from quitting; after all, the net result is that the staff member disappears into the clouds. But there is a difference, and it's indicated by the flow-regulators labeled as "transfer delay" on the pipelines emanating from the Rookies and Pros reservoirs. This corresponds to the real-world experience of many managers: When an employee quits, he or she disappears from the team immediately; but if someone tries to "steal" your team members by transferring them out of your team to a different project, you can usually delay the transfer for several weeks or months to ensure that work-in-progress is finished.

Finally, Figure 4.7 shows the complete human resource component of the Abdel-Hamid/Madnick model. The additional components shown in Figure 4.7 address the truly fundamental question that the project manager has to cope with on a daily basis: *How many new people should I hire onto my project team?* This involves a calculation in a different part of the model (one that is not shown here) to determine the "work force level needed," based on the productivity of the existing staff members, how close the project is to the deadline, and various other factors that affect the manager's "willingness" to augment the team. However, the "needed" work force may be limited by various constraints; in the top-right corner of Figure 4.7 is a bubble labeled "ceiling on hires" which involves some calculations about the number of new hires that can be accommodated by "full time equivalent" (abbreviated as FTE) members of the team.

Note also that the "work force gap" bubble serves as an *input* to "rookie transfer rate" and "pro transfer rate" bubbles in Figure 4.7. This reflects the fact that the project manager might determine that he has a surplus of project team members (perhaps because the team was more productive than expected, or because there were fewer defects to correct, etc.), and that he wants to initiate a transfer in order to trim the size of the team.

A common reaction to the model shown in Figure 4.7 is, "Well this is all very interesting, but it's *very* complicated. And I don't see what it has to do with the use of object-oriented technology and the latest programming tools that I'm using to increase productivity in my team." True—but it *does* provide more insight into the dynamics of team members joining and leaving the project team, which can often have just as large an impact on project success as the choice of programming languages.[6] And though Figure 4.7 looks a bit compli-

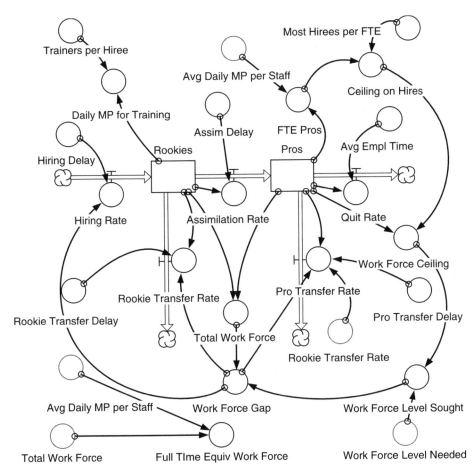

FIGURE 4.7 ABDEL-HAMID AND MADNICK'S
HUMAN RESOURCE MODEL, PART 4

cated at first, the visual notation is straightforward enough to make it digestible after a little study. Finally, keep in mind the consequences of the "head-in-the-sand" reaction to all of this: If the project manager

---

[6] Remember also that I've shown only a small portion of the Abdel-Hamid/ Madnick model here; other subsystems *do* deal with the actual "production" of software, where the project manager can experiment with different assumptions about the productivity impact of the latest whiz-bang CASE tools and programming languages. And other portions of the model also deal with additional "soft" human issues—e.g., what happens if the project manager discovers that he's behind schedule and decides to compensate by asking the project team to work overtime?

decides that the process illustrated in Figure 4.7 is so complicated that he doesn't want to think about it, that doesn't mean that it disappears. These issues exist in real-world projects, whether we want to acknowledge them or not.

4.3.2 Models of Software Maintenance

Figures 4.8(a) and 4.8(b) illustrate a model of an entirely different kind of software process: The process for software maintenance in a large IT department in a telecommunications organization [15]. Figure 4.8(a) shows maintenance requests arriving (note the "cloud" near the top-left corner of the figure) and going through a series of "proposal" and "approval" activities before moving on to the second part of the process in Figure 4.8(b). The second part of the process is a fairly traditional waterfall process of coding, unit testing, subsystem testing, etc.

A quick glance at Figures 4.8(a) and 4.8(b) again conveys the impression that these models are complex—though it should be noted that the full Abdel-Hamid/Madnick model has approximately three times as many variables and is actually far more complex than might be assumed from the brief discussion above. Also, it should be noted that the maintenance model shown in Figures 4.8(a) and 4.8(b) looks complex primarily because it is "flat"—i.e., it was developed in an older version of the iThink modeling tool that did not support the concept of "submodels" (roughly equivalent to the notion of "leveled" data flow diagrams).

And in any case, if the model is complex, it's usually an indication that the underlying process is complex, too; as noted above, the knee-jerk reaction that "this stuff is too complicated to understand" is a tacit admission that the software process is complicated. If that's the case, it *does* make sense to study it, in order to ensure that everyone understands it. And if it really is too complicated to understand, then maybe it should be thrown out and replaced.

In the past, we've attempted to "understand" such models by studying intricate diagrams like Figures 4.8(a) and 4.8(b) closely; but as I've noted several times in this chapter, diagrams like these are *static* representations of a process that is intrinsically *dynamic* in nature. The limitations of a printed textbook preclude any meaningful attempt to demonstrate the dynamics; and those same limitations plague most of our other modeling techniques, as well as the first-generation CASE tools that automated them.

To illustrate the importance of dynamics, look at the "pipelines" and reservoirs in the top-left corner of Figure 4.8(b): They're labeled "systems needing construction modification" and "systems needing requirements modification." This is part of the defect-detection and defect-correction activity that takes place in any real-world software process, regardless of whether the formal model of that process acknowledges it. It's important to note that such defect-related activities involve "cycling back" to an earlier stage of the process and that there can be significant time delays involved; an important study of defense-related software projects by Cooper and Mullen [8] found that an average of *nine months* elapse between the time a defect occurs and the time it is discovered. Furthermore, they found that an average of *seven cycles* of rework were required on many large defense projects to achieve a 95 percent probability of successful completion.

All of this suggests that the dynamic behavior of a software process—including such externally visible characteristics as the overall "cycle time" from the beginning of the process to the final delivery of finished results—can be very sensitive to such things as the defect rate and the time delays involved in detecting and correcting errors. Figures 4.8(a) and 4.8(b) were created as a part of a "real-world" modeling exercise for a large telecommunications firm, and it was startling to discover that if the defect rate was higher than a rather modest threshold, *no successful work-products would ever emerge from the process, no matter how many people were assigned to carry it out.* The dynamics of a high-defect software process are such that bad work will circulate, from the beginning to the end and then back again, forever.

One last point: The model illustrated in Figures 4.8(a) and 4.8(b) required approximately one person-month of effort to produce a demonstrable prototype, and three person-months to refine and expand into a fully developed model. When software processes are modeled in this fashion, the biggest job is usually that of discovering and documenting *what the process really is,* for it often turns out that the "official" software process bears little or no resemblance to the way work is really accomplished; in the case of Figures 4.8(a) and 4.8(b), the model represented an entirely new process that was about to be introduced as part of a process reengineering effort. It's also

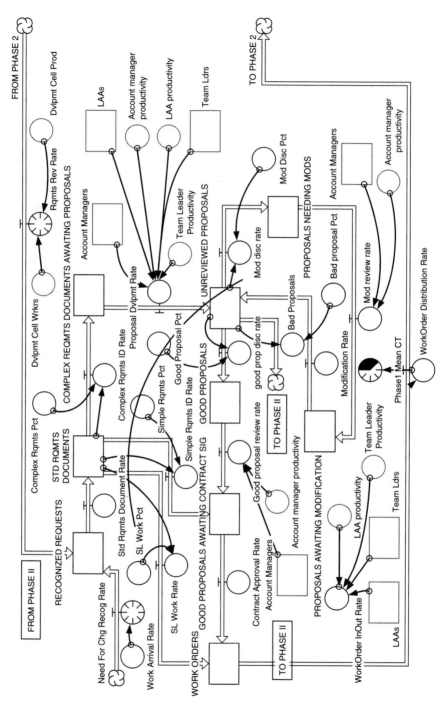

FIGURE 4.8(A) A MODEL OF SOFTWARE MAINTENANCE, PART 1

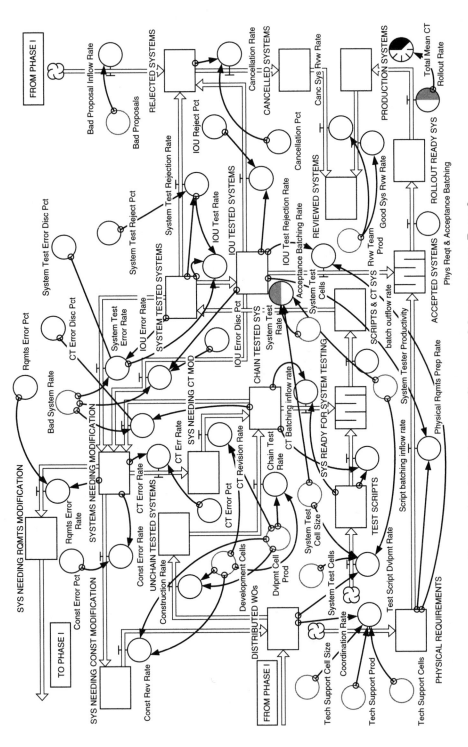

FIGURE 4.8(B) A MODEL OF SOFTWARE MAINTENANCE, PART 2

important to "calibrate" the model by supplying metrics for all of the flow rates and reservoirs; thus, the software metrics activity discussed in Chapter 3 is an essential ingredient for a successful modeling effort.

4.4 WAR GAMES

Assume for the moment that you've developed a system dynamics model of your software process, along the lines of the two examples discussed above. What then?

The primary use of such models is "what-if" planning and process improvement. As noted earlier, such visual representations allow us to capture the "mental models" of the successful project managers, so that a form of "organizational learning" can take place; such a learning process, as discussed by Abdel-Hamid [1], Senge [13], and others, is likely to have a much more fundamental, long-term impact on the IT organization than the short-term "silver bullet" phenomenon of a new programming language or CASE tool. Some commercial products that can help support this learning process include ProjectChallenge from the On Line Knowledge Group within MCI Systemhouse (http://www.systemhouse.mci.com/103e.html) and the project simulators from Fissure (http://www.fissure.com).

A particularly interesting form of organizational learning is the "war game." To the extent that the models discussed in this chapter are accurate and realistic, they can be used as the basis for a simulation of a project or an IT organization; teams of software professionals and/or project managers can then compete against one another, in mock battle, to see who can "win" by finishing their project on time, under budget, with minimal defects, etc. To make things interesting, the models should also contain some "random" events, such as unplanned changes to user requirements, budget cuts, political crises, and perhaps even the unanticipated departure of a key member of the team in the middle of the project. A post-mortem of the war game often serves as a "consciousness-raising" session by allowing the teams to articulate the assumptions and mental models they used when playing the game.

This may seem like an obvious, and therefore rather trivial, strategy—but it's often a surprise for the participants in the war game to see that they have entirely different mental models about issues they regard as "obvious," and that they are all equally convinced that their mental model is the best one. Figure 4.9 illustrates one such set of surprises, based on a war-game that involved 125 people in 19 competitive teams. In this war-game, the software development activities of an entire IT organization were being modeled, and the competitive teams had to decide how much money to allocate for annual salary increases, how much to invest in CASE tools, how much should be spent on training, etc. Nine "rounds" of the simulation were carried out; in each round, decision were made and then entered into the simulation model, and the results were printed out.

As the moderator of the war game, I imposed two rules: First, each team was allowed to see the results of the other teams during all the intermediate rounds of the competition. And second, any team was allowed to change its previous decisions if it decided that it had made a terrible blunder. Under these conditions, I expected that all of the teams would gradually converge on a common set of decisions, since they could recover from their errors and observe the successes of the other teams. Thus, it was quite a surprise to see the final results in Figure 4.9: In most of the categories, there was a 10-to-1 variance between the teams. The fourth column of data in Figure 4.9, for example, lists "PM tools" and represents the amount of money (in thousands of dollars) the team felt they should spend on project-management tools (e.g., tools like Microsoft Project) in a simulated organization with 200 developers. As you can see, team #1 felt that an appropriate expenditure was $400,000 while team #2 spent a miserly $20,000.

Even more surprising was the attitude of the various teams when it came to changing their decisions; indeed, with rare exceptions, *none* of the decisions were modified once they were made, regardless of the observed results of the other teams. The *only* category that was subject to constant change—indeed, different values were introduced in each of the nine rounds—was the decision about annual salary increases.

4.5 SUMMARY AND CONCLUSIONS

As noted in Chapter 3, many organizations are focusing on "process improvement" to achieve significant gains in productivity and quality; such efforts typically involve the SEI capability maturity model (CMM) or the ISO-9000 model. If your organization is still building conventional software applications, then the SEI-CMM can serve as

CASE War Games Cumulative Results at end of Round 9, with team-specified model changes

	Raises (%)	Office Cost	Partici-pation	PM tool K $$	PM Train $	PM Change	Mthdlg Tool $	Mthdlg Train $	Mthdlg Cust $$	Repoz-Tool $$	Repoz-Train $$
T01	5.0%	$810	1.00	400	1500	0.75	3000	1500	200	800	300
T02	2.0%	$1,050	0.85	20	100	0.80	1200	800	500	350	100
T03	4.0%	$700	0.75	200	300	0.95	1000	1500	200	0	0
T04	1.0%	$1,055	1.00	40	300	0.90	1000	1000	100	0	0
T05	2.0%	$950	0.95	200	200	0.30	1000	800	50	400	200
T06	3.0%	$900	0.90	200	150	0.80	1500	1000	0	300	350
T07	5.0%	$1,001	0.80	15	100	0.70	550	600	10	150	75
T08	1.0%	$1,000	0.95	50	750	0.50	4000	3000	1500	0	100
T09	3.0%	$900	0.65	40	60	0.95	3000	1760	500	60	100
T10	2.0%	$1,000	1.00	200	2000	1.00	1500	2000	500	800	500
T12	2.0%	$950	0.70	300	500	0.80	1000	2000	1000	100	50
T13	2.0%	$900	0.90	75	100	0.70	1500	1500	100	50	100
T14	2.0%	$1,000	1.00	100	200	0.80	1500	2000	100	250	500
T15	3.0%	$1,000	1.00	100	300	0.70	700	2300	200	400	1600
T16	2.0%	$1,200	1.00	200	500	1.00	2000	3000	250	200	300
T17	2.5%	$1,100	0.90	100	300	0.73	1000	2000	100	100	100
T18	2.0%	$950	1.00	40	25	0.85	1600	960	40	50	30
T19	1.0%	$1,000	0.75	100	50	0.30	1000	100	0	100	10
T20	2.0%	$950	0.55	60	1000	0.80	3000	1500	50	750	200
Avg	2.4%	$969	0.88	128	444	0.75	1634	1543	284	256	243

	Metrics Tools $$	Metrics Train $$	Metrics Group	SQA Tool $$	SQA Train $$	SQA Group	Reuse Tool $$	Reuse Train $$	Reuse Group	Size of Library	Re-Eng Tool $$	Re-Eng Train $$
T01	700.0	200	3.0	1600	500	5.0	500	300	3	400	600	400
T02	50.0	50	2.0	50	500	2.5	50	100	2.5	500	100	100
T03	100.0	30	3.0	10	140	3.0	50	250	2	500	100	150
T04	70.0	200	3.0	75	350	4.0	50	100	3	500	0	0
T05	10.0	5	2.0	100	600	3.0	200	300	10	1000	80	40
T06	100.0	55	3.0	50	500	3.0	150	250	10	750	300	50
T07	1.0	0.5	2.5	3	1.5	3.0	10	15	5	800	100	50
T08	75.0	25	4.0	100	250	5.0	10	10	2	300	0	10
T09	30.0	30	3.0	40	30	3.0	30	20	1	200	300	100
T10	300.0	300	3.0	500	1000	5.0	200	1500	3	500	500	500
T12	75.0	125	3.0	250	500	3.0	150	200	4	750	25	25
T13	75.0	100	3.0	75	100	3.0	100	200	5	500	50	100
T14	150.0	100	3.0	5	200	2.0	10	100	2	400	200	20
T15	600.0	1800	5.0	10	100	1.0	0	100	2	500	10	20
T16	100.0	200	3.0	200	400	3.0	200	400	4	100	100	200
T17	75.0	100	2.0	250	500	3.0	200	400	4	500	100	200
T18	10.0	6	2.0	10	6	3.0	30	20	4	1000	30	20
T19	100.0	10	2.0	500	1000	3.0	500	100	5	500	0	0
T20	0.5	100	2.0	300	1000	10.0	100	500	30	750	1000	1000
Avg	###	181	2.8	217	404	3.6	134	256	5	550	189	157

FIGURE 4.9 RESULTS OF A SYSTEM DYNAMICS WAR GAME

	Q turn-over (people)	percentage turnover (ANNUAL)	Rookies remaining in Q 20	Veterans remaining in Q 20	CASE Capi-tal $$ in Q 20	Develop. Budget in Q 20	Backlog in Q 20	What Quarter does backlog disappear?
T01	2	5.50%	4	148	9050	7376	18	12
T02	2	7.30%	3	149	16430	13194	18	12
T03	2	8.10%	21	147	16170	10043	41	30
T04	2	5.90%	2	148	16815	15399	18	11
T05	2	6.30%	8	148	15865	13440	18	15
T06	2	6.70%	12	148	15045	11562	18	16
T07	2	7.50%	0	146	18329	4369	18	11
T08	2	5.90%	4	148	11620	15355	18	12
T09	3	9.20%	27	137	14400	12618	18	19
T10	2	5.80%	0	148	8200	13766	18	10
T12	3	8.80%	21	137	14700	14332	18	17
T13	2	6.80%	10	148	15875	13711	18	16
T14	2	5.70%	2	148	14665	13375	18	11
T15	2	5.70%	0	148	9160	11632	18	10
T16	1	5.30%	0	147	12000	10404	18	8
T17	2	6.65%	2	148	14575	10670	18	11
T18	2	5.70%	0	152	17163	12328	18	12
T19	2	7.90%	12	148	16430	15224	18	16
T20	2	8.30%	24	144	9490	13618	88	when hell freezes over
AVG	2	6.79%	8	147	13999	12232	23	14

T01	productivity improvmts: 15% for PM, 17% for Meth, 1% for Repoz, 10% Metrics, 15% SQA, 2% Reuse & Re-Eng
T02	allowed hiring of veterans = 20% of rookies hired
T03	productivity improvmts: 15% for PM, 17% for Meth, 1% for Repoz, 10% Metrics, 15% SQA, 2% Reuse & Re-Eng
T04	no changes requested
T05	no changes requested
T06	reusable components can be created in one month, instead of taking 3 months
T07	rookies turn into veterans in one quarter; as a result, rookies vanish in Q 12
T08	no changes requested
T09	no changes requested
T10	reusable components created in 1 mo, instead of 3 mo—NO EFFECT NOTED, possibly inadequate tool $$
T12	meth customizing $$ double productivity impact of methodology—NO EFFECT NOTED
T13	no changes requested
T14	reusable components created in 1 month instead of 3 months—NO EFFECT NOTED
T15	max productivity improvement with no training reduced to 30%—NO EFFECT NOTED
T16	Rookies eliminated, company hires only veterans
T17	T17 asked for organizational "rate of learning" factor—too hard to implement at this time
T18	rookies turn into veterans in 6 quarters instead of 10
T19	training now has twice the impact on productivity increase of each type of tool
T20	NO CHANGES REQUESTED TO MODEL
AVG	

FIGURE 4.9 CONTINUED

an excellent road map for the transition from anarchy (level 1) to a repeatable process (level 2) to a formal, defined process (level 3).

But once the organization has reached level 3 and has begun focusing on the metrics activities associated with level 4, it makes eminently good sense to augment the effort with an investment in the kind of system dynamics models discussed in this chapter. And it should be regarded as an ongoing investment: The initial model will inevitably be a crude one, but it can be refined and "polished" until it becomes a highly sophisticated planning and experimentation tool for the organization.

REFERENCES

1. Abdel-Hamid, Tarek. "Organizational Learning: The Key to Software Management Innovation." *American Programmer*, June 1991.

2. Abdel-Hamid, Tarek. "Thinking in Circles." *American Programmer*, May 1993.

3. Abdel-Hamid, Tarek, and Stuart E. Madnick. "Impact of Schedule Estimation on Software Project Behavior." *IEEE Software*, May 1986.

4. Abdel-Hamid, Tarek, and S. E. Madnick. "Lessons Learned from Modeling the Dynamics of Software Project Management." *Communications of the ACM*, December 1989.

5. Abdel-Hamid, Tarek, and Stuart E. Madnick. *Software Project Dynamics: An Integrated Approach.* (Englewood Cliffs, NJ: Prentice Hall, 1991).

6. Aranda, Rembert, Thomas Fiddaman, and Rogelio Oliva. "Quality Microworlds: Modeling the Impact of Quality Initiatives over the Software Product Life Cycle." *American Programmer*, May 1993.

7. Chichakly, Karim J. "The Bifocal Vantage Point: Managing Software Projects from a Systems Thinking Perspective." *American Programmer*, May 1993.

8. Cooper, Kenneth G., and Thomas W. Mullen. "Swords and Plowshares: The Rework Cycles of Defense and Commercial

Software Development Projects." *American Programmer*, May 1993.

9. Diehl, Ernst W. "The Analytical Lens: Strategy-Support Software to Enhance Executive Dialog and Debate." *American Programmer*, May 1993.

10. Forrester, Jay. *Industrial Dynamics*. (Cambridge, MA: MIT Press, 1961).

11. Lin, Chi Y. "Walking on Battlefields: Tools for Strategic Software Management." *American Programmer*, May 1993.

12. Richardson, G.P., and G.L. Pugh III. *Introduction to Systems Dynamics Modeling with Dynamo*. (Cambridge, MA: MIT Press, 1981).

13. Senge, Peter M. *The Fifth Discipline: The Art and Practice of the Learning Organization*. (New York: Doubleday, 1990).

14. Smith, Brad, Nghia Nguyen, and Richard Vidale. "Death of a Software Manager: How to Avoid Career Suicide Through Dynamic Software Process Modeling." *American Programmer*, May 1993.

15. Variale, Tony, Bob Rosetta, Mike Steffen, Howard Rubin, and Ed Yourdon. "Modeling the Maintenance Process." *American Programmer*, March 1994.

16. Yourdon, Edward. "Simulating Software Projects." *Application Development Strategies*, March 1997.

5

PERSONAL SOFTWARE PRACTICES

Personality is only ripe when a man has made the truth his own.

Søren Kierkegaard, The Journals of Søren Kierkegaard: A Selection, *no. 432 (edited and translated by Alexander Dru, 1938).*

As I pointed out in Chapter 3, the Software Engineering Institute's Capability Maturity Model (SEI-CMM) has had a remarkable impact on many large software organizations by focusing their attention on the concept of "key processes" for achieving improvements in productivity and quality. The original CMM described by Watts Humphrey [3] has been refined and updated [6] after an exhaustive review, and is now in active use in hundreds, if not thousands, of software development organizations around the world.

But I also noted in Chapter 3 that the CMM has many critics, especially those that believe that it fails to meet the needs of software development organizations which operate in what James Bach [1] calls a "mad world." Bach's criticism has been rebutted by defenders like Bill Curtis [2], but the debate continues—and while it does, the

CMM tends to be used primarily in the larger IT organizations whose culture is comfortable with methodologies and formal processes; and it tends not to be used in the smaller consulting firms and software-product companies. Some of these smaller organizations revel in the notion of being "cowboys" with more emphasis on individuality and creativity than on an externally imposed process discipline; but as we will see in Chapter 7, the cowboy approach has evolved into a serious discipline known as "good-enough" software.

But many consulting firms and "body-shop" companies have a very different objection to the SEI-CMM. They frequently work on software development projects for a client organization, and they are well aware of the importance of meeting deadlines and budgets; and for competitive reasons, they very much want to improve their productivity and quality. The problem is that they don't have the resources to invest in the additional time, people, and planning associated with the SEI's process improvement approach. Having started and run several small businesses myself, I know that the problem is not restricted to software-oriented planning: Small companies often lack experience, the knowledge, the capital, and the non-financial resources to do *any* kind of serious, long-term planning; "long-term" means "after next week," or "when this contract is over and we really *will* do some serious planning."

Even within a large organization, there is often a hesitation to embark upon an SEI-style process improvement effort—especially in the small project teams that have sprung up within the end-user departments to develop Visual Basic applications in a rapid-prototyping fashion. If you're the project manager of such a project—and especially if your project team is embedded within a larger level-0 IT organization[1]—you probably don't have the time or the energy to embark upon a formal process-improvement initiative. The up-front investment in time and effort probably won't be appreciated by the end-user, and a cursory examination of the formal SEI processes often reveals the existence of processes that are relevant only if the entire IT organization follows them.

---

[1] In case you haven't heard of "level-0," it's an informal and unofficial characterization of the IT organizations that haven't even heard of the Software Engineering Institute and its five-level process maturity model. Wags have even proposed a level "-1" for the organizations that are philosophically opposed to the concept of levels.

5.1 THE CONCEPT OF PERSONAL SOFTWARE PROCESSES

These issues are not new; they've been discussed since the SEI model was first introduced in the late 1980s. As Watts Humphrey points out [5]:

> Many viewed the CMM as designed for large organizations and did not see how it could be applied to individual work or to small project teams.... The SEI thus started a process research project to examine ways individual software engineers could apply level-5 process principles. After several years of research, means were devised to adapt 12 of the 18 CMM key process areas to the work of individual software engineers.

The result is an important new process-improvement model, known as the *personal software process*, or PSP. Humphrey has described it in two recent books [4, 7], the first of which is 789 pages long and filled with intimidating mathematical equations. But if you believe software development is something more serious than extemporaneous coding in Visual Basic, then this is definitely a book that you need to understand, and whose advice and guidance you need to follow. At the time *this* book was being written, Humphrey's new text had been available for nearly a year; I've been rather distressed to see how few American software professionals are aware of it, and I'm hopeful that it will gradually become part of the "public consciousness" of the U.S. software industry. Of course, there's nothing to prevent the software industry in other parts of the world from grabbing Humphrey's new ideas, too; the only thing that may help us here is the preference that many non-U.S. software firms seem to have for the ISO-9000 process improvement model. Having seen the vintage-1989 version of the SEI-CMM and rejected it in favor of ISO-9000, there's some chance that our competitors may remain oblivious of the evolutionary improvements represented by version 1.1 of the SEI-CMM (as documented in textbook form in [6], and which is also available on the Internet[2]); and there's a somewhat greater chance they may remain completely unaware of Humphrey's important new work.

---

[2] To find a discussion of the SEI-CMM on the World Wide Web, point your browser at http://www.sei.cmu.edu/technology/cmm.html

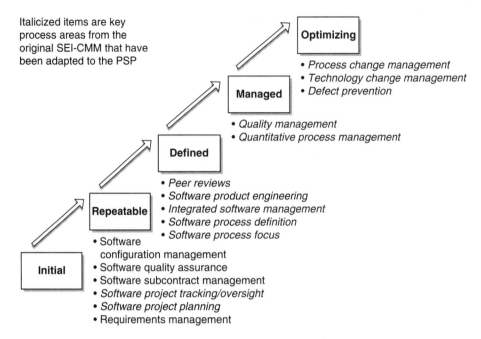

Italicized items are key process areas from the original SEI-CMM that have been adapted to the PSP

Optimizing
- *Process change management*
- *Technology change management*
- *Defect prevention*

Managed
- *Quality management*
- *Quantitative process management*

Defined
- *Peer reviews*
- *Software product engineering*
- *Integrated software management*
- *Software process definition*
- *Software process focus*

Repeatable
- Software configuration management
- Software quality assurance
- Software subcontract management
- *Software project tracking/oversight*
- *Software project planning*
- Requirements management

Initial

FIGURE 5.1 KEY PROCESSES IN THE PERSONAL SOFTWARE PROCESS

To understand what the PSP is all about, refer to Figure 5.1, which shows the five stages of the original SEI-CMM, with the 18 key process areas. To reach the "repeatable" level, or level 2, for example, an organization needs to implement such key processes as software configuration management, software quality assurance, software subcontract management, and requirements management. But as noted earlier, in many software projects, these activities are beyond the ability and the "charter" of the individual software professional and perhaps even the project manager: They only exist, and are only carried out in a repeatable fashion, if the organization defines the processes and assigns people and resources to carry them out.

But software project planning and software project tracking/oversight—two of the processes shown in Figure 5.1—are areas where personal processes *are* meaningful for the one-person project or for the activities of an individual within a larger project. Equally important, within the framework of Humphrey's PSP, they can be measured and monitored from a mathematical, statistical perspective. This kind of careful measurement and monitoring of one's own individual processes becomes the basis for improvement.

Here are a few other examples of processes that can be defined, formalized, standardized, measured, and improved—all on a personal basis:

- *Peer reviews* (level 3)—can be arranged and organized with your peers, on your own initiative; and they can be standardized as part of the activity for *everyone* within a small project team. Obviously, you have to decide for yourself that this is useful and worthwhile, but once you've made this decision, you can probably proceed without the approval or knowledge of the rest of organization—though I do know one project team that was forced to conduct all of its informal peer-level code reviews at the neighborhood pub, because the project manager was determined to use the discovery of each new bug as an opportunity to punish the programmer who created it. One of the obvious questions here is: How would you know, objectively, whether the time and effort invested in reviews and inspections are cost-effective for your work? That's where the notion of personal-level metrics becomes crucial; I'll discuss this in more detail below.

- *Software process definition and focus* (level 3)—you can define and document your own process, i.e., the process that you have been following. This assumes that you *do* have some kind of rational process for developing software, as opposed to the creative approach that says, "I have absolutely no idea how my software is created; I just sit at my workstation and wait for divine inspiration." It's pretty hard to improve if you don't have a good idea of what you're doing. The key point here is that the emphasis and focus of the software developer shifts away from the product (e.g., "How many lines of code did I write today?") to the process ("How did I go about creating that code? What were the steps I followed?").

- The process followed by an individual does *not* have to be a "brand-name" methodology from some famous textbook author. It does *not* have to be the version of information engineering or object-oriented analysis or structured design associated with some vendor's CASE tool. It may be an amalgamation of all of these concepts, or it might be something entirely unique that you've developed over the years. What matters is that it be organized and followed consistently; and within the framework of the PSP, what really matters is that its activities be measured and subjected to constant improvement.

- *Quality management and quantitative process management* (level 4)—i.e., documenting, measuring, keeping track of your own "cost of quality" (COQ) as the basis for improvement. Humphrey argues that COQ has three components: failure costs (the costs of diagnosing a failure, making necessary repairs, recompiling, re-testing the software, and getting back into operation), appraisal costs (the costs of evaluating the product to determine its quality level, including design/code reviews and inspections), and prevention costs (the costs associated with identifying the causes of the defects and the actions taken to prevent them in the future).

"Failure costs" are part of the everyday life of a typical programmer: Bugs have to be identified and tracked down when a program aborts or produces the wrong output or behavior. Modifications to the original program have to be made, and the modified program has to be compiled and tested again. Programmers may have an intuitive sense of how much or how little effort goes into these tasks, but they rarely measure these tasks carefully; part of the PSP is concerned with focusing attention on all of this, so that it becomes evident whether significant improvements are needed. To simplify the record-keeping of a PSP initiative, Humphrey suggests that "because the defect-free compile and test times are typically small compared to the defect-present times, they are included in failure costs."[3]

Similarly, "appraisal costs" involve such everyday activities as testing and prototyping, as well as the more controversial activities of inspections and walkthroughs. But while some programmers might complain that walkthroughs take a lot of time, there is rarely any conscious measurement of the actual effort involved or whether that effort might have been preventable by spending more time in preliminary analysis and design activities.

Similarly, prevention costs are rarely measured, and often involve little more than some casual thinking along the lines of,

---

[3] *A Discipline for Software Engineering*, page 281.

"Next time, I'll have to remember not to make that stupid mistake."

- *Process change management* (level 5)—an organized strategy for using feedback from level-4 management to accomplish changes and improvements to one's own process. When these efforts are carried out by the entire IT organization, they can involve concepts as advanced and sophisticated as the system dynamics models discussed in Chapter 4. But they can be carried out at the individual level, too—either in the form of incremental process improvements or by making substantial changes to one's methodological approach. An example of a "substantial change" might be the decision to begin using a new methodology such as object-oriented design; this may entail a considerable investment in reading textbooks, attending training seminars, and practicing with unfamiliar ideas, before they become well entrenched.[4]

- *Technology change management* (level 5)—an organized strategy for determining when and how to inject new technology (e.g., CASE tools, visual programming languages, object technology) into your own software development process. Of course, if the entire organization is at level 5, then this issue would be part of an organizational strategy; but as we know, most organizations are still languishing at level 1 or level 2, so the technology change is typically haphazard, arbitrary, and disconnected from the personal needs and the personal process of the individual software engineer. Indeed, many organizations have such a large capital investment in older technology that they are reluctant to upgrade and begin using the newest tools, languages, operating systems, and workstations. A self-employed consultant can make his own decisions about when, where, and how to

---

[4] In 1994-95, I published a monthly newsletter called *Guerrilla Programmer*, which argued that many software professionals must take responsibility for their own professional advancement in areas like these, because their employers are unwilling or unable to do so, or (in the worst case) simply unaware of the changes taking place around them. During this period, I received hundreds of e-mail messages from software professionals around the world who confirmed my opinion, and who told me that in many cases, they had been forced to invest their own time and effort in learning new methods and techniques because their employers were actively opposed to such new ideas!

make such investments; and the individual software professional in a large organization may also have some flexibility when it comes to introducing new tools (after all, if the organization is really at level 1 on the SEI scale, anarchy prevails anyway!). And most commonly, the project leader on a small application development project has a considerable degree of latitude—especially in many of today's organizations, where "downsizing" and "empowerment" are in vogue—when it comes to introducing the best technology to fulfill the project requirements.

• *Defect prevention* (level 5)—a measured, controlled effort to modify one's software development process to prevent errors from occurring, rather than investing more effort in testing the software to find the errors after they have been inserted. An example of this is a process called causal defect analysis (which I discussed in detail in *Decline and Fall of the American Programmer*): During walkthroughs and inspections, the software engineer can stop after each defect has been discovered and ask, "How did this defect occur? What was it about the process that made it happen?" Supported with appropriate metrics, this provides the basis for formal "feedback" to modify the process to prevent such errors from occurring again.

5.2 THE PRACTICALITY OF THE PSP

Does the PSP concept work? Humphrey's experiments with veteran software professionals, summarized in his *American Programmer* article [5] and shown in Table 5.1, are impressive; again, remember that these are improvements experienced by individuals, not by the organization as a whole. Perhaps that's why the reaction from some of the software engineers who have gone through Humphrey's training and put the ideas into practice is, "I'm doing this for me, not for the organization."

Of course, that doesn't mean that it's easy to introduce a PSP approach—just as most of us find that it's not easy to introduce a sense of discipline in other aspects of our daily lives, such as proper diet and exercise. As Humphrey observes: [5]

TABLE 5.1   Improvement Statistics from Watts Humphrey's
PSP Experiments

Measurement Area	Group A	Group B	Group C	Group D
Productivity improvement	82.4%	22.9%	136.0%	61.6%
Defect reduction	53.4%	45.8%	55.1%	80.1%

...the problem is compounded by the fact that software engineers are rarely able to experiment. Everything they do is for delivery on a short and demanding schedule. An experiment would thus entail considerable risk. Not surprisingly, their reaction is to defer experimenting with new methods until they have some free time. Unfortunately, they never seem to have free time.

And the problem is compounded further by the imposing formality that surrounds the published PSP approach; as noted earlier, Humphrey's textbook is too long to read casually during the weekend, and the mathematics are likely to overwhelm those who can barely remember their college calculus courses.[5] But there *is* hope: PSP has been deliberately packaged as an educational offering, and I am optimistic that it will gradually be introduced in university courses and industry-oriented training for software professionals. To assist in that effort, Humphrey [5] points out that:

If you're an educator, it's also worth noting that additional support materials are available. A support diskette is available for the modest price of $14.95; it contains copies of the forms illustrated in the book, plus data analysis spreadsheets for the exercises. An instructor's guide and instructor's diskette are also available, with notes, lecture slides, and spreadsheets to review and analyze student data.

Even if you overcome the problem of finding the time to learn the PSP, there are likely to be other difficulties—especially the cul-

---

[5] To avoid discouraging you completely, I should point out that much of the mathematics is deferred until the appendices—and the appendices fill the last 300 pages of the book. That still leaves 486 pages of serious reading, but the determined software professional can manage a first reading in one or two weekends. Nevertheless, a full mastery of the PSP is likely to require a one-week intensive seminar, and possibly even a one-semester university course. If you don't have time for such a full-scale effort, consider reading Humphrey's *Introduction to the Personal Software Process* [7], which summarizes the concepts in 278 pages.

tural and political problems that we all face in our organizations. Naturally, it's easier to engage in a personal-improvement campaign if the rest of the organization is also involved in a similar effort; in simple terms, PSP is likely to be more successful in an organization that has reached level 2 on the SEI scale than in the level-1 shop. As Humphrey notes:

> When you are the only person using a PSP, your biggest problem will be maintaining a consistent discipline. This is hard to do under the best conditions, and it is particularly difficult to do by yourself. While your peers will likely be interested in what you are doing, they also will be skeptical. Normal statistical fluctuations will take on greater significance and the occasional poor results, instead of being a learning experience, will seem like a major reverse. Your friends may laugh at your discomfort and you will likely regret ever discussing the PSP. If you are not sure of the PSP's benefits, you could have trouble continuing to use it without support. Hence your initial focus should be on building a performance record. Don't worry about convincing anybody else of the value of the PSP until you have convinced yourself.[6]

And for the project leader who wants to introduce a PSP process within the project team, there are similar obstacles and problems to overcome. As Humphrey notes:

> The PSP is not something people can pick up casually. Unless there is strong motivation to do the work, few will be able to do it...

> If there is interest in your organization in introducing the PSP, insist that it be done as part of the job. It should be a team commitment with an instructor, allocated time, assigned support, and an established schedule. The managers must be involved and the PSP must be treated as an important job commitment. Engineers quickly learn to concentrate their energies on what their managers are interested in and they judge their managers' interest by what they ask about. To motivate the engineers to do the PSP work, the managers should ask them about it at least once a week.[7]

---

[6] *A Discipline for Software Engineering*, page 474.
[7] *A Discipline for Software Engineering*, page 475.

5.3 SUMMARY AND CONCLUSIONS

As you can imagine, the complete details of the PSP would require a far more elaborate discussion than I've provided in this brief chapter—but rather than providing more details by doubling the length of this chapter, I would prefer that you get your hands on a copy of Humphrey's book and digest all of the details yourself. The full PSP includes detailed suggestions for:

- Baselining your existing personal software process.
- Developing a planning process for your software development.
- Measuring software size as part of the planning process.
- Estimating software size in advance.
- Estimating the required schedule and resources for software.
- Conducting appropriate measures of one's process.
- Conducting meaningful design and code reviews.
- Performing software quality management.
- Performing software design in a more formal fashion.
- Verifying the design, using methods such as object state machines, program tracing, etc.
- Scaling up the PSP to larger problems.

Whether any of this will seep into the organizational consciousness of large IT organizations is debatable—but it's also irrelevant to some extent, for this is a personal software process. As Humphrey argues at the end of the formal presentation of the PSP:

> ...When you trust your life to someone, you want them to behave professionally.
>
> Now consider your professional life. Should you entrust it to someone who is out of date? If you were looking for career guidance, would you ask someone who had not cracked a technical book since college? Probably not. The skill, knowledge, and ability you bring to your job will determine your future. Your future is in your hands.[8]

Amen!

---

[8] *A Discipline for Software Engineering*, page 485.

REFERENCES

1. Bach, James. "The Immaturity of the CMM." *American Programmer*, September 1994.

2. Curtis, Bill. "A Mature View of the CMM." *American Programmer*, September 1994.

3. Humphrey, Watts. *Managing the Software Process.* (Reading, MA: Addison-Wesley, 1989).

4. Humphrey, Watts. *A Discipline for Software Engineering.* (Reading, MA: Addison-Wesley, 1995).

5. Humphrey, Watts. "A Personal Commitment to Software Quality." *American Programmer*, December 1994.

6. Paulk, Mark, Charles Weber, Bill Curtis, Mary Beth Chrissis, et al. *The Capability Maturity Model: Guidelines for Improving the Software Process.* (Reading, MA: Addison-Wesley, 1995).

7. Humphrey, Watts. *Introduction to the Personal Software Process.* (Reading, MA: Addison-Wesley, 1997).

6

BEST PRACTICES

Custom, then, is the great guide of human life.

David Hume, An Enquiry Concerning Human Understanding, *sct. 5, pt. 1 (1748).*

A few years ago, one of my children asked for a tennis racket for his birthday. It sounded like a reasonable request, except that he had his heart set on a particular racket endorsed by tennis star Andre Agassi. Aside from the fact that it was substantially more expensive than the "plain-vanilla" racket I had intended to buy, it wasn't available in any of the local neighborhood stores. Exasperated, I made the awful mistake of telling my son that it really didn't matter which racket I bought him, since he was only 11 and couldn't play very well anyway. He burst into tears, and a minor family crisis ensued; I eventually gave in and bought the Agassi racket. And as far as I'm concerned, he still doesn't play a particularly good game of tennis.

I see a similar situation quite often as a software consultant, visiting project teams to offer advice on how they might improve their "game" of application development. When I ask the software designers and programmers how they're going about their job of building a system, the answer is most often described in terms of particular tools. "This is a PowerBuilder project," the senior designer will tell me. Or, "We want to use the latest technology, so we're doing the whole thing in Delphi."

Well, that's fine—at least we haven't reached the point where Andre Agassi has his name on a CASE tool; but the use of a particular programming language or CASE tool doesn't guarantee success. Similarly, I cringe when I hear project teams describe their approach entirely in terms of a "brand-name" methodology. "This is a Booch project," the systems analyst will tell me; or, "We debated using Coad/Yourdon, but we decided to go Jacobson all the way." I live in fear of the day when Madonna or the Rolling Stones attach their names to a software engineering methodology.

Obviously, we all want to use good methods and good tools: To use the tennis metaphor, if you're a good player, then a superior racket will make a difference. But my son's Andre Agassi racket didn't make it possible for him to beat his old man when he was 11, and when he finally did beat me for the first time a couple years later, it was with a borrowed, nondescript racket at Club Med. The Agassi racket had been relegated to a closet at home; it wasn't worth the effort to bring along on the vacation trip.

If name-brand tools aren't the answer, then what is? You can imagine the kind of answer a tennis instructor would give to that question—and there are similar answers that we can offer in the field of application development. The term "best practices" is roughly equivalent to the collection of guidelines and advice we would give a tennis neophyte about posture and form, the essence of a good tennis stroke, the lessons of tactics and strategy, and so forth. In the software field, a possible example of a best practice is, "Every good project has a risk management plan, which the project manager updates weekly."

Many IT organizations focus on new tools, languages, and workstations as their "silver bullet" for improving productivity and technology; they want to buy the Andre Agassi equivalent of a CASE tool or programming language. But in this chapter, I want to focus on the notion of "best practices" for application development. What are they, and how do they differ from "standards" or "methodologies" that you can read about in a textbook? What are some examples of best practices? And, perhaps most important, how can you go about developing your own best practices for your own organization and your own project team?

6.1 WHAT ARE BEST PRACTICES?

James Bach, whose controversial views on the SEI process maturity model [2] have stirred quite a lot of debate recently, tells an apocryphal story of an assignment he had been given a few years ago at Apple Computer: He was instructed to develop a set of standards and procedures for testing software products. Since testing is obviously not a new concept, it occurred to him that perhaps one of his predecessors had already developed a set of standards that could be used as a starting point. But his inquiries proved unsuccessful—all of his colleagues told him that no such standards existed—until he happened to burrow through the contents of a desk that had been used over the years by numerous transient Apple employees. There in the desk, he found not one set of testing standards, but seven; and the colleague who had been most strenuous in his claim that no such standards existed was the very person who was the present occupant of the desk.

Faced with such a situation, most of us would immediately ask the following question: Since we don't want to reinvent the wheel, which of the seven sets of standards, developed by generations of well-meaning standards evangelists, should we choose? The "best practices" answer, in this case, is: *none of them*. After all, none of them were being used; indeed, the organizational culture was entirely unaware that they existed! But presumably some testing *was* being done at Apple, and presumably some products were better tested than others, because some groups were using different approaches than others. So one could argue that the best standards for testing were the ones that were already being used and that worked "best."

This may seem like an obvious point, but it's quite contrary to what I see in most application development organizations, where someone is convinced that he or she knows better than anyone else what tools, methods, and techniques should be used. Such a person usually has good intentions and may have the additional advantage of experience, talent, intellect, and political power. In the simple case, such a person is the project leader in an organization where each project can set its own rules regarding tools, methods, etc. But in some cases, this person, together with his or her colleagues, are members of the Standards Department or the "Methods and Procedures" department—or, to be *au courant*, the Process Improvement Department. Regardless of its name, the group typically feels that its job is to invent the practices to be adopted and standardized within the organization. It's a noble gesture, but it's often doomed to failure: Even if the Standards/Methods group is blessed with superior knowledge and experience, the recommendations typically turn out to be heavy-handed and unpopular, and the group acquires the reputation of being the "Process Nazis." Sooner or later, the well-intentioned advice about methods, tools, and procedures ends up in a desk drawer—along with the previous six generations.

"Best practices" are thus less concerned with invention and creation than they are with archaeology. If the Standards/Methods/Procedures group wants to rename itself as the Best Practices Group, then it should realize that its job is to act like social scientists visiting an alien race deep in the forest: observing behavior, documenting existing practices, and offering advice on which practices have been observed to produce good results—e.g., higher levels of quality.

6.1.1 Top-Down versus Bottom-Up

There's another characteristic of best practices: They tend to percolate up from the bottom of the organization, rather than being rammed down the throats of software engineers from the top of the organization.

Think about it. The traditional Standards/Methods group is typically chartered by senior management to develop the "official" tools, practices, and procedures. The output produced by the group often has an air of religious authority, and the materials sound like the Ten Commandments: "Thou shalt always and forevermore develop a logical data model before embarking upon the programming phase of they project."

Best practices, on the other hand, reflect what the "workers" *are* doing, rather than what the bosses think they *should* be doing. In the best of all worlds, there may be a substantial amount of overlap between top management's official proclamations about the way software is supposed to be developed, but it's almost certain that many of the "official" rules are ignored, modified, or sabotaged. And more important, there are likely to be quite a number of practices that senior management simply doesn't know about. Senior management, after all, wouldn't know a software process if they fell over one in most organizations; they have a tendency to delegate the issue of software practices and processes to one of the in-house groups, or they simply buy one from an external consulting firm.

This notion of best practices coming from the "grass roots" part of the organization is consistent with the prevailing trend of downsizing, elimination of middle management, and empowerment of the working-level people at the bottom of the organization. On the other hand, I suspect that it may run afoul of the efforts under way in many organizations to increase their "process maturity" by achieving a level-3 SEI assessment—those efforts tend to be imposed from the top of the organization, often with an iron hand.

But the iron-handed approach typically doesn't work. The people who are supposed to be carrying out the practices observe that management sends out inconsistent messages—by demanding short-term deliverables ("We can't afford to miss this deadline!") while simultaneously preaching the need for long-term improvements. In the worst case, a cynical group of workers will point out that senior management doesn't follow the officially proclaimed practices themselves—so why should the workers?

6.1.2 Where Do Best Practices Come From?

It would be wonderful if there was a "universal" set of best practices that every organization could use; in the next section of this chapter, I'll summarize just such a set—which, if nothing else, could be useful as a starting point in your own organization. But ultimately, each organization needs its own. Best practices within Microsoft are hardly likely to have much resemblance to best practices for the software in an air traffic control system. Even within the same industry, it's unreasonable to expect that company A's best software practices will be the same as company B's.

Here's another point to consider: Each generation of software professionals needs its own best practice—even if it means "rediscovering" the best practices used by the previous generation and articulating those practices with a new set of words and images. From a technological perspective, the approaches that worked well for mainframe applications may well be the worst possible approach for today's GUI-oriented, client-server projects. Sounds obvious, doesn't it? But ask yourself: Who are the folks heading up the Standards/ Methods department? Typically, it's a bunch of middle-aged old farts who got tired of working on high-stress projects and who feel that they're in a good position to tell the young whippersnappers the way things ought to be done. Alas, strategies of functional decomposition for COBOL programs may not be relevant for the design of event-based Visual Basic programs.

On the other hand, many of the project management practices that the old fogies are trying to impose upon the organization *are* still valid. The elements of planning and controlling the details of a project are almost universal; the principles of leading and managing people are the same today as they were 30 years ago. But today's young whippersnappers don't believe it and don't want to hear it; even if they understand it intellectually, they want to experience it themselves and formulate their best practices in their own vocabulary.

6.2 BEST PRACTICES AT DOD

The U.S. Defense Department has initiated a "Best Practices" project for its software development efforts; its objectives are summarized nicely in a letter written in July 1994 by Noel Longuemare, the under secretary of defense for acquisition and technology, and Emmett Paige, Jr., the assistant secretary of defense for common control, communications, and intelligence to the secretaries of the three military services and the vice-chairman of the Joint Chiefs of Staff:

> Current DOD software acquisition practices have not proven to provide an effective framework for managing the acquisition of large-scale software development maintenance programs that are an essential part of our increasingly complex weapons systems. Although many excellent practices for effectively managing such programs exist in both industry and government, their under-

standing and use within our software acquisition programs is not widespread. The April 6, 1994, memorandum...alerted service acquisition executives to the importance of integrating these practices into their software acquisition processes.

We share these concerns, and together have established the Software Acquisition Best Practices Initiative to improve and restructure our software acquisition management process. The purposes of this initiative are to:

- Focus the defense acquisition community on employing high-leverage software acquisition management practices;

- Enable program managers to focus their software management efforts on producing quality software, rather than on activities directed toward satisfying regulations that have grown excessively complex over time;

- Enable program managers to exercise flexibility in implementing best practices within disparate corporate and program cultures; and,

- Provide program managers and staff with the training and tools necessary to effectively use and achieve the benefits of these practices.

The Best Practices Initiative has brought together a group of consultants and advisors, which has been dubbed the Airlie Software Council after its meeting place in the Virginia countryside; the participants are listed in Table 6.1. The Council has had three meetings during the past year, and though I've only had a chance to attend a portion of one of those meetings, I've been quite impressed with the interim results. As of January 1995, the list of best practices was up to 170 and was still growing; it will continue evolving and will eventually be disseminated through DOD.[1]

Several colleagues have commented that 170 is far too large a number to deal with realistically. It's hard enough to remember the Ten Commandments in our day-to-day life, and most organizations would be well advised to begin with an equally concise list of best practices for their software projects. With more experience, and per-

---

[1] The best-practices initiative is now part of the Software Program Manager's Network, and a complete set of practices is available on the World Wide Web at http://spmn.com Organizations are encouraged to join the network; to find out how to do this, send e-mail to member@spmn.com

TABLE 6.1   Participants in the DOD Airlie Council
Best Practices Initiative

Victor Basili, University of Maryland
Grady Booch, Rational Software Corporation
Norm Brown, DOD Software Best Practices Initiative
Tom DeMarco, Atlantic Systems Guild
Mike Evans, Computers and Concepts
Capers Jones, Software Productivity Research, Inc.
Tim Lister, Atlantic Systems Guild
John Manzo, U.S. Robotics
Lou Mazzuchelli, consultant
Tom McCabe, McCabe & Associates
Frank McGrath, Logicon
Roger Pressman, R.S. Pressman & Associates, Inc.
Larry Putnam, Quantitative Software Management
Ed Yourdon, consultant

haps with the assistance of on-line tutorials, expert systems, agents, and other razzle-dazzle technology, we might be able to take advantage of more such practices—but not at the beginning.

Fortunately, the DOD group has been thinking along the same lines. After its January 1995 meeting, the Airlie Software Council narrowed the list down to nine "principal" best practices; these are shown in Table 6.2.

TABLE 6.2   Airlie Software Council's
"Principal Best Practices"

1. Formal Risk Management
2. User Manual As Specification
3. Inspections, Reviews, and Walkthroughs
4. Metrics-Based Scheduling and Tracking
5. Binary Quality Gates at the Inch-Pebble Level
6. Program-Wide Visibility of Project Plan
   and Progress Versus Plan
7. Defect Tracking Against Quality Targets
8. Separate Specification of Hardware
   and Software Functionality
9. People-Aware Management Accountability

Note that the practices shown in Table 6.2 do not represent the official policy of the U.S. Defense Department, and it's not clear that they ever will be official policy. Equally important, the practices were not conceived by DOD software people, nor are they intended to be used only on DOD projects. As you can tell from the names listed in Table 6.1, the Airlie Software Council consists of consultants, software product vendors, metrics gurus, methodologists, academics, and defense contractors. The practices recommended by this group come from the collective experience of projects in both the private sector and the public sector; with one exception (practice #8), every item on this list is (in my opinion) universally applicable.

That does not mean that you should rush right out and carve these practices onto a stone tablet called "The Nine Commandments of Software Projects." As discussed earlier, best-practices initiatives are usually most successful when they consist of a bottom-up process of documenting of what already works in your organization. Nevertheless, it can't hurt to have a list of best practices that have worked for a wide range of other organizations. You may have to toss out a couple of the items in Table 6.2 and no doubt you'll want to add a few of your own, but the majority of them should be applicable—and they may help accomplish a "consciousness-raising" activity if your organization doesn't have a clear idea of what works and what doesn't work. This is especially common in SEI level-1 organizations, where there are no formal processes in place and where the behavior and outcome of one project is likely to be dramatically different from the next one. In such an environment, the projects that do succeed are often as much of a mystery as the ones that fail. What makes them succeed? The instinctive answer given by the project team is often something like, "We had very talented people, and we all worked very hard." But was that all it took? What else did the project team do? Perhaps by reviewing the items in Table 6.2, the successful project teams can begin to articulate practices that they've followed unconsciously, instinctively—and from which the other project teams can begin to learn.

6.2.1 Practice 1: Formal Risk Management

Risk management is arguably the most important of the best practices identified by the Airlie Software Council. In the summary of its January 1995 session, the council states:

This discipline requires at the very minimum:

- Appointment of a Risk Officer whose principal responsibility is Risk Management
- Inclusion in the budget and schedule of a calculated Risk Reserve Buffer of time, dollars, and other key resources to deal with risks as they materialize
- Compilation of a database for all non-negligible risks
- Preparation of a profile for each risk including: probability, cost impact, schedule impact, earliest expected visible symptom, action plan(s) to be invoked upon detection, probability weighted contribution to Risk Reserve
- Continuously updating and monitoring risk plans to account for new potential and manifest risks

Admittedly, risk management may not seem worth the effort on small projects—especially those that have the luxury of infinite amounts of unpaid overtime on the part of a small, highly motivated staff. On such projects, whatever risks do exist can typically be overcome by brute force. And even if the risks prove to be insurmountable, the financial consequences are typically small enough that they can be overlooked

But on large projects, a healthy respect for significant risks is often the difference between success and failure; and on the large projects, the financial consequences—as well as the legal, social, and political consequences—can be devastating. Risk management was the topic of a special issue of *American Programmer* in March 1995; in the introduction for that issue, I wrote:

> I'm often asked to visit an organization to provide advice on some technical aspect of a project they're working on. In many cases, I have no background information about the company or the project, and the fact that they've called me in several months after the project has gotten under way is sometimes a sign that disaster is looming. So my first question, when I walk in the door, is typically, "May I see your risk management plan?" To which the typical response is, "Say what? A risk *what*?"

Lack of awareness of risks—and/or a nonchalant attitude toward risks—may be one example of the generational problem I mentioned before. If you're a 22-year-old application developer and you're working on your first project, it may not have occurred to you that there are dozens of potential risks (e.g., bankruptcy of the vendor providing a critical piece of proprietary software) that could sink your project. And if you're a typical 22-year-old macho cowboy programmer, you may truly believe that any such risks that might emerge can be overcome, because you're real smart and you're willing to work real hard. And you may be working in a macho management environment where the suggestion of anything to the contrary is akin to treason—e.g., "Real men can overcome problems; only wimps and cry-babies spend a lot of time worrying about risks."

Note that the Airlie Software Council recommends the appointment of a person whose primary responsibility is management of risks. Again, this isn't relevant for small projects, but it's a strategy you should seriously consider if you have a project involving 50+ application developers. If you have a medium-sized project, you might regard the role as a half-time position, and you might be tempted to incorporate it into the job description of the quality assurance group—or you might regard it as something for the project manager to do, along with all of the other activities associated with project management. But remember that there are issues of psychology and politics here: To some extent, the Risk Officer (or whatever you name you give this person) is the "loyal opposition"—i.e., someone who identifies, assesses, tracks, and articulates the various reasons why things might not work, when everyone else on the project team (including the project manager!) desperately wants to believe that things will work. Putting this activity into the hands of the project manager increases the chances that it will be given short shrift.

Note also the Council's recommendation of a "Risk Reverse Buffer" to deal with risks. This is hardly a radical idea, and it's one that many of us instinctively include in our schedules and budgets, sometimes under the heading of "Miscellaneous" or "Contingency Factor." Indeed, this will probably be something that the various project managers in your organization will instinctively agree is a "best practice"—and the absence of such a buffer will be unanimously agreed upon as a major reason why the unsuccessful projects get into such trouble.

The Council's suggestion that a "profile" be developed for each risk is fairly straightforward, but it includes a couple of interesting items. In addition to estimating the likely share of the risk reserve buffer that the risk might consume, the Council also recommends identifying the earliest expected visible symptom—i.e., "what's the first evidence that we will have that this risk is in the process of occurring? How will we know that it's happening?"

This suggestion reflects the perspective of Capers Jones, one of the Council members, in his landmark book, *Assessment and Control of Software Risks* [9]. Jones has argued for some time that we should catalog software risks in the same way the U.S. Health Service catalogs communicable diseases: by identifying symptoms, causes, cures, and the like.

Similarly, the Council's recommendation that the project team continuously update and monitor its risk plans is an obvious one—and many organizations have adopted a simple "best practice" articulated by Barry Boehm: A "top ten" list of relevant project risks can be accumulated and updated periodically (e.g., whenever regular project status reviews take place); the risks can be color-coded as "green" when they have been eliminated; "yellow" when they are reaching a level where attention and caution are required; and "red" when they have reached a critical stage.

Although risk management isn't practiced as widely as it should be, it's comforting to know that a substantial amount has been written on the topic. In addition to the March 1995 *American Programmer* and the textbook by Capers Jones, there are also some excellent books by Robert Charette as well as technical reports providing a checklist, or taxonomy, of common risks for IT projects; see the references at the end of this chapter for details.

6.2.2 Practice 2: User Manual As Specification

One of the major risks for any software project is the lack of precise, accurate, and testable specifications. If you don't know what the software is supposed to do, how can you build it?

There are various "best practices" that one might propose for dealing with this problem: Indeed, the efforts that we've made in this area over the past 25 years offer some useful insights into the difference between "best practices" and "standards."

A typical approach in many application development organizations throughout the 1970s and 1980s, for example, was a formal standard that said, "Thou shalt not begin writing any code for a development project until a compete, detailed functional specification of user requirements has been created and until the user has signed every page of the specification in blood." The standard often dictated the form of the specification as well, using such popular approaches as data flow diagrams, entity-relationship diagrams, and so forth. The idea was that graphical models of the "essence" of the system requirements would be more successful than turgid, thousand-page narrative tomes that were usually obsolete by the time they were written.

Unfortunately, such approaches often didn't work—no matter how well intentioned they were and no matter how scrupulously the standard was followed. We've gradually learned the reasons for this: sometimes users are simply incapable of articulating what they want; sometimes they don't even know what they want (even if they could articulate it); and sometimes their requirements change so fast that by the time we write it down, in detail, the requirements are obsolete.

And this has led to a de facto best practice in some organizations that has become almost a religious battle-cry: Don't write *any* requirements documents! Instead, spend some time discussing requirements with the user, then build a prototype. If the prototype is thoroughly unsuccessful, then throw it away and build another one. If the prototype is moderately successful, then refine it and evolve it until it is completely acceptable to the user. The fact that this violates the standards manuals and flies in the face of many of the software engineering textbooks of the 1970s and 1980s doesn't matter to the best-practices person; what matters is that it works. Period.

The Airlie Software Council has proposed a different kind of best practice: Insist that a complete set of user manuals be generated before the earliest design and implementation activities begin, and that these manuals become an integral part of the system specification.

The fact that the Airlie Council has made such a proposal doesn't mean that it will work for you—your users may not even ask for user manuals. But while small projects often have the luxury of extemporaneous prototyping from the beginning until final delivery to the customer without ever producing a user manual, large projects behave differently: inevitably, ponderous tomes are written to describe the requirements and functional capabilities of the system. This is endemic within government projects (not just DOD), and many members of the Airlie Software Council reported on their experiences in post-mortems of such large projects that had collapsed without delivering *anything*; in almost every case, the specifications were utterly unintelligible.

Microsoft uses a variation of this approach: coding is not allowed to begin until the testing department has approved the specifications for a product—which, in many cases, are the user manual. The practice arose from the complaints of the testing groups, whose efforts are supposed to occur in parallel with the coding efforts of the developers. "How can we figure out what kind of test cases to create," the testing department asks, "if we don't even know what the software is supposed to do?" (As noted earlier in this book, Microsoft also has a Best-Practices initiative, and is disseminating several such practices throughout the organization.[2])

6.2.3 Practice 3: Inspections and Peer Reviews

Breathes there a programmer anywhere on earth who has never heard of inspections, reviews, and walkthroughs? This practice has been part of the culture of the software community forever, and it has been recommended and endorsed by methodologists, consultants, and quality assurance professionals for at least 25 years. It's built into the SEI's capability maturity model as a "key process area": to reach level 3, the organization needs to have a formal mechanism for inspections and reviews.

- Induce uncertainty, don't "swallow" it. The rest of the organization wants you to announce a delivery date with 100% certainty, but that's not realistic: Make the rest of the organization *adapt* to your uncertainty. Tell the marketing department that they'll be the first to know once you know when your product will be finished.

- As project manager, you're the greatest expert in the world as to when your project will finish. If *you* don't know, then why should anyone else in the organization think they know? Why should anyone else even presume to think they can make an estimate more accurate than yours? The quality assurance group articulates the status of the project; this is the group that induces

---

[2] Several of the Microsoft "best practices" have now been documented in textbook form [10, 11, 12]. Here are a few tidbits of "best practices" advice that Jim McCarthy, head of Microsoft's Visual C++™ product group, presented at a recent software conference.

honesty in the project. Don't expect it from the rest of the troops; programmers are dreamers and optimists, dealing with fuzzy stuff. As a project manager, you want them to dream and to be optimistic; depend on QA for honesty.

- It's very important to prevent someone on the team from "going dark"—McCarthy's phrase for disappearing into a dark room and closing the door, so that the manager can't tell how much progress is being made. To prevent that, many managers try to "micro-manage" the activities of their people, insisting on daily deliverables. A better approach is to create a "project ecology," so that there are interdependencies between *everyone* on the team, and so that everyone depends on everyone else for his or her day-to-day progress. Then the team members will all micro-manage each other, rather than the boss giving daily orders.

- The importance of having small milestones or "inch-pebbles" in a project is that the team can learn from its mistakes and maintain its optimism—rather than blowing a *big* deadline and getting so bummed out that they quit.

- Take away the moral baggage associated with schedule slips. Slips aren't bad; they're a normal sign of dealing with a problem. When dealing with schedule slips, don't succumb to the temptation to trade one bad date for another; as McCarthy points out, if your team misses a deadline, users and upper management will come to you and say, "Okay, you missed the deadline for milestone X; when *will* you reach that deadline?" It's very tempting to feel somewhat guilty and inadequate and blurt out something like, "Well, I'm really confident that we'll reach milestone X by next Tuesday." The fact that you've just missed the deadline strongly implies that you fundamentally *don't know* when you'll actually reach the milestone.

Many organizations interpret this practice in terms of code walk-throughs alone. But the Airlie Software Council recommended:

Peer review[s] should be conducted on designs at all levels (particularly detailed designs), on code prior to unit test, and on test plans.

This still leaves a great deal of latitude as to when the reviews should take place, how they should be conducted, who should be invited to attend the reviews, and what results should be reported outside the peer group. This is clearly an area where your best-practices team has to conduct some field studies and anthropological research to find out what does work within the culture of your organization. You may find that the best project teams in your organization follow Microsoft's "mentor" approach, where the inspections involve one-on-one discussions between junior developers and a designated mentor. Or you may find that a more traditional form of peer reviews is conducted, but a set of practices has evolved over time covering details of the who/what/where/when questions.

All of this implies a "worst practice," too: The projects that fail have a much higher incidence of outright refusal on the part of key technical personnel to participate in such reviews. "This is my code," the super-programmer will announce arrogantly, "and nobody gets to see it until I say so." Though the Airlie Council didn't explicitly indicate that the converse of their best practices would indeed constitute worst practices, they did identify a number of other worst-practices; I'll discuss them later in this chapter.

6.2.4 Practice 4: Metric-Based Scheduling and Tracking

The Airlie Software Council made the following recommendation regarding scheduling and tracking:

> Statistical quality control of costs and schedules should be maintained. This requires early calculation of size metrics (function points, for example), projection of costs and schedules from observed empirical patterns of past results, and tracking of project status through the use of captured result metrics. Use of a parametric analyzer or other automated projection tool is also recommended.

As with the previous practices, this one needs to be compared with your organization's current operational practice, rather than being implemented blindly. The successful project leaders in your organization may balk, for example, at the notion of "statistical quality control" of costs and schedules—but if they're successful, how do they control the cost and schedule fluctuations that occur in a project? What you're likely to hear is an argument against the "crash diet" syndrome: just as many of us have to admit to ourselves that we become overweight one day at a time, one ounce at a time, so we also have to admit that our projects become late one day at a time, and over budget one dollar at a time. It doesn't happen all at once, even though some project managers seem to be blissfully unaware of problems until the day before the deadline, at which point their programmers suddenly announce that they're a year behind schedule.

The recommendation of an early calculation of size metrics is one that your best project managers probably are carrying out. How can you estimate the cost and schedule for a project if you don't have a good estimate of its size? How do your successful project managers estimate size? Are the estimates still based on lines of code, or can you detect a movement toward language-independent metrics like function points among the successful managers? Indeed, what you may find is that the successful managers have a "breathalyzer test" to see if the project team members who carried out the estimating function were at least in the right ballpark. One manager I know has a very simple scheme for the on-line, transaction-based systems that his project teams typically develop: He simply counts the number of data-entry screens, inquiry screens, and output reports that the project team is planning to implement—and then multiplies those figures by a set of parameters, acquired from previous projects, in order to obtain a ballpark estimate of schedule and costs. As long as this crude estimate is within 50 percent of the "official" estimate derived by his project team, he feels comfortable.

There really are two key points here:

- The most successful project managers estimate their schedules and costs, rather than negotiating a politically acceptable deadline and budget for a fixed amount of functionality. Unsuccessful project managers are far more likely to accept an arbitrary date and/or an arbitrary budget and then hope that superhuman efforts will allow a miracle to occur. In the worst case (which one typically sees in an SEI level-1 organization), nobody believes any of the estimates anyway—everyone assumes that when the deadline is reached, the project will simply continue as long as necessary, until it *is* finished. Savvy project managers realize that schedules and budgets do have to be negotiated in many cases, but they also ensure that such variables as functionality, quality, and resource levels are part of the negotiation.

- Successful managers track the status of schedule, cost, and other critical project variables on a daily or weekly basis—so that if things begin to slip, they know about it right away. It's unconscionable for a project manager to be in a state of ignorance about the project's true status until a week before the deadline, when the programmers suddenly inform him that they're going to be six months late.

6.2.5   Practice 5: Binary Quality Gates at the Inch-Pebble Level

Tracking project status on a daily basis doesn't help if you allow "partial credit" for activities—e.g., the infamous status report of "90 percent done," which most programmers will claim on the second day of the project, and then continue claiming until six months after the deadline has passed. As the Airlie Council put it:

> Completion of each task in the lowest level activity network needs to be defined by an objective binary indication. These completion events should be in the form of gates which assess either the quality of the products produced, or the adequacy and completeness of the finished process. Gates may take the form of technical reviews, completion of a specific set of tests which integrate or qualify software components, or project audits. The binary indication is meeting a pre-defined performance standard (e.g., defect density of less than four per function point). Activities are closed only upon meeting the standard, *with no partial credit* (emphasis added).

Check with the successful projects in your organization, and you're likely to see some form of this notion of "binary" completeness: A task is either completely done or it's not done at all, from the perspective of project control. Microsoft and several other software companies accomplish this by means of a "daily build," where all of the components of a software product are compiled, linked, and integrated into a new version every day. This requires a daily, binary "moment of truth" for each member of the project team: Either the module that you've been working on is sufficiently finished that you can submit it to the daily build, to be assembled together with all the others—or it's not. As Microsoft's Jim McCarthy (head of the Visual

C++ product group) says, "The daily build is the heartbeat of the project; it's how you know the project is alive."

6.2.6 Practice 6: Program-Wide Visibility of Project Plan and Progress versus Plan

The Airlie Software Council didn't mince words with this recommendation:

> The main indicators of project health or dysfunction—the Control Panel indicators—should be made available to all project participants. Anonymous channel feedback (response by program participants without identifying themselves) should be encouraged to enable bad news to move both up and down the project hierarchy.

The notion of a "project control panel" was another of the Council's recommendations; it consists of a set of "fuel gauges" to indicate resources that have been consumed by the project, as well as progress indicators, risk gauges, warning indicators, and quality indicators. Several metrics consultants—e.g., Howard Rubin and Council member Capers Jones—have been advocating these highly visual "dashboard" control panels for some time, and I've seen them implemented as a "best practice" in organizations like Andersen Consulting.

Regardless of whether you use a control panel, the main issue here is visibility. Again, don't take my word or the Airlie Software Council's word for it; ask your own project managers for their opinion. You may find some who argue against the idea of an anonymous communication channel, or who argue that certain forms of bad news ought to be hidden from the team in order to keep them from getting distracted or discouraged. The "need to know" mentality is still alive and well in some organizations, especially (ironically) within the Defense Department.

On the other hand, if your organization is eliminating layers of middle management in a downsizing effort and project teams are being reduced in size, then you don't have much choice in this area. Whether you like it or not, more and more information is available to the project team members—and they're not stupid. A project manager who lies or deliberately withholds important information about the project status quickly loses the trust and credibility of the team members; and while they may not mutiny overtly, they probably won't be willing to add the extra ounce of effort that might be necessary to ensure success.

What about bad news discovered by the bottom-level team members? What mechanism is there for communicating that news to the project manager, to end users, and to others outside the team? What mechanisms are in place to prevent the well-known phenomenon of "shooting the messenger"? There are many ways of accomplishing this, including high-tech variations on anonymous e-mail and low-tech ideas such as old-fashioned suggestion boxes. What constitutes a "best practice" in your organization depends not only on the technology, but also on the culture, leadership style, and politics.

6.2.7 Practice 7: Defect Tracking against Quality Targets

The Council had this to say about defects:

> Defects should be tracked formally at each project phase. Configuration management enables each defect to be recorded and traced through to removal. In this approach, *there is no such thing as a private defect*, i.e., one that is detected and removed without being recorded (emphasis added). Initial quality targets (expressed, for example, in defects per function point) as well as calculations of remaining or latent defects are compared to counts of defects in order to track progress during testing activities.

In simple terms, successful projects are typically fanatical about tracking defects—and not just at the end of the life cycle, when programmers are frantically fixing bugs while the testing people are uncovering new ones. The best-practices approach that members of the Airlie Council have observed in projects all over the world involves identifying and tracking defects in all of the project phases, including requirement analysis, design, documentation, and so on.

Note the emphasis on making all defects public. As you can imagine, this is culturally unacceptable in many organizations, especially where defects have a pejorative connotation—e.g., the culture where the programmers mutter to themselves, "The boss is keeping track of the bugs, and she's gonna remind us how many we had during our next performance review." In such a climate, developers work hard to find and eliminate defects in private or during peer reviews where the defects are not reported as long as they can be fixed on the spot. But in the "best of the best" projects observed by the Airlie team in their various consulting experiences, every defect is recorded—to facilitate better tracking of schedules and budgets and also to facilitate process improvement for subsequent projects.

Note also the emphasis on configuration management; many organizations languishing at level 1 on the SEI scale don't have such a practice, and it's a critical one. By the way, keep in mind that configuration management and formal tracking of defects almost always require automated tools for medium- and large-sized projects. So in addition to the glamorous, visually oriented programming tools that you're buying, make sure to buy some good tools for configuration management and defect tracking; several of the new client-server testing products, for example, also have some excellent defect tracking components.

6.2.8 Practice 8: Separate Specification of Hardware and Software Functionality

Readers of this book are typically not developing both hardware and software. But if you are, here's what the Airlie Council recommends:

> For projects developing both hardware and software, a separate software specification must be written with an explicit and complete interface description consisting of:
>
> - Full census of inputs and outputs between the software and all its externals
> - Definition of each input and output down to the data element level.

6.2.9 Practice 9: People-Aware Management Accountability

The Council's advice here is quite succinct:

> Management must be accountable for staffing qualified people (i.e., those with domain knowledge and similar experience in past successful projects), as well as low staff turnover.

This is straightforward advice, but many Council members report that they have seen it violated again and again: neophytes are sent to a 2-day introductory seminar on a critical technology (e.g., object-oriented programming) and are then thrown into a mission-critical project where nobody on the team has any experience on previous projects. No wonder the project fails.

Even worse, we often see large projects where a large percentage of the project staff (often including the project manager and his or her key subordinates) has little or no "domain knowledge" about the application area. Some software consulting firms are guilty of this practice, hoping that the people they've assigned to the project can fake it long enough to pick up enough knowledge to get by. Within IT and MIS organizations, the reasons are predictable: politics, a desire to use idle staff, and a naive belief that "software is software, it doesn't really matter what the application area is."

Note also the Council's emphasis on low staff turnover. I've known managers who developed a reputation for delivering software on time and under budget—but in so doing, they burn out their staff and develop so many enemies that they're forced to quit and move on to another company. A "best practice" articulated at Microsoft is, "A good project delivers good software *and* a good team that's ready and willing to work together on the next project."

High staff turnover at the end of a project is bad enough; but high staff turnover during the project can be a disaster, especially on large projects that may last for 3 or 4 years. In such scenarios, the team members who make all the key decisions at the beginning of the project are typically gone by the middle of the project; and the people who join the project midway through the coding effort have the same feeling of befuddlement that we've all experienced walking into a movie theater in the middle of a two-hour movie: *What's going on here? Why is everyone behaving this way?*

Obviously, some turnover is inevitable—and some of it is entirely beyond the control of the project manager and may have nothing to do with the project environment (e.g., marriages, divorces, or other personal factors). But if the turnover rate is high, it's often an indication that something has made the disgruntled team members lose faith in the project and/or the manager—e.g., the manager is trying to cope with schedule slippage through massive overtime.

6.3 WORST PRACTICES

The emphasis on best practices is a natural one, especially in the typical U.S. organization that focuses on triumph and victory, success and winning. But if the organization can identify its best practices, wouldn't it also be a good idea to identify *worst* practices? For the conservative organization, it may be politically preferable to concentrate on avoiding the practices that have consistently led to failures.

There's another reason why it may be useful to focus on worst practices: Some organizations may find it extremely difficult to identify or reach a consensus on best practices. This is especially common in SEI level-1 "cowboy" organizations where individuality and artistic freedom are highly cherished. Thus, the project manager and/or the technical project team members may react to all of the suggestions in the previous section of this report by saying, "We have our own way of doing things, and the 'best practices' you've identified just wouldn't work for us." That's fine—but it's still useful to summarize those practices that have been consistently associated with project failures. If nothing else, the cowboy project team should be aware that it is going out on a limb, flaunting the organization's tribal folklore, if it insists on following such approaches. And such practices may form the beginning of a risk management plan (i.e., a taxonomy of major risks in your organization) discussed earlier as part of the best-practices approach.

The Airlie Software Council identified nine worst practices that its members had observed in projects; they're listed in Table 6.3. As with the best practices discussed earlier, these are not intended to be universal truths to be imposed unthinkingly upon your development organization; you should use them as a starting point, match them against your own organizational experience, and devise your own customized list. You may completely disagree with some of the items on the list, and you'll probably find some of them irrelevant (e.g., worst-practice #7 and #8, involving hardware-software trade-offs). And some of them may lead to "aha!" reactions, focusing attention on issues that had previously been ignored.

A key point, by the way: The people in the trenches are often the best source of information about worst practices—simply because they're the ones who have to cope with such practices, overcome them, and clean up the mess that they cause. Don't ignore these folks!

TABLE 6.3 Airlie Council "Project Caveats" of Worst Practices

1. Don't use schedule compression to justify usage of new technology on any time critical project

2. Don't specify implementation technology in the RFP.

3. Don't advocate use of unproved "silver bullet" approaches.

4. Don't expect to recover from any substantial schedule slip (10% or more) without making more than corresponding reductions in functionality to be delivered.

5. Don't put items out of project control on the critical path.

6. Don't expect to achieve large, positive improvements (10% or more) over past observed performance.

7. Don't bury all project complexity in the software (as opposed to the hardware).

8. Don't conduct the critical system engineering tasks (particularly the hardware/software partitioning) without sufficient software expertise.

9. Don't believe that formal reviews provide an accurate picture of the project. Expect usefulness of formal reviews to be inversely proportional to the number of people attending beyond five.

6.3.1 Caveat 1: Don't Use Schedule Compression to Justify Usage of New Technology on Any Time Critical Project

This caveat is likely to cause great controversy in some organizations—because new technology (especially new application development tools and languages) are frequently justified in the mid-90s precisely because they are promised to help "compress" the project schedule by a substantial amount. Thus, one of the reasons that many application development organizations are using Visual Basic, Smalltalk, Delphi, PowerBuilder, and other similar tools is precisely because it appears to be possible to reduce 3-year development schedules to 3 months.

So what on earth does the Airlie Council have in mind with this caveat? Well, consider the following:

- The first time that a new technology is used, it often takes more time than if the technology had not been used at all—simply because of the overhead of training, as well as the lost time caused by confusion, experimentation, and arguing among project team members about how best to use the technology. If you're lucky, the project schedule will be approximately the same as before and the benefits will be measured in terms of quality improvements; the benefits associated with schedule compression and higher levels of productivity will begin to occur on the second or third project.

- If it is indeed a time-critical project, then there will be enormous pressure upon the project team to reduce training and eliminate any open discussion and arguments about how to use the technology. And if the first-time usage of the new technology causes overhead despite these efforts, then there is a serious risk that other forms of quality reduction (e.g., diminished testing, cancellation of peer reviews, skimpy documentation) will take place in order to maintain the schedule. All of this is likely to lead to a less successful (or even unsuccessful) result, and the problems are likely to be blamed on the new technology. This is exactly what we have seen in recent years with CASE technology, object-oriented methods, structured methods, and many other useful new technologies.

- The schedule compression benefits of the new technology are often touted by the technology's vendors—who often fail to point out that the compression only occurs in the life-cycle phase where the technology is being used, not in the overall life cycle. The classic example is the new programming language that compresses coding activities by a factor of three, but doesn't have any impact on testing, documentation, design, and analysis—and since programming is likely to represent only 10 to 15 percent of the schedule of large projects, the new technology may not have any significant impact on the overall ability of the team to meet the time-critical schedule.

6.3.2 Caveat 2: Don't Specify Implementation Technology in the RFP

This should be an obvious caveat; it doesn't require any explanation. But end users are increasingly involved in the creation of RFPs for new systems, and they often innocently stipulate the use of various hardware platforms, operating systems, programming language, and DBMS products. Politics may intrude here, too, as in the case of the MIS manager who says, "We're a Windows/Visual Basic shop now, and we'll say so explicitly in the RFP, because we don't want any of those Communist perverts sneaking in with their Macintoshes and Smalltalk solutions."

6.3.3   Caveat 3: Don't Advocate Use of Unproved "Silver Bullet" Approaches

This caveat is a variation of #1; a typical justification for the use of unproved "silver bullet" approaches is the desperate hope that it will provide the schedule compression and/or productivity improvements that the project team desperately requires.

This doesn't mean that the Airlie Council members—or anyone else urging caution at the use of silver-bullet technologies—are intellectual Luddites. Experimentation with interesting, potentially exciting new approaches and technologies is fine; that's what pilot projects are all about. But unproven silver-bullet technologies are often used on mission-critical projects that are already trying to cope with several other risks, such as tight schedules and budgets. An even worse situation is the organization that mandates the use of such unproven methods and technologies for all projects, based on the hysterical optimism of the "technology champion" who has typically just recently achieved a position of political power.

6.3.4   Caveat 4: Don't Expect to Recover from Any Substantial Schedule Slip (10% Or More) without Making More than Corresponding Reductions in Functionality to Be Delivered

Discuss this one honestly with the project managers in your organization. If, say, a 12-month project is 3 months behind schedule, what are your options? The worst-practice option is a denial of reality—i.e., a desperate hope that things will get better, that the schedule slippage to date was caused by unique circumstances, and that the lost time will somehow be recouped. Other possible strategies include adding more people to the project, eliminating testing and documentation activities, gently requesting the project team to engage in a "death march" of double-overtime until the project is back on schedule, etc. Do any of these tactics work—or, as the Airlie Council members have found, do they just postpone the inevitable and sometimes make matters even worse?

If the deadline is nonnegotiable and the project is now substantially behind schedule, the one strategy that typically does have a chance of working is to reduce the functionality of the delivered system—assuming, of course, that the system has been designed in a sufficiently modular fashion that individual features and functions can be added or removed without causing serious side-effects. But inevitably, there will be side-effects caused by this kind of midcourse change—if not in the software itself, then within the project team, as assignments are juggled, partially developed components are shelved, and so forth. Inevitably, some partially completed work is going to be scrapped, some egos are going to be bruised, and some additional time is going to be spent debating which pieces of functionality will be kept and which pieces will be postponed or eliminated. Thus, you'll need a disproportionate reduction in functionality in order to recoup the schedule slippage.

6.3.5   Caveat 5: Don't Put Items Out of Project Control on the Critical Path

This caveat is so obvious that one wonders why it was included on the list. The reason is simple: The Council members have observed the phenomenon over and over again in their consulting and project-audit activities.

To put it another way, many project managers instinctively identify, assess, and manage the project risks that are under their control—e.g., technical risks and personnel risks. But there are frequently additional risks outside the manager's sphere of influence that are far more serious—e.g., risks associated with litigation, politics, changes in government regulations, and sole-source vendors teetering on the edge of bankruptcy. If those risks are on the critical path, the project manager needs to be in a position of authority to control them; otherwise, the risk is essentially unmanageable.

6.3.6 Caveat 6: Don't Expect to Achieve Large, Positive Improvements (10% or More) Over Past Observed Performance

Some organizations will regard this as a pessimistic caveat—indeed, almost defeatist in nature. It also argues against the notion of "breakthrough performances": an explicit strategy that some organizations have used in order to consciously, deliberately achieve large (e.g., factor-of-ten) performance improvements. But sudden, large improvements rarely occur as a result of managerial fiat or wishful thinking; the more likely experience is slow, steady improvements—which have enormous benefits in the long run, but perhaps not enough to accomplish a miracle in the current project.

If you decide to ignore this caveat—i.e., if you're serious about achieving a "breakthrough performance," my strong advice is to get some help, or at the very least, make sure that the project manager is someone who has achieved breakthrough performances under similar conditions in the past.

6.3.7 Caveat 7: Don't Bury All Project Complexity in the Software (as Opposed to the Hardware)

This caveat obviously pertains to projects where hardware and software are being developed concurrently; as mentioned earlier, I've assumed this situation doesn't occur for most readers of this book, so I won't comment on it in more detail.

6.3.8 Caveat 8: Don't Conduct the Critical System Engineering Tasks (Particularly the Hardware/ Software Partitioning) without Sufficient Software Expertise

This, too, pertains primarily to the DOD projects where hardware and software are being developed concurrently.

6.3.9 Caveat 9: Don't Believe that Formal Reviews Provide an Accurate Picture of the Project. Expect the Usefulness of Formal Reviews to Be Inversely Proportional to the Number of People Attending Beyond Five

The last caveat on the Airlie Council's list is an intriguing one, especially since peer reviews were emphasized as a desirable best practice. But "formal" reviews are something entirely different; in most projects, they are elaborate political affairs, attended by various "outsiders" (auditors, quality assurance personnel, members of the user organization and senior management, observers from other projects, and rabble-rousers who have nothing better to do with their time) whose political agenda may be entirely different than that of the project team.

There is a natural tendency to assume that if a project survives the "trial by fire" of a formal review, then everything must be in good shape; after all, if the skeptics, critics, and enemies of the project can't manage to sabotage the project, what could be wrong? In short: everything! Precisely *because* it's a political exercise, the project team may unconsciously withhold information and hide all the bad news. And though the skeptics and critics will be looking diligently for flaws, they usually have only superficial knowledge of the project details; indeed, many of them have little or no knowledge of the technology used by the project. So the savvy project managers should remember that they must form their own "picture" of the project status.

6.4 IMPLEMENTING BEST PRACTICES

Throughout this report, I've cautioned you not to accept the Airlie Council's recommended best practices as "stone tablets" to be implemented as rigid standards. You've got to develop your own; and even more important, you have to introduce them into the organization so that they'll be accepted by the culture. There are several ways of doing this:

- Project post-mortems.
- Informal meetings and discussions.
- Electronic dissemination.

6.4.1 Project Post-Mortems

Post-mortems are familiar to veteran application developers in large MIS organizations; alas, they are a vanishing phenomenon, especially as application development is being dispersed through the user organizations.

A post-mortem should not be a boring exercise of checking off boxes on a list of procedures provided by the quality assurance department. What's needed is the frank discussion of what worked and what didn't work; what needs to be documented are the blunt statements from exhausted project team members who blurt out, "If I ever work on another project like this, I would never do X again..." But all too often, the surviving team members of a successful project are whisked away to begin the next project; and the victims of a project failure are fired, banished, or humiliated into abject silence. By the way, rather than writing the post-mortems in the form of a turgid report that no one will read, consider videotaping them. Let the rest of the organization see the passion with which the project team articulates its best practices.

A variation on this theme is to conduct post-mortems during a project, rather than waiting for it to finish. As Tom DeMarco points out in a recent book [8], most post-mortems don't accomplish much; even though the advice from the post-mortem group is sincere and practical, nobody pays much attention—because they're already deeply involved in some other project. But if a project team does a post-mortem of its successes and failures at each milestone (e.g., after each prototype is delivered to the customer), then it can "eat its own dog food" by putting its own advice into practice for the next stage of its own project.

6.4.2 Informal Meetings

Brown-bag lunches, Friday afternoon brainstorming sessions, quality circles, and a variety of other informal forums are good ways to share experiences, discuss best practices, and develop a consensus about their use throughout the organization. Indeed, these informal meetings evolve in some organizations without any formal management attention or approval—which I consider healthy, but which some managers find quite threatening. If you find that upper echelons of management in your organization begin voicing disapproval of these informal meetings, it's a good sign that the whole concept of "best practices" is doomed and that management is intent on forging ahead with a top-down dictum of what "must" be done in application development projects.

6.4.3 Electronic Dissemination

Electronic mail, internal Web sites, Lotus Notes bulletin boards, on-line databases of "frequently asked questions" (FAQs), and other mechanisms for widespread dissemination of best practices are appropriate in large, dispersed development organizations. This is especially useful as the list of best practices grows beyond the limited number I've discussed in this report; it's handy to have searching and browsing mechanisms, with hypertext navigation mechanisms, to access as much detail as might be needed.

But don't get carried away with high-tech approaches; if you're not careful, a new "standards" empire will emerge, intent on *telling* you what the best practices should be, rather than documenting observed practice.

6.5 SUMMARY AND CONCLUSION

Ours is an industry constantly faced with new tools, programming languages, hardware, operating systems, and concepts. It's only natural that we're prepared to abandon old technologies that are no longer relevant and take advantage of exciting new technologies.

But there's a bedrock of experience—especially involving basic project management principles—which does *not* change all that rapidly. One of the best ways to improve application development in your organization is to discover, document, and articulate the best practices of your best people—so that every team, and every project, can be a winner.

REFERENCES

1. *American Programmer,* special issue on Risk Management: March 1995.

2. Bach, James. "The Immaturity of the SEI CMM." *American Programmer,* September 1994.

3. Betts, M. "Feds Debate Handling of Failing IS Projects." *Computerworld,* November 2, 1992, p. 103.

4. Boehm, Barry. "Software Risk Management: Principles and Practices." *IEEE Software,* January 1991, pp. 32-41.

5. Carr, Marvin J., Suresh L. Konda, Ira Monarch, F. Carol Ulrich, and Clay F. Walker. *Taxonomy-Based Risk Identification.* Technical Report CMU/SEI-93-TR-006 (Pittsburgh, PA: Software Engineering Institute, June 1993).

6. Charette, Robert N. *Application Strategies for Risk Analysis.* (New York: McGraw-Hill, Intertext, 1990).

7. Charette, Robert N. *Software Engineering Risk Analysis & Management.* (New York: McGraw-Hill, Intertext, 1989).

8. DeMarco, Tom. *Why Does Software Cost So Much? and other puzzles of the information age.* (New York: Dorset House, 1995) ISBN: 0-932633-34-X.

9. Jones, Capers. *Assessment and Control of Software Risks.* (Englewood Cliffs, NJ: Prentice Hall/Yourdon Press, 1994).

10. Maguire, Steve. *Debugging the Development Process.* (Redmond, WA: Microsoft Press, 1994) ISBN: 1-55615-650-2.

11. Maguire, Steve. *Writing Solid Code.* (Redmond, WA: Microsoft Press, 1993) ISBN: 1-55615-551-4.

12. McCarthy, Jim. *Dynamics of Software Development.* (Redmond, WA: Microsoft Press, 1995) ISBN: 1-55615-823-8.

13. Yourdon, Edward. *Structured Walkthroughs,* 4th edition. (Englewood Cliffs, NJ: Prentice Hall, 1989).

GOOD-ENOUGH SOFTWARE

Always do right—this will gratify some and astonish the rest.

Mark Twain, Message, February 16, 1901, to the Young People's Society, New York City.

7.1 THE CONCEPT OF "GOOD ENOUGH"

Industry scuttlebutt informs us that Microsoft® Windows™ 3.1 was shipped in 1992 with some 5,000 known bugs. But it was "good enough"—look how many millions of copies were sold over the years and how the operating system ridiculed by Apple's grumpy programmers as "a thing on a thing" became the foundation for an entire segment of the computer industry before eventually being replaced by

Windows 95™.[1] On the other hand, some would argue that Apple started the trend when it shipped HyperCard® in the late 1980s with some 500 "open" bugs; but HyperCard was good enough, too. Meanwhile, Intel allowed the Pentium® floating point bug to exist for several months before acknowledging it publicly, presumably on the assumption that it was good enough. Despite the subsequent uproar and the fact that Intel had to write off $475 million in related costs, Intel stock traded at an all-time high within a few months, and jaded observers have commented that it was a cheap price to pay for the name recognition that "Pentium" now commands.

Some other companies have had problems, too. Intuit, the developer of Turbotax and MacInTax (yes, the very same company Microsoft attempted to acquire) acknowledged in early March 1995, that when importing data from its Quicken™ financial software program, it dropped every 30th item. The company apparently knew about the bug since late December 1994, but kept shipping the product anyway. Is that good enough?

Bugs are one characteristic of "good enough," but not the only one. The uproar over the Macintosh® version of Microsoft Word™ 6.0 (to which Microsoft has finally responded by announcing a "maintenance release" to registered owners in March 1995) suggests that functionality is another important aspect: If a software product, or an application program, is too big, too slow, too ugly, or too limited, it will be judged *not* good enough. Microsoft thought it was "good enough" to produce a new word processor with—as the company put it—ten times the functionality and three times the amount of code as the earlier version, with the expectation that it would run

---

[1]Windows 95 was released in August 1995; though the entire industry has apparently decided, *a priori*, that it is "good enough," it may be some time before we discover how many bugs it contains. Metrics guru Capers Jones gave a keynote presentation at the Fifth International Software Quality Conference in Austin, Texas, in October 1995, in which he said that (a) the number of "latent" defects in a typical software system could be estimated by raising the size of the system (as measured in function points) to the 1.2 power, and (b) that Windows 95 represents approximately 80,000 function points. If this estimate is correct, it would suggest that Windows 95 had approximately 1,345,434 latent bugs (i.e., bugs injected during the development process, and which had to be exorcised through inspections, code review, in-house testing, and beta testing). If all of these testing activities removed 99 percent of the defects, that would still leave 13,454 to be uncovered after the software was released.

approximately as fast on widely available vintage-1995 68040 Macintoshes as the previous version (Word 5.1) ran on 68030 Macs. But it wasn't clear that the marketplace was prepared for the hundreds of new features, especially when a few critical features, including the all-important feature of booting up the word processor, were significantly slower; subsequently, many people (including me) abandoned Word 6.0 for the "good-enough" functionality of Word 5.1.[2]

Functionality, quality, and schedule are the three most important elements of "good-enough" in most software today; they form a triangle, as illustrated in Figure 7.1. The key point, of course, is that all three dimensions are interconnected: If you change the schedule for a software project, the functionality and the quality are likely to change. There are additional dimensions of cost and staffing, too, but we'll leave them out of this discussion; the trade-off between people and time has already been discussed eloquently by Fred Brooks in *The Mythical Man-Month.*

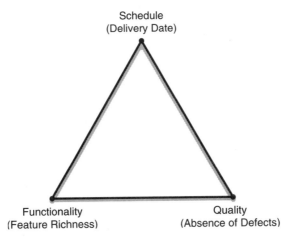

FIGURE 7.1 THE "GOOD-ENOUGH" TRIANGLE

The trade-offs between schedule, functionality (or "feature richness," as Microsoft likes to call it), and quality are never easy to calculate; Larry Putnam has explored the topic in *Measures for Excellence*

---

[2] I finally switched to Word 6.0.1 in August 1995 (nearly a year after its initial release) to take advantage of its features while writing the hardcover edition of this book. But it still had bugs: when adding this footnote to the text of the chapter, Word inserted the wrong footnote number.

[8], and has demonstrated mathematically what we all know intuitively: It's not a linear relationship. If you double the number of required features for a software product and hold the quality constant (as well as cost and manpower), then the schedule is likely to more than double.

There are a couple of key points to keep in mind about all of this:

- It's the *customer* who determines what the proper balance of schedule, functionality, and quality should be—not the programmer or the quality assurance department obsessed with its ideal of "zero-defect" programming.
- The balance between schedule, functionality, and quality shifts dynamically during a project. It has to be reevaluated by the customer and the project manager, often on a daily basis, and the changes have an impact on the design and programming of the software, as well as testing strategies, risk management, and managerial assignment of staff resources to various programming tasks.

Intellectually, much of the discussion makes sense, but many of us who have worked in the software field for a long time have trouble with it. As a recent article in *Business Week* [5] put it:

> Free technology demands that engineers learn a whole new discipline: wastefulness.... It's hard on designers who take pride in writing tight code and building efficient systems. But why waste time and effort making efficient use of something that isn't scarce?... Microsoft's Windows 95 will be huge and slow on today's PCs. But Microsoft knows that customers will simply buy new computers or add memory to their old ones.

It remains to be seen whether Windows 95 will be good enough in terms of size and speed, but most software professionals do agree that for the typical application, it's not worth wasting time and effort within the project schedule to save a few microseconds and bytes of memory. But where we *really* have trouble is the idea that it's not worth spending more time in the project schedule to reduce the number of defects, or perhaps even eliminate them altogether.

Obviously, we don't want *any* bugs in the software for a pacemaker or a nuclear reactor or the air traffic control system for commercial airline flights. And in the best of all worlds, our users would like us to develop software instantly, at no cost, and with no defects. But that's just not possible in today's world; in more and more application domains, we've been forced to accept the fact that the reengineering slogan of "faster, cheaper, better" really means "fast enough, cheap enough, good enough." As noted earlier, the uproar over the Pentium bug suggests that it was deemed *not* good enough, while the surprisingly large numbers of defects that are publicly acknowledged in popular shrink-wrapped software products—e.g., word processors, spreadsheets, tax calculation programs, and PC operating systems from a variety of the best-known software companies—suggest that those products *are* good enough. And if a vendor offers the marketplace an alternative set of products with a different combination of functionality, quality, cost, and availability (i.e., the ability to buy it *now* rather than waiting an extra six months for it), it's not always obvious which one will succeed.

Software projects for nuclear reactors and pacemakers will probably continue focusing on zero-defect software, but the shrink-wrap software industry and the corporate MIS application software industry are clearly shifting toward a new paradigm that says, "It's okay to have bugs as long as you can give me the software *now* with the basic features that I need." All of this is beginning to challenge some of our basic assumptions about software development, and I believe that it will lead to some fundamental changes in the way we manage software. Some purists—especially the long-time veterans with university degrees in Computer Science or Software Engineering and who regard themselves as "professionals"—may express horror at the "flight from quality." But I think it will lead to more rational software development projects and a more rational way of negotiating the criteria for successful projects with our customers and managers.

I grew up in a software industry that regarded *all* bugs as bad, and where zero-defect software was the Holy Grail that we labored to achieve. I still believe bugs are bad, and I still believe that if I can deliver a software product with the same functionality as my competitor, with the same delivery schedule and the same cost, but with ten times fewer defects, then my product will prevail in a competitive, free-market economy. And I still believe that process improvement efforts are likely to improve my software development efforts so that I'll produce software faster *and* cheaper *and* better than my cowboy competitors.

But I can't ignore the increasingly vocal complaints from my customers that it often takes me twice as long as my competitor to produce software with ten times fewer bugs—and time is more important to them than bugs. As industry observer James Bach says [1], "It's okay to have bugs in the software you ship—but you should choose *which* bugs you ship." And as Microsoft's chief technologist, Nathan Myrhvold, argued in a recent interview [2]

> We've gone from 27,000 lines of code [for the first version of Microsoft Word] to 2 million lines of code [for the current version] for the same money. If I say I've got two version of Word—that old one from 1982 that's perfect, with zero defects; or the new one that's got all this cool new stuff, but there might be a few bugs in it—people always want the new one. But I wouldn't want them to operate a plane I was on with software that happened to be the latest greatest release!

What impact does all of this have on us when we plan and organize our software development efforts? It seems to me that in the past, we often negotiated critical project success parameters *once*, at the beginning of the project, and then attempted to optimize a few other parameters that the customer was often unaware of. For example, the functionality, schedule, budget, and staff resources were typically negotiated in terms of political constraints: We were told that our task was to deliver a software system with a certain amount of functionality (which was often ambiguous, misunderstood, and poorly documented) within a certain schedule and budget (which was based on hysterically optimistic estimates or simply imposed by managerial fiat), and with a relatively fixed staff of developers. Within those constraints, the developers often attempted to optimize such features as maintainability, portability, reliability, and efficiency. Thus, the battle cry for many projects was: "We'll deliver high-quality, bug-free software on time, within budget!"

For an important class of software projects, that battle cry is still relevant—as previously noted, nobody wants to fly on an airplane whose guidance control software has as many bugs as the word processor we bought at Egghead Software. Nobody wants their telephone system or their bank's ATM system to crash as often as their desktop operating system. But for another class of software projects—which is arguably far larger today than the class of "critical" software systems— rapid delivery of the software to the customer is sometimes more important than the number of defects it contains. In other situations, "feature richness" may be the dominant factor; in still others, cost might be the only thing the user cares about.

Much of the shift that we're now experiencing is associated with the fact that information technology is now a consumer commodity: Unit costs are low, and everyone can have it. In the past, most of us worked on customized, proprietary, one-of-a-kind systems with schedules measured in years and budgets measured in millions of dollars. Today, some of us are still employed by organizations who want customized systems—but the schedules and budgets have shrunk considerably. And the customers will often point out to us that they can achieve almost the same results by lashing together a jury-rigged combination of Microsoft Word, Lotus Notes, and Borland Quattro®, which they can obtain from a mail-order discount catalog. The shrink-wrapped software may be clumsy and limited in its functionality for the user's application, but it's cheap—and it can be put into service tomorrow morning.

There's also an issue of inertia that we have to cope with, especially in the consumer-level desktop marketplace. Suppose, for example, that you have no word processor on your desktop PC and the time has come to acquire one. You have a choice among products A, B, and C. Product A costs $500 and it comes with a money-back guarantee; product B costs $100 and comes with a long legal disclaimer at the front of the user manual that basically says "caveat emptor." Meanwhile, product C costs only $50 and has twice as many features as A and B, and its developers are so confident of its quality that they're bragging about their double-your-money-back guarantee—the only problem is that it's vaporware, and despite all of the glowing reviews in the trade magazines, it won't actually be available for six months. Assuming that you need a word processor *now*, presumably you would make a rational choice between A and B, based on your assessment of the importance of cost versus defects.

But suppose that you already have a word processor—perhaps product B—installed on your computer, and you've been using it for the past year. Some of its features are slightly annoying, but it's adequate for accomplishing your mundane, daily word processing tasks. And suppose that it has become evident to you that the quality isn't all that great; it crashes once a day, and you've become accustomed to saving your documents every 15 minutes to avoid losing work in progress. Now vendor C finally delivers its product to the market-place, and it really *does* cost only $50, and it really *does* have a level of quality ten times higher than your existing product. Would you bother switching? Maybe—but maybe not. What if product C required you to convert all of your existing word processing docu-ments to a different format? What if it required you to switch to a dif-ferent operating system? You might well conclude that product B was "good enough"—and the project manager for product B might well have outsmarted the project manager for product C, even though C was pursuing a set of goals that we would all admire as software professionals.

The point is that the software project manager has to be aware that *each* of the project parameters—cost, schedule, staffing, functional-ity, and quality—is potentially critical today, and it is up to the cus-tomer (which may be the end user for an in-house system, or the marketing department for a software product company) to decide what the proper balance is. It's also crucial to remember that the bal-ance between the parameters is a dynamic one and may need to be readjusted daily. After all, the business environment is likely to change in a dramatic, unpredictable way—and this can easily change the cus-tomer's perception of the importance of schedule, cost, and so forth.

As a mental abstraction, any intelligent customer—especially one who has survived in today's tumultuous business times—is aware of the need to make trade-offs and to balance priorities. But customers are often naive about the details; for example, it may not occur to them that defects (aka "bugs") are an aspect of the software that we have to consciously plan for, and for which we have to establish trade-offs in terms of other parameters. And, of course, they may not want to make cold-blooded, rational, calculated decisions about those trade-offs: It's understandable (even though immensely frustrating) for a customer to demand a software system in half the time and half the cost, with half the staff and twice the functionality, and half as many defects as the developers believe is technologically possible.

What does this mean for the project manager? If we can assume for the moment that we're dealing with rational customers and that a rational negotiation can determine the criteria for project success, then it is incumbent upon the manager to be as forthright and detailed as possible about *all* of the relevant success criteria. Thus, instead of just *assuming* that zero-defect quality is required, the project manager should be able to say something like, "Our standard approach for developing the software you've described will require X number of people and Y units of time, with a cost of Z dollars; we'll deliver P units of functionality, with a defect level of Q bugs per function point."

Chances are that the proposed combination of X, Y, Z, P, and Q will *not* be acceptable to the customer; the likely response might be "You can't have Y units of time; we need to have the software in half that much time." A less rational response might be, "We want twice as much functionality as you proposed, but you can only have half as many people, half the time, and half the cost." This is possible, assuming (unrealistically, most likely) that the customer completely relaxes the constraint on the number of defects; after all, I can deliver an infinite amount of software, with an infinite amount of functionality, in zero time—if it doesn't have to work at all. The least rational response of all, from our customers, is one that constrains *all* of the project success parameters to some level that is demonstrably unachievable.

It *is* perfectly rational for our customers to challenge our proposal for X, Y, Z, P, and Q—particularly if we can get them to focus their attention on one parameter at a time. If the user wants the software in 0.5 units of time, then it's incumbent on us to provide a counterproposal that shows the impact that such a change will have upon one or more of the other parameters. Some twenty years ago Fred Brooks reminded us, in *The Mythical Man-Month*, that time and staff-resources are not interchangeable in a linear relationship; if we reduce the project schedule in half, it will *more* than double the required staff. Or we can cut the schedule in half, keep the staff constant, and increase the cost in a nonlinear fashion (e.g., by having the constant-level staff work extraordinary levels of overtime).

The mathematics of the relationships between X, Y, Z, P, and Q are something we don't know enough about at our present level of software engineering. Larry Putnam and Ware Myers have explored this in their book, *Measures for Excellence*, but much more work is necessary. Similarly, some of the commercial estimating packages allow for some exploration of the trade-offs between these parameters when establishing the initial project estimates and plans—but they rarely allow for dynamic renegotiations once the project has commenced. Renegotiation may not be all that important in a project that only takes three months; but in a project that extends over a year or two, it's almost inevitable in today's turbulent business environment.

While the precise nature of the mathematical relationships has yet to be developed in detail, we have enough information today—especially from the work of such metrics experts as Larry Putnam, Howard Rubin, and Capers Jones—to provide a reasonable basis for a rational discussion of the issues with our customers. The biggest difficulty, I believe, will be one of politics and management. Getting our customers to engage in such a rational negotiation will probably require some extensive education, but getting our project managers to negotiate in this fashion will be equally difficult.

It will be indeed difficult to say to our customers, "I'm going to deliver a system to you in six months that will have 5,000 bugs in it—and you're going to be *very* happy!" But that is likely to be the world many of us are likely to live in for the next several years. As James Bach argues [1],

> ...we have some idea what software quality is, but no certain idea. We have some methods to produce it and measure it, but no certain methods. Quality is inhibited by the complexity of the system, invisibility of the system, sensitivity to tiny mistakes, entropy due to development, interaction with external components, and interaction with the end user. In summary, creating products of the best possible quality is a very, very expensive proposition, while on the other hand, our clients may not even notice the difference between the best possible quality and pretty good quality.

7.2 WHAT PREVENTS US FROM BUILDING GOOD-ENOUGH SOFTWARE?

None of us want to build "shoddy" software; on the other hand, sometimes we become obsessed with building "perfect" software. What is it that prevents us from satisfying our customers by delivering what they regard as "good-enough" software? I've already hinted at some of the reasons; here's a more complete list:

- We have a tendency to define quality only in terms of defects — and we assume that fewer defects mean better quality and that "mo' better" quality is always preferred by user. At the 5th International Software Quality Conference in Austin, Texas, in October 1995, metrics guru Capers Jones showed the results of a survey of senior management opinions about quality. "Defects" typically ranked fourth or fifth in a list of ten items; issues like cost and time to market were typically among the top three priorities.

- We define quality (defect) requirements/objectives once, at the beginning of the project, and keep it fixed. This makes sense in a stable environment, but nothing about today's development projects is likely to be stable—including the technology that we use, the vendors we rely on, and even the members of our project teams.

- We've been told for such a long time that processes are crucial, that we often forget that processes are "neutral." Processes don't build high-quality software; they merely provide a framework for good people, supported with good tools and technology, to do good work. But ISO-9000 and the SEI-CMM don't help if you have incompetent people: A fool with a "process-tool" is still a fool. And the wrong process can be a disaster, too; as Abraham Maslow once observed, "If your only tool is a hammer, all your problems look like a nail."

- We pursue quality with a fixed process that we define once, at the beginning of the project—or, even worse, for all projects in the whole company. This is one of the more common mistakes that I see when I visit project teams. Many well-intentioned organizations apply process improvement principles at the end of a project, so that the next project will follow a better process—but they won't allow the project manager to modify the process (or in the extreme case, scrap it entirely) during a project. But common sense tells us that we might need to do just that, and a project manager needs to know that it's acceptable to change the game plan if necessary, without being visited by the process police. Suppose, for example, you've adopted an object-oriented development process for your project—but two months into the project, when your first prototype is being demonstrated to the user, you learn that (a) the run-time performance is miserable and has no chance of scaling up for larger volumes of processing, (b) the two key OO wizards on your project team fell in love, got married, quit, and have left for a honeymoon in the Himalayas, (c) the OO

CASE vendor you were depending on has just gone bankrupt, and (d) two months of experience has demonstrated that nothing about the project really required the OO paradigm anyway. Do you really want to be compelled, by organizational mandate, to continue using an OO approach?

- We underestimate the nonlinear trade-offs between such key parameters as staff size, schedule, budget, and defects; at the "macro" level of planning, which usually occurs in the early stages of the project, our users naively assume that the relationships are all linear. IT professionals intuitively understand the nonlinearity, but typically don't have any quantitative alternatives they can show the user. There are several good, commercial estimating packages to assist in this kind of planning, but only a small percentage of projects use them.

- As I suggested in Chapter 4, we ignore the dynamics of the processes: time delays, feedback loops, etc. This usually happens at the "micro" level of planning, later in the project, when the project managers says, "If we decide now to drop function X from the development plan, it will save us 3.14159 work days of effort..."—but there is almost always a "ripple effect" associated with these decisions, and most organizations lack a system-dynamics modeling approach that would make it practical to study the consequences of those ripple effects.

- We ignore the "soft factors" associated with the software development process, such as morale, adequacy of office space, and the like. It's very hard to build good-enough software if your project team members are demoralized, grumpy, and exhausted. This still comes as a surprise to some managers!

7.3 DEFENDING GOOD-ENOUGH SOFTWARE

Here are some typical objections and complaints about the good-enough software approach. Some of these concerns may have occurred to you while reading this chapter; in any case, I guarantee that someone in your IT organization will articulate them:

- *This is just an excuse to build mediocre software.* No, no, NO! Professional software developers don't want to develop mediocre products. But even if we define "perfect" software and even if that definition didn't change during the course of the project, the reality in most projects today is that we won't be given the optimal resources to do the job "right." Given sub-optimal resources, it's our responsibility to make sure that we and the user understand what's going to be sacrificed: schedule, functionality, defect-reduction, practices or some combination of the three.

- *This may be relevant for Microsoft and other shrink-wrap software producers, but not for us.* Oh, yeah? Ask your users what they think about it. Don't presume—as IT professionals often do—that you know what's "best" for the user.

- *We build high-reliability systems, so this approach isn't relevant for us.* Wrong! The approach is still valid—but the balance between schedule, feature richness, and defects is skewed more heavily in favor of defect reduction. Unless your project team is staffed by Ph.D. computer scientists capable of developing a mathematical proof of correctness and unless your project involves fewer than a thousand lines of code, it's virtually impossible to guarantee that there will be zero bugs in the software. There is always a trade-off between time, functionality, and defects.

- *This will lead to anarchy.* In the worst case, true—but it's even more likely if you put your developers and/or your users into a situation where they're forced to follow completely irrational and unrealistic software processes. Good-enough software can be, and should be, a carefully managed, proactive risk-management approach.

- *Maybe you're right, but my managers won't accept it.* Well, is that good enough for you? If all else fails, vote with your feet.

7.4 BUILDING GOOD-ENOUGH SOFTWARE

As noted above, those who feel that the concept of good-enough software is heresy often describe it as a "flight from quality" or an acceptance of mediocrity on the part of an IT organization in its people, its products, and its processes. And indeed, there is a very real danger of falling into this kind of mind-set: Whether it's in software development or any other profession, we sometimes see people responding to projects and deadlines and customer requests by delivering the least amount of value they can get away, at the last possible moment. Under normal circumstances, most of us would prefer to think that we had delivered the most amount of value that we could manage with the limited resources available to us, and that we did so as early as possible in order to be proactive rather than reactive.

And good-enough software can be approached in this fashion: as a conscious, aggressive, proactive strategy to deliver the best possible combination of functionality, low defects, and quick delivery—given that we have limited resources and a great deal of uncertainty about every aspect of software development. James Bach [1] argues that there are five "key process ideas" involved in creating good-enough software. I discuss these ideas below.

7.4.1 A Utilitarian Strategy

Bach describes a utilitarian strategy as the "art of qualitatively analyzing and maximizing net positive consequences in an ambiguous situation. It encompasses ideas from systems thinking, risk management, economics, decision theory, game theory, control theory, and fuzzy logic."

What does this mean in practical terms? Obviously, it means that the classic waterfall strategy for developing software should be tossed out; but more than that, it means that any fixed, rigid, authoritarian methodology, or life cycle approach, for developing software should be tossed out the window. Some organizations follow a software development approach that allows the project team to customize the life-cycle and the overall development process at the beginning of the project; that's a good beginning, but as we'll see below, we even need to allow customization during the software project.

Some organizations follow a rapid-prototyping approach, or variations on the iterative, spiral, or evolutionary lifecycles that have been described by methodology gurus like Barry Boehm over the years: An even more interesting variation is the SCRUM methodology, which has been popularized recently by Ken Schwaber (virman@aol.com) at Advanced Development Methods in Burlington, Massachusetts. A good summary of these methodologies can be found in *Wicked Systems* by Peter DeGrace and Leslie Stahl (Prentice Hall, 1990).

7.4.2 An Evolutionary Strategy

Bach notes that "evolution is discussed [in the literature] mainly in regard to the project life cycle. What I'd also point out is that we can take an evolutionary view of our people, processes, and resources."

A moment's thought will convince you that this kind of evolution does happen in the real world, whether or not we want to acknowledge it. A project might begin, for example, with a team of ten people and a set of resources consisting of workstations, offices, conference rooms, funds for research and training, and so forth. But as the project continues, we might find that some of the project team members leave, while others acquire more experience and skills. The resources will increase or decrease, depending on the economic fortunes of the enterprise. And the development processes used by the team can change in an evolutionary way, too, depending on the availability of technology, people, and resources.

Typical elements of an evolution strategy include the following:

- Build good-enough versions of the deliverable system in self-contained stages, using some form of a time-box approach. Among other things, this practice will give you and the customer an opportunity to see which combination of feature richness, defect elimination, and rapid delivery characterizes "good enough."

- Acknowledge at the beginning of the project that you won't be able to plan everything—i.e., that some aspects of the project are essentially unknowable until you've actually carried them out. (This is the definition of a "wicked system" in the DeGrace and Stahl book.)

- Integrate early and often; Microsoft's "daily build" approach is a good one to emulate here—i.e., generate source code, compile it, install it, and build an operational, working prototype of your application every day.

- Reuse, purchase, or salvage existing software components wherever feasible.

- Record and review the experiences that occur during the project. This is another aspect of the dynamic, evolutionary approach: The few organization that I've seen carrying out such evaluations refer to them as post-mortems, a term originally used to describe a medical examination of a dead body. A post-mortem of a completed project—whether or not it was a success—is typically nothing more than an exercise in recording vaguely remembered bits and pieces of history. As Tom DeMarco points out in his new book, *Why Does Software Cost So Much?*, the post-mortem has little or no effect on subsequent projects. "We really made a terrible mistake when we did X," the project team will write in their post-mortem report. "We should resolve never to do X again on any future project." But by then, everyone is already working on another project, and since nobody pays much attention to the details of a dead project, X has already been done again. But what about a post-mortem review during a project—i.e., at the end of each deliverable version? It doesn't have to be a protracted exercise; a half-day, or full-day meeting (preferably off-site, away from the office) gives the team a chance to review its recent activities while it still matters. Lessons learned can be applied to the next deliverable version; processes, tools, and even personnel assignments can be modified to increase the chances of success for the next milestone.

7.4.3 Heroic Teams

Bach describes heroic teams as "not...the Mighty Morphin Genius Programmers,...[but]...ordinary, skillful people working in effective collaboration." The assertion that development of good-enough software requires "heroic teams" is almost as controversial as the idea of good-enough software itself. You can imagine the arguments and complaints: Heroes are cowboys. Heroes are unmanageable. Heroes are obnoxious, and they insult our customers. Heroes are arrogant loners, and they're not team players. Heroes don't document their code. Heroes write *terrible* code that nobody else can maintain. And besides, there aren't many heroes; even if we wanted them, we couldn't find them, and our management wouldn't let us pay the kind of salary they want.

Yeah, yeah, yeah...all of this is true, to a greater or lesser extent. And it's easy to see how these characteristics would be regarded as unacceptable in the typical IT organization—particularly if it's a large IT organization (with several hundred people) embedded within a larger enterprise. Ironically, even though the majority of business enterprises around the world today depend utterly and absolutely on their IT systems to survive, and even though they are in the "information processing" business to a greater or lesser extent, they don't think of themselves that way. If you ask any manager or any knowledge worker of the Acme Widget Company what business he's in, he'll reply "widgets!" without a moment's hesitation; thus, the most valued employees in the enterprise are those who invent widgets, manufacture widgets, sell widgets, distribute widgets, fix widgets, or count widgets. The CEOs of such companies are likely to tell you proudly about their early days in the company, when they sold widgets door-to-door and when they knew every nuance of every model of widget the company manufactured.

The heroes in such companies are "widget-masters," regardless of their official title—"chief designer," or "creative director," or "senior bond trader." And they are revered for their talents; to the extent that they have shortcomings, these are excused as part of the psychological makeup of the widget-master. Sure, people will complain that their widget-masters are cowboys and that they're largely unmanageable; they'll acknowledge that widget-masters are sometimes obnoxious, and they insult the customers. Widget-masters are arrogant loners, and they're not team players. They don't document their plans, designs, and ideas...but since the company's entire being depends on their talents, their shortcomings are accepted as a necessary part of life.

Of course, one could argue that this is no longer an accurate picture of today's modern enterprise: Banks, insurance companies, financial services companies, airlines, and dozens of other industries are so "information-intensive" that it's dangerously misleading to portray them as being in the "widget" business. Nevertheless, the culture of these companies is often based on a long tradition—which may stretch back over decades or even centuries—and it's strongly influenced by middle managers and senior management who began working in the company in the pre-IT world of the 1950s and 1960s.

As a result, even though software is likely to be crucial to the widget company's day-to-day operations, it's still a mystery—and it's still an expensive, frustrating overhead item in the company's profit-and-loss statement. The cultural consequence is pretty obvious: Nobody wants any software heroes, and everyone who has risen to a position of power in the corporate culture resists the idea of glorifying and rewarding a software hero. It may be necessary to tolerate a few of them from time to time, but everyone is delighted when the time comes that they can be pushed out the door.

One of the places where this attitude is clearly not present is the "shrink-wrap" PC-software-product companies; software is the very essence of the business, and its senior executives are frequently the ones who developed the company's initial software product. And given the demands for surviving—as a world-class competitor—in such a business, it's not surprising that the shrink-wrap software companies are the ones who have developed, articulated, and championed the concept of good-enough software. Other companies that are beginning to recognize the crucial value of software heroes are the multimedia companies, the software-game companies, the interactive-entertainment companies, the information service-providers, and, yes, even a few banks and insurance companies and stodgy old widget manufacturers.

The impact of all this on our profession is both subtle and profound, and it's particularly evident in the published literature. The situation could be compared to the art of warfare: Though I haven't done a literature search, I suspect that far more books have been written about waging war with conventional armies and navies than the relatively few books that have been written about strategies for commandos and guerrilla soldiers. In our field, everyone knows about the startup software companies that are clearly populated by heroes, and whose activities may be highly successful, but are also highly risky and uncertain. But while we sometimes do see books about these software heroes [4, 6], there is rarely any formal discussion about the process they use for developing successful software products; Jim McCarthy's book [8] about software development at Microsoft is the closest thing that I've seen to an overt discussion of strategies for developing good-enough software.

What we *do* see in the software literature is an enormous amount of discussion about software processes as the key "driver" in developing world-class software; the SEI's capability maturity model (CMM) is a very visible and important example of that school of thought. I believe that there are some excellent concepts embodied in the SEI-CMM, and I believe that Humphrey's new PSP, which I discussed in Chapter 5, contains some important new additions to those ideas. But there are some potentially serious weaknesses in such process-driven approaches, particularly in today's topsy-turvy business environment, for it creates an environment where people can abdicate personal responsibility by delegating everything to the process.

For example, consider the adage that says, "If there's a defect, don't blame the person; blame the process that led to the defect." Well, that's fine: It preserves the software professional's ego and sense of self-worth, and we can presumably modify the process so that we won't have the same problem on the next project. But meanwhile, what about this project? Whose job is it to recognize that the process failed on this project? Whose responsibility is it to forge ahead, solve the problem, and find a work-around to the faulty process? Whose job is it to *get the job done?* And as for the next project: How do we know that the modified process will work?—after all, the environment is likely to have changed again, so that a different set of conditions will be encountered by the next project team.

James Bach [1] observes another problem with conventional software processes, especially the ones that are developed and documented and enforced in large organizations:

> Orthodox methodologies don't fly with good enough software companies for one reason more than any other: they're boring. Bored people don't work hard. They don't take initiative, and they avoid ambiguous problems instead of tackling them with gusto. Take care to create an exciting environment that fosters responsible heroism, and great software will follow.

This doesn't mean that we should abandon all processes and resort to complete anarchy or uncoordinated efforts by individual superheroes; a good-enough software team *does* have processes, but as noted above, those processes are dynamic, and they operate within an evolutionary framework. It's a question of degree: If you're fighting a war with an army of a million people with average talents, you use one set of tactics. If you're waging war with a guerrilla army of a few dozen or a couple hundred people, you need a different caliber of people and a different set of tactics. Good-enough software, combined with software heroes, is just such a combination.

Much of the exciting, successful software that we've seen in our industry in the past 30 or 40 years has indeed been developed by such guerrilla teams, typically involving fewer than a dozen people. On the other hand, the trend during much of the 70s and 80s for most

IT organizations was the creation of ever-larger software armies, sometimes leading to projects involving thousands of people. Some of those projects did succeed, but many of them resulted in spectacular failures; such projects have been banned in many large enterprises, and they no longer represent the dominant trend in software development. Nor are they necessary in many cases today: The power of modern programming tools often makes it possible for a small team of five to accomplish the same results as a team of 500 people using an older generation of technology.

7.4.4 Dynamic Infrastructure

Bach describes dynamic infrastructure as the antithesis of bureaucracy and power politics. An IT organization with a dynamic infrastructure is one in which upper management pays attention to projects, pays attention to the market, identifies and resolves conflicts between projects, allows the project to "win" when there are conflicts between projects and organizational bureaucracy, and one in which project experience is incorporated into the organizational memory.

Note that the "best practices" approach discussed in Chapter 6 is a good mechanism for documenting and evangelizing such project experiences. But the key point here is that good-enough software development probably won't succeed in the highly political environment that we still find in many IT organizations today. If the organizational climate is characterized by back-stabbing, empire-building, and following rigid procedures because "that's the way we've always done things around here," then good-enough software can still be developed in isolated circumstances, but typically only when a fanatically devoted project team finds a way to sneak off and carry out a "skunk-works" project.

7.4.5 Dynamic Processes

Bach describes dynamic processes as those that change with the situation—"processes that support work in an evolving, collaborative environment. Dynamic processes are ones you can always question because every dynamic process is part of an identifiable metaprocess."

He suggests that three key attributes of dynamic processes are portability, scalability, and durability:

- Portability: How can the process be shared with others, applied to new problems, and carried into meetings for discussions with others?
- Scalability: Can the process be carried out manually by one person on a small project, as well as being carried out with automated support on a big project—so that it's applicable across a broad range of projects taking place within the organization?
- Durability: Can the process withstand misuse and neglect?

7.5 THE IMPLICATIONS FOR AMERICAN SOFTWARE

Why should any of this be cause for celebration? What does it have to do with my sense of a "rise and resurrection" in the American software industry?

Like everything else about the software industry, there are no secrets here; there is no magic. There is no reason why a software organization in Kuala Lumpur or Cairo couldn't follow the same strategy that we see in Redmond, Washington, or Cambridge, Massachusetts. Indeed, one could argue that the pragmatic, utilitarian "good-enough" strategy is universally practiced in small startup software companies around the world.

On the other hand, the good-enough approach to software works well in an American culture and is less successful in various cultures that emphasize top-down authoritarian management styles and those that favor a group consensus over individualistic decision-making. I'm certainly not a professional sociologist, so my observations should be read with some caution—but I think it's a safe generalization to suggest that European cultures and some Asian cultures may be less comfortable with the good-enough software strategy than the "cowboy" culture that prevails in many American software companies.

On the other hand, remember that the pragmatic aspect of good-enough software is driven by competitive market pressures; many of the emerging software companies in the developing countries of Asia, Africa, and Latin America are keenly aware of such pressures.

Indeed, the pressures are often far greater than those faced in U.S. startup companies, because the lack of capital, technology, and infrastructure support is often much more severe than that faced by American software entrepreneurs who build their first software product in the relative comfort of a well-heated garage with a state-of-the-art Pentium PC.

As noted above, our opinions about good-enough software are often evident in the published literature in our field. I find it interesting, for example, that Europe and much of Asia embrace the ISO-9000 approach to software quality, while the U.S. favors the SEI-CMM. Ignoring the details of these two schools of thought, there is one fundamental difference: ISO-9000 certification is binary, whereas the SEI model has five "levels" of process maturity. In the ISO-9000 scheme, an organization is either certified or it's not; in the SEI scheme, an IT organization might well decide that level 2 is "good enough" for the kind of software it develops and that level 5 is an unnecessary objective.

This is somewhat akin to the arguments about quality that we began hearing in the 1980s, when the U.S. approach was often compared to the Japanese approach. Many Japanese companies argued that quality was an absolute: You either had it or you didn't. And many American companies argued that it was relative: you either had a lot of it or not very much of it. In a mature, relatively stable environment, one might prefer the "absolute" school of thought—if for no other reason than the pressure from competitors who are achieving it, in the form of zero-defect "six-sigma" quality.

But the software industry is far from mature or stable. For many software organizations, everything changes chaotically every day. The hardware technology changes abruptly on a regular basis; one day we hear that our favorite hardware chip doesn't do floating-point arithmetic correctly, and the next day we hear that the same vendor now has a chip ten times more powerful. The competition changes equally abruptly, as do the economy, the government regulations, the weather, and the desires of an eminently fickle marketplace. In such an environment, cowboys prevail and good-enough software reigns supreme.

Keep in mind that the stakes are not trivial for many software organizations that pursue the good-enough approach. If you're an application developer building an in-house customer-information system, your success or failure may be terribly important to you and your end user, but it's typically not visible to the rest of the world. But if you're Microsoft, Borland, Lotus, Computer Associates, or one of the other large software-product companies, you're dealing with a marketplace that involves millions of customers and millions of copies of your product. Indeed, this raises an entirely different issue that contributes mightily to the success of software organizations today—marketing—which I'll discuss in Chapter 10.

7.6 SUMMARY AND CONCLUSIONS

Whether or not you agree with all of this, the concept of good-enough software has clearly become part of the daily operating strategy in many of the successful software-product companies today. It has also become part of the *sub rosa* strategy for application development in many conventional IT organizations. While they continue to promote and support conventional ideas about zero-defect software, process improvement, and formal methodologies, the reality of today's high-pressure business environment simply forces application development teams to adopt the more utilitarian approach discussed in this chapter. In this regard, the difference between a Silicon Valley software-product company and an in-house Visual Basic application development team is that the Silicon Valley programmers know what they're doing and are proud of it; and they're also rewarded explicitly for following such a strategy, whereas the in-house Visual Basic team often feels guilty that it adopted a pragmatic approach that required it to "cut corners" when dealing with the official company methodology.

As noted above, the good-enough software approach does not mean abandoning all processes and discipline; but it does mean shifting the emphasis from the process (and the higher-level managers who invent the process) to the individuals who are responsible for delivering successful results. And to some extent, this represents a career choice for all of us as software professionals. To use an analogy: would you rather be a soldier in the U.S. Army or a commando in the Green Berets?

So what should you do about all of this? Here are some suggestions for IT managers:

- Convene a group of your most thoughtful, articulate people on this topic and see what they think about it. Take them off-site, and give them a few drinks to loosen their tongues—otherwise, they're likely to continue chanting the corporate mantra, "Methodologies are good. Our methodology is the best. We will always strive to deliver perfect software on time, under budget, may God have mercy on our souls." You're going to find some violent disagreements on the concepts discussed in this chapter; you need to get this debate out in the open, and see if you can arrive at a consensus.

- Convene a group of your key end users and senior managers and engage in a similar discussion with them. Do they even understand what the trade-offs are between functionality, defects, and speed of delivery? Do they agree that it's something that has to be negotiated rationally at the beginning of a project, and then reevaluated dynamically during the project? If you operate in a highly competitive business environment, there's a good chance that your users are ahead of you in this area.

- Review your existing methodologies, software development life cycles, standards, and training to see whether they're compatible with the good-enough approach. Chances are they're not compatible, and chances are that the group that developed all of it (e.g., the standards group, the quality assurance group, the process improvement group, or whatever you call it) will strongly oppose any efforts to change things.

And here are some thoughts for IT professionals:

- If you're having trouble with the concept of good-enough software, imagine that your software project was your own business, and the revenues it generates are the only thing that will pay the salary and the rent each month. With that perspective, how would you change your approach to developing software?

- Make sure your managers read this chapter, since it will summarize what might otherwise take you an hour or two to explain. It will also give them a chance to mull over the issues in private, rather than being forced to give you an on-the-spot answer to a verbal presentation.

- Make sure you stay abreast of ongoing discussions and debates about good-enough software. Web pages mentioned elsewhere in this book, as well as Internet discussion groups, are a good source; as this book was being written, a lively debate on the topic was taking place on the CompuServe® CASEFORUM.

- If you encounter strong resistance from your IT managers and/or the various groups in charge of defining official company standards and policies (which is highly likely), then incorporate this into your own career-oriented risk management plan. If you work in an academic research institution or a government monopoly, then perhaps you can afford to ignore everything in this chapter; but if your IT organization is part of a business enterprise in today's competitive environment, then ignoring the good-enough approach is putting your career in peril.

REFERENCES

1. Bach, James. "The Challenge of 'Good Enough' Software." *American Programmer*, October 1995.

2. Brand, Stewart. "The Physicist." *Wired*, 3.09, September 1995, p. 154.

3. Brooks, Frederick. *The Mythical Man-Month*. 20th anniversary edition. (Reading, MA: Addison-Wesley, 1995).

4. Coupland, Doug. *Microserfs*. (New York: HarperCollins, 1995).

5. Gross, Neil, Peter Coy, and Otis Port. "The Technology Paradox." *Business Week*, March 6, 1995.

6. Kaplan, Jerry. *Startup*. (Boston, MA: Houghton Mifflin, 1994).

7. McCarthy, Jim. *Dynamics of Software Development*. (Redmond, WA: Microsoft Press, 1995).

8. Putnam, Larry, and Ware Myers. *Measures for Excellence: Reliable Software on Time, Within Budget*. (Englewood Cliffs, NJ: Prentice Hall/Yourdon Press, 1992).

9. Yourdon, Edward. "When Good Enough Software Is Best." *IEEE Software*, May 1995.

Part Three

THE BRAVE
NEW WORLD

SERVICE SYSTEMS

A new world is not made simply by trying to forget the old. A new world is made with a new spirit, with new values. Our world may have begun that way, but today it is caricatural. Our world is a world of things.... What we dread most, in the face of the impending débâcle, is that we shall be obliged to give up our gewgaws, our gadgets, all the little comforts that have made us so uncomfortable.... We are not peaceful souls; we are smug, timid, queasy and quakey.

Henry Miller, The Air-Conditioned Nightmare, *Preface (1945).*

8.1 WHY DO WE RECREATE THE SAME OLD STUFF?

The concepts and techniques in the preceding seven chapters are important ones for those of us who are involved in building the information systems that keep our companies running. Whether it's an order-entry system using the latest user-interface paradigm or a process control system using distributed processors to keep a manufacturing plant running, or a decision support system that will *finally* provide senior management with the information they need—our customers and end users never seem to tire of asking for more and more and *more* software from us. And to cope with the competitive pressures of a global software marketplace, we need to produce this software faster, cheaper, and better than ever before.

I've been an active participant in the software industry for over 30 years now, and I'm constantly amazed by the tendency of the marketplace to keep asking for the same kind of applications, over and over again. Haven't we already built payroll systems and order-entry systems and process control systems? Do we really need another decision support system for our senior executives—after all, if they didn't use the last system, should we really be so optimistic that they'll use this one?

Of course, there's a good argument that says the first generations of information systems, as well the "products" built around those systems were pretty crude. George Basalla [1] and Henry Petroski [4] have observed that many of the artifacts of technology that we take for granted today underwent numerous iterations, sometimes over a period of centuries, before becoming well-polished; even the lowly paper clip went through seven generations of refinement and improvement. There's no doubt that the information systems of the 1960s and 1970s were pretty crude beginnings; indeed, even the systems of the 1980s were mediocre in many respects. So perhaps we *do* need to keep building the same old systems, over and over again, just to make them adequate for their intended purpose.

Meanwhile, we're placing that software inside hardware units that have improved by some six orders of magnitude during my lifetime. Even if we had not changed a single program statement in the application software written in, say, 1965, the effects would be astounding—for the same old application software would now run thousands of times faster, and the storage capacity for the data associated with those applications would be thousands of times greater. Computing results that used to take hours or days now take seconds or less—and this in itself would be sufficient for revolutionary changes in the way we do business, though nobody would thank the software industry for making it possible.

But with the exception of a few ancient government systems and perhaps a few moth-eaten application programs in a few insurance companies and banks, we have *not* kept the same old software that we first wrote in 1965; we have rewritten our applications over and over again, not only to make them more suitable for the user's real needs, but to take advantage of the ever-increasing hardware power in order to add new functionality and new ways of interacting with the software. Most computer professionals are familiar with Moore's Law, published in 1965, which observed that the number of components on a microchip had doubled every year since 1959 and that the trend would continue until at least 1975; Microsoft's chief technologist, Nathan Myhrvold, argues that the same thing is happening with software:

> ...it turns out that like hardware, software also has to undergo something like Moore's Law. I did a study of a variety of Microsoft products: I counted the number of lines of code for successive releases. Basic had 4,000 lines of code in 1975. Currently, it has perhaps half a million. Microsoft Word was at 27,000 lines of code in the first version. It's now about 2 million. So, we have increased the size and complexity of software *even faster* than Moore's Law. [2]

Myrvold's two examples are intriguing, for they illustrate the advantages and disadvantages of this hundred-fold increase in the size and complexity of software that has occurred during the past twenty years. While there may be some die-hard reactionaries who remember the good old days of the early versions of Basic on vintage-1975 microprocessors (as well as the earlier versions that date back to Dartmouth's time sharing Basic in the 1960s), most of us would agree that today's version of Visual Basic has opened up a whole new world of computing possibilities for many organizations. While it would be an exaggeration to say that Visual Basic created the client-server revolution, it certainly has added a considerable momentum to that revolution.

But as for Microsoft Word—and, by extension, the comparable word processors from Lotus and Corel and other suppliers—it would be difficult to find a wide consensus that we're a hundred times better off than we were twenty years ago, or even ten times better off than we were a decade ago. This book, for example, is being written with the very latest version of Microsoft Word, and while it does have a few nifty features that I've grown to love (such as the "auto-correct" feature that handles all of the transpositions of "i" and "o" as I type), my "gut" instinct is that it's only incrementally better than the version of Microsoft Word that I used on my first Macintosh in the summer of 1985 to write *Nations at Risk*. The hardware is obviously much better—I didn't even have a hard disk on my first Mac—but the functionality within the software is still, for my purposes, pretty much the same.

But if Microsoft has increased the size of Word by a factor of a hundred, surely they must have done something besides enhancing the user interface (which was already pretty good on vintage-1985 Macintoshes!). And indeed, a brief tour through the pull-down menus makes it obvious that there are dozens, if not hundreds, of new features in the current version. A grammar checker, a thesaurus, macros, hyphenation, sophisticated mail-merge support, etc., etc.—the list goes on and on. Presumably, someone out there in the marketplace needs all these new features; as for me, I'm enough of a technology junkie that I typically upgrade to new versions of software products whether I need to or not. On the other hand, many people proudly and defiantly announce that they are continuing to use word processors or spreadsheet packages one or two versions behind the vendor's latest release, because they can't stand the "feature bloat" in the products they now refer to as "fatware."

All of this reminds me of the automobile industry. In the 1950s and 1960s, when the U.S. automobile industry reigned supreme, the marketplace was enticed to buy cars that became ever larger, heavier, and gaudier. It's not clear to me that the tail-fins and the vast amount of chrome on that generation of cars made us drive any more quickly or safely, but the TV commercials insisted that we would be happier with them. And then came the Japanese imports in the 1970s: In addition to being cheaper and higher-quality, they were also smaller, leaner, simpler, and more fuel-efficient. Could there be a lesson here for the software industry?

8.2 CORE SYSTEMS, INFRASTRUCTURE SYSTEMS, AND SERVICE SYSTEMS

Many people reading this book will argue, "That may be relevant for Lotus, Borland, and Microsoft—but I'm not building word processing packages. What's this got to do with me?"

Indeed, there are some special consequences of this trend for software-product companies, which I'll discuss in Chapter 11. But even if you're building conventional order-entry applications, there is an important lesson: *Software is becoming a commodity.* Word processors are *obviously* a commodity: You can buy them at the corner store, and they're all pretty much the same. While your choice of WordPerfect® versus Microsoft Word might be based on the underlying functionality of the two products, it's equally likely that your choice will be based on a combination of price, service, support, convenient access (do they have it in stock at the corner deli?), and the power of the advertising message from the respective manufacturers. These are also the factors that have a dominant influence on your purchase of automobiles, television sets, and toothpaste.

And by the same argument, most conventional business application software is also a commodity. Notwithstanding the fact that almost all application software has gotten faster and better and sexier during the past twenty years, the key point to remember is that our customers now have multiple choices and multiple vendors. *They can get the software anywhere.* Remarkably sophisticated accounting systems and payroll packages can be purchased for $100 from Egghead Software; more elaborate business applications can be purchased for larger sums of money from well-established software firms such as SAP and Peoplesoft. And if the user requirements are particularly unique, our customers have now learned that they are no longer constrained to have the software developed in-house. They are no longer captive victims: They can outsource the development work to local consulting firms or to offshore programming shops on the other side of the world.

What does this mean for those of us who want to make a living developing software? In simple terms, it means that if we continue working on conventional business applications, we're going to have to accept the fact that we're in a commodity business—where pricing and cost-control and marketing and distribution may well turn out to be the driving forces of the business. The functionality and quality of the product will be important, too, but it will be expected as a "given," as a condition for doing business. And within that commodity marketplace, we may find that there are some dramatic shifts as the customers decide that they no longer want bloated fatware and that smaller, leaner systems are what they really want.[1]

But there's more to it than that. The basic message of this chapter is that if we're *really* going to be competitive, and if we're really going to have fun (why else work in this industry, anyway?[2]), then we need to find something beyond commodity software to develop. My colleague Rob Thomsett suggests that a good way to think about this is to distinguish between *core* systems, *infrastructure* systems, and *service* systems. Most of us have spent our career working on core systems and infrastructure systems, and it is these two categories that have become commodities. The "new world" that we should be focusing on is the service systems; systems built around the information highway, which I'll discuss in Chapter 9, are one good example of such systems.

Core systems provide the fundamental business processing requirements of an organization, and they're typically unique within an industry—e.g., network management systems in a telecom company, reservation systems within the airline industry, and checking-

---

[1] There's a straightforward technology solution to this for many conventional PC applications: *component-based* software. We already see small signs of this with the installation options available from some of the major vendors: The full set of software comes on a CD-ROM, and we have the option of installing a "full set," a "typical set," or a "minimal set" of the software onto our machine. But the flexibility is quite limited; it usually involves little more than the choice of whether to install the tutorials and help files and printer-drivers, *not* the composition of the basic software itself. I would like the option of installing my word processor and specifying, "No, I don't want the grammar checker and I don't want the thesaurus, and I never use mail-merge, and you can also leave out functions X, Y, and Z...". The result would hopefully be a piece of software that takes only half as much RAM and hard disk space, and runs twice as fast as the piggish full-featured package.

[2] This is not a frivolous remark. Business organizations tend to become serious, no-nonsense cultures, especially when they become large and worry about answering to the shareholders. And for the individual, there are times when we're serious, and we worry about paying the bills and keeping our jobs. Indeed, some of us have to worry about the possibility of having no job because of the competitive pressures discussed in detail in *Decline and Fall of the American Programmer*; but most of us assume that in the worst case, we could always get a job maintaining COBOL core systems for a brain-dead government agency somewhere. But who wants such a job? They're *boring*! Assuming that we have any control over our destiny, why not find something in our chosen profession that's fun and challenging, that gets the adrenaline going? You know that it's time to move on to a new job when your manager says to you, as A.P. Herbert said in "Is it a Free Country?" (*Uncommon Law*, 1935), "People must not do things for fun. We are not here for fun. There is no reference to fun in any act of Parliament."

account systems in the banking industry. But there's less and less competitive advantage associated with these systems; given the current state of technology, most large competitors have approximately the same core systems. This makes sense, particularly in light of the discussion above: These were the first systems that most large organizations automated in the 1960s and 70s; they have been refined and improved, not only to take advantage of new hardware technology, but also to match the features of the competitors within that industry. From the consumer's perspective, it's difficult to see any significant differences between the airline reservation system offered by American or United airlines; and if I changed my checking account from Citibank to Chase Manhattan, I would expect to deal with fundamentally equivalent information systems.

And the business executives within these organizations are beginning to develop a similar perspective: These core systems are essentially all the same. Because of that, they can be treated as a commodity, and they can be acquired from the suppliers of such commodity systems—whether it's a software-package company, or a "body shop" of programmers in Bangkok. This still leaves a lot of room for competitive distinctions and differentiation: Even if Bank A and Bank B purchase the same checking-account system from a vendor of checking-account packages, the two banks don't have to install it the same way, or service and support it in the same fashion. And, more important, that checking-account system will accumulate vast amounts of data during the day-to-day operation of the bank; how the bank decides to use that data can be a *very* unique decision and can be the basis of the service systems described below.

But before we can focus on the service systems, we need to have "infrastructure systems" in place. Infrastructure systems are the portfolio of applications required to maintain the organization as a financial and human resource unit; thus, they include such well-known applications as payroll, general ledger, and personnel systems. This, of course, is another area that has consumed an enormous amount of software talent during the past 30 years—and even today, many software professional are still spending their time working on new versions of such systems. Unfortunately, the infrastructure systems don't offer much competitive advantage here, either: Is company A going to beat company B in the marketplace because its accounts receivable system is better? It's more likely that A and B will use commodity-style accounts-receivable packages; if one package is better than another, then it will gradually dominate its marketplace, or the competitors will work frantically to match the same level of functionality, support, pricing, and so forth.

There is one form of infrastructure system that *could* provide a competitive advantage for the next few years: groupware-based systems, ranging from electronic mail to Lotus Notes. But here again, we're looking at commodity solutions: Nobody in his right mind would develop customized in-house e-mail software today, nor would any rational organization attempt to replicate Lotus Notes for its own in-house use. Installing and deploying such systems is where the competitive differentiation is based, together with the massive changes to the organizational culture required to take advantage of such systems. As a systems analyst or as a general-purpose information technology consultant, this is a very exciting area to work in; but as a software engineer, designer, or programmer...well, installing and configuring cc:Mail™ is hardly very exciting, and even writing Lotus Notes scripts can get pretty boring after a while.

The real competitive advantage in the next few years, according to Rob Thomsett, will come from an "outer" layer of systems that he refers to as *service* systems: the systems whose purpose is to build extremely close and open relations between the organization and its clients. Have you seen the software package that Federal Express provides its customers, so that customers can track the status of their packages from their own PCs?[3] Can you imagine the Post Office (in *any* country) providing that kind of service? Do you wonder why we all avoid using the Post Office whenever possible, and trust our *really* valuable packages to FedEx, DHL, and UPS?

The important thing about the service systems is that they are proactive and individualized. In the past, companies have used information gleaned from their core systems to anticipate market trends

---

[3] The FedEx service is now available on the World Wide Web. I found out about this during a presentation at an Internet conference in November 1995, where the speaker joked, "Can you imagine how primitive it would be if Federal Express actually made you get a copy of their software and run it on a hardware/software platform that they specified?" Indeed, that's exactly what they did do when the service was first offered; but things move quickly in this field, and FedEx is already further ahead of its competitors with the WWW service though both UPS and the U.S. Post Office now have Web sites for tracking packages.

and patterns; this has enabled them to develop new products, offer new services, open new markets, and so forth. And this continues to be a useful activity, enhanced today by the power of supercomputers that identify "microtrends" like the tendency of customers to buy a bag of pretzels whenever they buy a six-pack of beer in the local grocery store, and the tendency for such purchases to occur within three hours of a televised football game. But even if such information-based marketing strategies have been refined from a shotgun blast to a rifle shot, they're still not personalized—nor are they proactive and interactive.

One could argue that today's information systems are much more "responsive" and that they provide more opportunities to offer services to the customer. True, but they tend to be passive: They only respond when the customer pokes them. If I happen to notice that the monthly fees on my checking account have increased, I might have the initiative to call a customer service representative at my bank (which proudly announces that I can do so seven days a week, 24 hours a day, on the assumption that I might have had a spontaneous burst of energy at 3 A.M.). I can ask the customer representative if there are any alternative arrangements that could lower my monthly fees, and I might be delighted to learn that if I deposit $5,000 in a savings account, I can write all the checks I want at no additional cost. But if I never thought to ask, the bank would never have told me. This is a key point: The bank might have attempted to inform the world at large, through massive expenditures on advertising campaigns, of its full range of checking-account services. But it didn't tell *me*, and it didn't point out that my unique combination of account balances and transaction-activities entitles me to a more appropriate kind of relationship.

Thus, the service systems that we're beginning to see are the ones that "reach out and touch someone" through the form of a personalized mailing, or a phone call, or an electronic communication via e-mail. In many cases, the objective is not necessarily an immediate sale with an immediate opportunity for revenue and profit (though, of course, that may be possible), but rather an opportunity to forge and enhance a *relationship* with the customer. If my bank were to call me tomorrow morning to offer me a new form of checking-account, I would be pleased at the thought of saving a few dollars in monthly fees or earning a slightly higher interest rate—but what would linger on, long after the phone call, would be the sense that the bank was actually paying attention to me.

There is, of course, something we need to keep in mind: Service systems are built on a foundation of core systems and infrastructure systems. The bank can't begin to provide a service of contacting me to offer a unique, personalized service if it doesn't have the appropriate data available from its core systems; and the knowledge workers within the bank are less likely to collaborate, communicate, and coordinate their efforts in such services if they don't have good infrastructure systems in place. But once those foundations are in place, there are almost unlimited opportunities—at least for the next 5–10 years—to create innovative service systems.

8.3 STRATEGIC IMPLICATIONS

Why does all of this matter? Partly because that's where the action will be. Thomsett argues that over the next few years, we'll begin to see a shift in the development efforts of large IT organizations; as Figure 8.1 illustrates, more and more effort will be devoted to service systems.

But there's a more important reason to pay attention to this trend: The smart organization will consider outsourcing its core systems over the next few years in order to free up its resources and intellectual energy to focus on the service systems; the dumb organizations will do

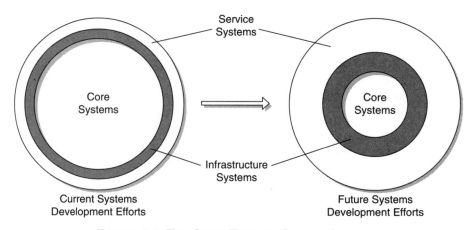

FIGURE 8.1 THE SHIFT TOWARD SERVICE SYSTEMS

just the opposite. And that should give you a clue as to your own career prospects: If you're still working on your company's core applications, you're not where the action is; not only that, your CIO is probably trying to figure out how to outsource all of that work to a body shop in India or Indiana. Will your job be saved when the company shifts its resources to the service systems of the future? Not unless you start playing an active role in preparing for that future.

This assumes that CIOs have some control over the future of their IS department. Ernst & Young's Center for Business Innovation [3] conducted a study of leading IS/IT organizations in early 1994 and concluded that most of them have to perform the processes shown in Figure 8.2 below. The organizations characterized by the E & Y researchers as "level-1"(not to be confused with the SEI's CMM levels!) are still having trouble supporting and operating their core systems; no wonder senior management wants to outsource them to someplace on the other side of the planet! Even the level-2 organizations are struggling, for today's end users are demanding more and more rapid delivery and evolution of both new and existing applications.

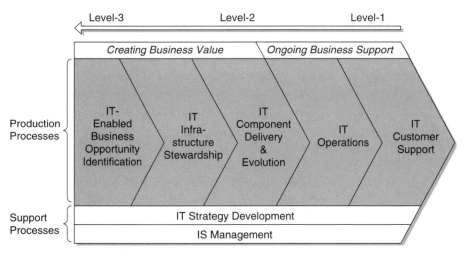

FIGURE 8.2 THE ERNST & YOUNG IT LEADERSHIP MODEL

As the IS/IT organization moves from level-2 up to level-3, it has an opportunity to begin focusing on the infrastructure systems discussed earlier—but if you can't even provide adequate support for your user's core systems (order entry, billing, etc.), why would the users trust you to reengineer all of their business processes, install automated workflow processes, and connect everyone via Lotus Notes?

It's only the organizations at the high end of level-3 that have achieved a sufficient track record of performance with the core systems and the infrastructure systems that will be trusted by senior management to participate in the Ernst & Young notion of "IT-Enabled Business Opportunity Identification," which is roughly comparable to Thomsett's service systems. That's where *you* want to be, if you're working in a typical company; if you see that your IS organization is languishing at the bottom end of level-1 on the Ernst & Young scale, you're in trouble.

8.4 THE IMPACT ON THE AMERICAN PROGRAMMER

Assuming that service systems are the wave of the future, why should this make us feel more optimistic about the prospects for the U.S. software industry? After all, it doesn't involve any magic or secrets, and we don't hold any monopolies on technology for creating such systems. It's not even clear to me who thought of the idea first, though I picked it up from my Australian friend and colleague, Rob Thomsett.

Indeed, *anyone* can build service systems, and the leading companies in Australia, Europe, South America, and North America are probably doing so at this very moment. As explained above, the essence of these systems involves building relationships with one's customers—which, to a large extent, means Australian customers for Australian companies, European customers for European companies, etc. True, we're operating in a global marketplace, but 50 to 80 percent of the customers for most organizations today are still within the local domestic region. To the extent that an organization has set up operations in other regions and marketplaces, it will need service systems to deal with those customers; but the first wave of service systems are likely to take place on the company's home turf.

And in that context, the notion of offshore programming becomes less attractive. True, the *software* for such systems can be developed offshore, just like any other kind of software. But deciding what *kind* of systems need to be built is going to require close interactions between a company and its customers—probably much closer than they've attempted before. It's going to require a deep understanding of the politics, trends, preferences, and cultural nuances of those customers in order to build an effective service system. The hypothetical banking system that I described above is a good example: I'd like to have my bank call me to offer attractive services, but not while I'm in the middle of eating dinner or taking a shower. It would be *very* easy for the bank to get me so annoyed with such calls that I withdraw my business and move to another bank.

As mentioned in Chapter 1, one of the arguments against my premise in *Decline and Fall of the American Programmer* was that offshore programmers would find it difficult to interact with the end users of an information system, especially in today's world of rapid prototyping and iterative development. Now the end users are not even located within the company building the system—they're out there in the marketplace, and it's even more difficult to reach them. Consequently, I think it will prove to be a boon for indigenous programmers in every country, at least in the short term: The Indians will build Indian service systems, the Irish will build Irish service systems, and the Americans will build American service systems. It will be a few more years before a U.S. firm decides to build a service system to develop closer relations with its customers in India and Ireland—and at that point, there will be stiff competition from the local software people who can probably do a better job at such things than our programmers in Illinois and Indiana.

Note that this still does involve a "shift" in skills, which ultimately does involve the "traditional" programmer whose demise I lamented in *Decline and Fall*. Building service systems will involve Visual Basic and client-server technology and a lot of other traditional software skills; and it's also likely to involve the Internet and the World Wide Web, which I'll discuss in Chapter 9. But the *real* skills required to build an effective service system are those of systems analysis. Who are the *real* users, what do they want, what do they need, how would they use the information we can give them, etc., etc.—these are the kinds of questions we'll have to ask when building our service systems, and the answers to those questions don't require a deep understanding of C++.

Bottom line: Assume that the core systems and infrastructure systems in your organization have become commodities and begin shifting your skills and your energies to the service systems.

REFERENCES

1. Basalla, George. *The Evolution of Technology.* (New York: Cambridge University Press, 1988).

2. Brand, Stewart. "The Physicist." *Wired*, 3.09, September 1995, p. 154.

3. Doctor, Mary Silva, and Richard W. Swanborg, Jr. "Attaining Top-Level IS Performance." Ernst & Young, January 1994.

4. Petroski, Henry. *The Evolution of Useful Things: how everyday artifacts—from forks and pins to paper clips and zippers—came to be as they are.* (New York: Alfred A. Knopf, 1993).

9 THE INTERNET

Demographic tests...show that the person least likely to buy Wired *magazine is an American schoolteacher.*

Paul Kegan, *"The Digerati,"* New York Times Magazine, *May 21, 1995.*

9.1 WHO CARES?

Like American schoolteachers, IT departments in many large companies studiously ignored what Kevin Kelly calls "the largest working anarchy in the world" during its first 20 years of existence [6]. The official reason for avoiding the Internet—which, in one large insurance company I visited in 1995, included a ban on access to e-mail to and from the outside world!—usually has something to do with security. The official explanation is that those awful hackers might actually be able to access their corporate data (which even their best software engineers haven't been able to make any sense of), but the *real* reason usually involves the fear of anarchy. If we let everyone in the company get on the Internet, who will be in control?

The last time we heard that kind of logical reasoning from the masters of the IT empire, the "threat" was personal computers. The official reasons for IT organizations banning PCs in the early 80s usually emphasized technical inadequacies: They're too small and they don't have enough storage capacity; you couldn't build any *real* applications on them because they don't run MVS, JCL, IMS, and COBOL; they don't read EBCDIC. But the real reason was generally something very different: If we let everyone have a PC, how will we control everything?

History may be about to repeat itself in the second half of the 90s. Remember what happened with the PC revolution? The mainframe empire withered and died in many organizations, and a lot of COBOL programmers are now suffering the fate I warned of in *Decline and Fall of the American Programmer*. But a new generation (and a few hardy survivors from the previous generation) have built new careers and new empires from the technologies associated with PCs. The same thing is going to happen again: The pervasive influence of the Internet and the World Wide Web will render even more of the old-fashioned technologies and the old-fashioned IT empires obsolete and irrelevant—but it will create new careers, new job titles, and new opportunities for those willing and able to pursue them. Far more than *any* of the technologies, languages, tools, concepts, and techniques discussed in the first eight chapters of this book, the Internet is responsible for the rebirth, the rise, and the resurrection of the American programmer. And for the moment, as I'll argue below, it *is* an American phenomenon; that will almost certainly change within the next five years, but we have an opportunity to build a lead in this industry.

A recent article by Ray Valdés [13] says that traffic on the World Wide Web (WWW) increased 1800 percent in 1994; and the May 1995 issue of *Internet World* reported that the number of Internet sites increased by 26 percent during the fourth quarter of 1994, and that WWW-registered host computers now constitute the most numerous commercial hosts on the Net. Indeed, it's hard to open any newspaper, business magazine, or computer trade journal today without seeing yet another article indicating that the entire Internet phenomenon, and especially WWW-related technology, is growing like crazy.

It's possible that I've gotten a little too excited about all of this—but if you think I'm excited, take a look at Timothy Leary's comments on the impact of the Internet [9]. On the other hand, if you've gotten the impression from my remarks at the beginning of this discussion that the information highway is mankind's greatest invention ever, it's useful to read Clifford Stoll's *Silicon Snake Oil*. Stoll achieved guru status a few years ago when he tracked down a series of computer hackers who had broken into his university computer system, a tale related in *The Cuckoo's Egg*. Now he's back to cast a jaundiced eye at everything from e-mail to the Usenet to the introduction of computers into the classroom and home. In his closing chapter, he argues that:

> The heavily promoted information infrastructure addresses few social needs or business concerns. At the same time, it directly threatens precious parts of our society, including schools, libraries, and social institutions... For all the promise of virtual communities, it's more important to live a real life in a real neighborhood. [12]

I found myself mentally arguing with many of Stoll's points, muttering, "Well, yes, this issue could be a problem if you adopted a simplistic, one-sided attitude of the Internet as 'infinitely good,' but most of us recognize that technology has disadvantages, too, and that it has to be used in an evenhanded fashion." Alas, most of us don't articulate the risks and disadvantages of our sexy technology, and we get so carried away with its benefits that we forget that the general public isn't aware of them. And in some cases, we don't realize that we've created a solution for which there is no urgent problem; a few years ago, for example, I was also convinced that pen-based computing was going to revolutionize the world. I still have my defunct AT&T® EO machine, but EO has shut down and pen computing has essentially become a niche technology.[1]

Maybe the Internet craze will fizzle in a few years, too, but the initial market reports certainly don't look that way; I don't think this is going to be a dead-end technology, and I'm more inclined to agree with the revolutionary prophets who say it will change our world. Nevertheless, I'm not suggesting that you invest your life savings in the technology by buying stock in an Internet start up company; and

---

[1] Apple's Newton® and Sony's MagicLink™ have managed to sell a hundred thousand units or so, but it's not a revolution: the marketplace seems more inclined to view these products as interesting gadgets but not the solution to any pressing problem. One could argue that what the world *really* wants is a Newton with voice recognition. Keep the pen, Apple—let me talk to my Newton.

I would urge caution if you decide to leave your safe big-company environment to work for a start up Internet service provider. But it's a small risk indeed to look for opportunities to become a "champion" of the technology within your existing organization, as I'll discuss below.

9.2 WHY THIS MATTERS TO THE AVERAGE PROGRAMMER

So what? What's this got to do with your career? Very simple: My strong belief is that this technology is going to provide the next wave of hot software jobs, just as client/server technology and Visual Basic fueled a software boom in the late 1980s and early 1990s. If you're still trapped in your mainframe COBOL shop, this is your way out.

Most discussions of the opportunities associated with the Internet and the WWW are aimed at start up businesses and entrepreneurial opportunities. If you have entrepreneurial instincts, you may be thinking of several possibilities, all of which are exciting but risky:

- Content providers are trying to package useful information on the WWW, in an attractive fashion, that consumers are willing to pay for. The concept is simple, but the implementation is usually far from obvious. Thus far, the most successful example seems to be *HotWired*, the on-line version of *Wired* magazine, in which advertisers pay princely sums for the privilege of posting advertisements that Web-surfers may or may not decide to click on.

- Service providers (ISPs) are the companies that provide the "on-ramp" to the information highway. New ones pop up every day, providing various forms of niche services to localized geographical areas or special segments of the marketplace. I suppose there's still room for more of these, and it's a lot more fun than programming in COBOL; but the market is already very crowded, and from an entrepreneurial perspective, it strikes me as a game of Russian roulette. The trade press is predicting a shakeout, and many of the small, mom-and-pop service providers are already finding it more difficult to compete. As a recent newspaper report [8] put it, "The mom-and-pop Internet access providers will for the most part be gone within the next three to five years." In their place will be massive service-providing operations from AT&T, MCI, Sprint, all of the regional Bell companies, cable TV operations (e.g., Continental Cablevision and Tele-Communications, Inc.)—plus such online service providers as America Online®, Prodigy®, and CompuServe.

- Tool providers are inventing various browsing and searching tools, as well as special-purpose utility software, security software, etc. If you were lucky enough or prescient enough to join one of the start up companies in this area, you're already rich: Netscape, of course, is the example that everyone in the computer field drooled over when the company went public in the summer of 1995 and created megamillionaires overnight. And Netscape wasn't the only example: Spry was acquired by CompuServe for $100 million; Booklink Technologies was acquired by America Online for $30 million; and Pipeline was acquired for $10 million by PSI. There may be a few more gold mines like this, but I think the main flurry is over.[2]

- Web site developers are creating ever more sophisticated sites for their clients, incorporating multi-media, forms, databases, and elaborate textual content. In addition to highly technical areas of expertise (network design, security, etc.), these projects are often using the very latest Internet tools and programming languages. The project teams are typically multi-disciplinary, with a majority of team members sometimes coming from outside the traditional computer field; and as a general rule, the project teams work under substantial pressure, with tight deadlines.

If you can join one of these entrepreneurial start up companies, that's great—but what if you want something a little more stable? What if you're one of those folks who just wants to make a decent living, with the possibility of a 20 percent bonus at the end of the year? The answer, I believe, is simple: sooner or later, *every* company will want to jump onto the Internet and hook into the WWW. They're going to need a lot of in-house talent to do that, and nobody has written the job descriptions yet.

---

[2] A special category of "tools" for the Internet and World Wide Web are the new application development languages such as Sun's Java. I'll discuss these in Chapter 10.

Here the kinds of things you can be doing in your company:

- Figure out how to set up an Internet site in your company, with your own domain name and all of the associated software that goes with a site—accounting software, security firewalls, Web browsers, and the usual assortment of FTP, Telnet, Archie, Eudora, and so forth.

- Figure out how to link your company's in-house LAN and in-house mail system(s) to the Internet. You've already got cc:Mail or Microsoft Mail (or both), and the folks in your company want to use that as the mechanism for launching mail on the Internet.

- Become a WebMaster. Help the marketing department design sensible home pages, using graphics and text, which will require you to learn the intricacies of formatting languages like HTML. Most of the Web pages available today are amazingly trite and superficial; and those that try to take advantage of graphics and hypermedia tend to go way overboard—much like the documents that we produced when we were first given laser printers and multiple fonts.

- If you see yourself as a systems analyst or business analyst, rather than a programmer, then help your marketing department (and your engineering department, and your finance department, and every other end-user department) find sensible business opportunities on the WWW. The straightforward opportunities today are Web displays of product information, PR information, etc. By mid-1996, there should be adequate security mechanisms on the Web to facilitate some degree of electronic commerce. Making this succeed in your company is not so much a technological challenge as a business challenge; there are tremendous opportunities to help your end-user departments avoid disasters in this area.

- On a simpler level, you can start helping people find things on the Web and become recognized as an Internet "resource" in your organization. The application development organization may not understand or appreciate what you're doing, because they only care about churning out more Visual Basic programs more quickly. But you might earn the undying gratitude of the folks in the marketing department who have decided (rightly or wrongly) that the WWW is crucial to their future plans, but who have no idea how to navigate it. You might help them download a copy of Mosaic or Netscape onto their computer—and then, even if your company has no Internet node of its own, you can show your end-users how to zoom onto the Web through CompuServe, America Online, or Prodigy. Once they're on the Web, you can keep them up to date about interesting Web pages they should know about (*Internet World* is a good source for these tidbits). For example, one of my favorite on-line services is the "HeadsUp" electronic news from Individual, Inc., which delivers news summaries on user-specified topics directly to your e-mail in-box each morning; now the company is on the WWW with a hypertext "NewsPage briefs" product, which you can check out at http://www.newspage.com

I could add more to this list, but you get the idea: This is an exploding technology that many people feel they must have (notwithstanding Clifford Stoll's concerns, which I'll discuss below), and they need help gaining access to the technology. It reminds me very much of the early days of the PC "revolution" in the early- and mid-1980s: End users were buying PCs, and they couldn't even figure out how to format their floppy disks or turn on their printer. While the mainframe MIS department sneered at them, they paid hefty consulting fees to the first generation of guerrilla programmers to help them gain access to the technology, set up some simple applications, and show them how to create spreadsheets. Today, of course, end users don't need help with such simple things, but the guerrilla programmers from the 1980s now have a nice consulting business building small and medium-sized client-server systems ... because the users can't figure out how to install NetWare®, and they don't want to write their own Visual Basic programs for the departmental applications they have in mind.

The next wave will involve integrating the Internet into their enterprise computing environment. They will expect to be able to access information resources on the Internet from within their word-processing program and their spreadsheets; WordPerfect and Microsoft have already developed extensions to their word processors to allow them to generate Web pages in HTML script and also to function as ersatz Web browsers When the first generation of these products are introduced, the end-user community probably won't be able to figure out how to use them—and while your in-house application development department sneers that all of this is just a "toy," you can grab the opportunity to become a hero to your end users. For a more conventional view of a career as the in-house Internet wizard, take a look at Alan Radding's article, "Life on the Internet." [11]

It won't take long for people to realize that a lot of other skills are required to really take advantage of the Internet within their corporate environment—to build Intranets, "extranets," and full-scale Internet applications.

- They're going to want to provide access to corporate data currently stored in Oracle, Sybase, DB2, or (shudder) IMS. Connecting the Web to these kinds of mainframe and client-server databases is going to require a lot of traditional skills from database designers, data administrators, and the like. In a similar fashion, they'll want to connect their Lotus Notes documents to the Internet and the Web; someone has to help them do that.

- They'll want to *create* new databases, on the fly, by allowing Internet-based customers to create orders, fill out survey forms, enter name-and-address information, and so forth. This will involve some front-end editing and processing before the information is stuffed into a database; thus, there will have to be an interface between the Web front end that the end user sees and a collection of more-or-less traditional application programs written in Visual Basic or COBOL. However, I think we'll see an entirely new wave of programming languages specialized for the Internet—languages like Sun's Java, IBM's VisualAge for WWW, ParcPlace's VisualWave, and so forth—which I'll discuss in Chapter 10.

- As organizations begin building up a Web site consisting of thousands of pages of information, cross-linked with hundreds of hypertext URL pointers, it will suddenly occur to the Web administrators that version control and configuration management are important. Gosh! Where have we heard that before? There's a reasonably good chance that the professional IT community has some decent skills in tackling this problem.

- As companies embark upon projects to build Web sites and various new forms of products and services based on the Internet, they're going to need some traditional systems analysis and project management skills. Someone will have to interview the end-users to determine their requirements—e.g., what do we *really* want to put on the Web, and how do we plan for that information to be accessed and used? Someone will have to put together cost-benefit calculations and explain the project rationale to senior management. Someone will have to oversee the intricate details of merging graphics and text and databases and multimedia and application software networking technology into a coherent system. The interesting thing is that none of this involves COBOL or mainframes, but it still *is* very much like the issues in classical systems development. And it will quickly escalate beyond the interest or ability of the end-user departments to do it by themselves—unless, of course, the IT department abandons them altogether, in which case they will build up their own expertise, just as they did with PCs a decade ago.

- It will involve evaluating and installing new versions of familiar products—e.g., the Internet-savvy versions of word processors—as well as evaluating exciting new products from entirely new organizations, such as Web browsers, server software, HTML editors, and new programming languages like Sun's Java. Much of this will be too technical for end users to properly evaluate; but equally important, it requires evaluation of such issues as vendor service and support, vendor reliability and stability, adherence to standards, the ability of the proposed new product to interface with existing products and systems within the organization, and so forth. Traditional IT organizations know how to do this, too.

So, what should you do next? The first requirement, of course, is to master some of this technology yourself. You've got a PC and a modem at home, of course; but you've probably been using your spare time teaching yourself how to program in C++ and Delphi. Put that aside for a while, and make an investment in the Internet and the WWW.

The next step is to start reading about the technology. Magazines like *Internet World* are quite useful, and there are books, too; indeed, your local bookstore not only has all of the entry-level Internet books that you first saw a year ago, but is now overflowing with books like David Angell and Brent Heslop's *Mosaic for Dummies: Windows Edition*

[1], and Ian Graham's *HTML Sourcebook* [5], and Larry Aronson's *HTML Manual of Style* [2], and Laura Lemay's *Teach Yourself Web Publishing with HTML in a Week* [7], and *Running a Perfect Web Site* by David Chandler, Bill Kirkner, and Jim Minatel [3]. There are also conferences devoted to this new technology. If you've been saving your money and your vacation time to invest in your own training, perhaps you should skip the client-server and visual programming conference this year, and check out Digital Consulting's *Web World* conference, or Mecklermedia's *InternetWorld*, or *The Internet Conference*.

9.3 WHO'S GOING TO WIN THE INTERNET RACE?

In the spring of 1995, while visiting Rio de Janeiro, I wrote an article in *Guerrilla Programmer* in which I complained about the primitive state of telecommunications in countries outside North America and argued that it would impede the ability of these countries to take advantage of the information highway. A Brazilian reader of *Guerrilla Programmer*, Josef Manesterski, wrote to me (by e-mail, of course) and disagreed with my argument:

> The telecom system in Brazil is far from what you imply. Being a poor country, the per-capita number of phones is small, but those that are installed do work. I can lift my receiver right now and talk to Kalamazoo or Timbuktu with equal ease. Being a frequent user of international phone calls, I think this statistic is not without meaning. Also, the national packet-switching network will transport your data over public X.25 lines from anywhere to anywhere in the country safely and reliably—it only takes a couple of phone calls to large companies using the system to verify this.

> What you probably did not notice is that our phone rates are one of the cheapest anywhere. I was in France a few weeks ago and paid the equivalent to $20 for a 100-unit phone card, one unit being about three minutes of local call...Well, the same amount of calling in São Paulo costs precisely...US $3.30 or one-sixth the price. I have two phone lines at home, and the bill for one of them, used more infrequently, was a staggering $3.50. The other was closer to $12.

> As for Internet, excuse me for fueling your concerns, but if all it takes for Brazil to compete is access to the Net, then you are indeed

in trouble. I have full PPP access, Web and everything, and so have a few hundred Brazilians. Many thousands still use shell accounts at the universities, but if this catches on as fast as cellular phones did (did you notice like everybody seems to have one?) by the end of this year the density of Internauts will rival many European countries...By the time, five to ten years down the road, when the Internet or whatever really does become Al Gore's superhighway we will be on it as easily as I am writing this.

Manesterski also emphasized that he had been using CompuServe successfully for a couple of years in Brazil, in contrast to the largely unsuccessful attempts that I've had with e-mail in Brazil and several other parts of South America in the past couple of years. If he's right—and it makes sense to assume that he has more extensive experience regarding Brazilian telecommunications than I do—then the race to master the technology of Internet and WWW may be more intense than I had thought.

And in some ways, it's obvious that Manesterski *is* right. Telecommunication privatization efforts are big news in many parts of the world, and it may dramatically speed up access to the information highway in the advanced countries of Europe and the developing nations of South America. Peru, for example, privatized its telephone system in 1994, and the change is astounding: It used to take twelve *years* to get a new phone line installed under the government monopoly, but the waiting time when I arrived for a visit in April 1995 was down to one week with the new privatized service (which is being operated by a telecommunications firm from Spain).

Nevertheless, I still believe that both Europe and South America are far behind the U.S. in terms of the information highway. They've heard of it, and they understand it intellectually; they have access to e-mail within their companies, and some of them have corporate access to the Internet. As Manesterski argued, it's possible to access the WWW in Brazil, if you have access to a university Internet node. And as Nicholas Negroponte points out in *Being Digital* [10], the fastest growth in Internet sites last year was in developing nations in Argentina, Iran, Peru, Egypt, the Philippines, the Russian Federation, Slovenia, and Indonesia.

To which my response is: *Bah, humbug!* Yes, I know there are Internet sites all over the world—but I remain convinced, after watching the phenomenon in my travels these past few years, that in no other country has the Internet become as pervasive as in the U.S.

Take a look around you: The movie ads in the daily newspaper now point to a WWW page for viewing video clips; the TV announcer on the evening news program invites you to send your comments by e-mail to the station; in New York City, billboards on the side of public buses display URL addresses in letters two feet high; the President of the United States invites you to observe the antics of his cat on line, and both political parties are now providing more Internet-based information about the day-to-day operations of government than we've ever seen before. And when you show the Web to your kids, they're likely to give you a bored, condescending look (as my son did a few months ago) and say, "Yeah, so what? We've been using this stuff in school for the past year."

All of this is rapidly being woven into the fabric of our society—just like the fax machine 5 years ago and simple e-mail 2 or 3 years ago—and it's happening much more rapidly in the U.S. than any other country I've visited. My impression is that the information highway is an order of magnitude less pervasive in other parts of the world: People don't send e-mail from home, their kids aren't on the Internet, the Internet hasn't been installed in schools below the university level, and they haven't yet begun to think about how their businesses might operate differently with access to the World Wide Web. The speed with which the technology is spreading is partly due to the U.S. telecommunications infrastructure; we may consider it chaotic and inefficient in many ways, and it may be no more advanced technologically than, say, Scandinavia, but I believe that it is livelier and more innovative, energetic, and entrepreneurial overall than anywhere else in the world.

Among other things, it's going to cause a profound change in the way we distribute and ascribe "value" to information. A common cultural belief on the Internet is that information is "free," and that once a piece of information is placed on the Internet, it has effectively been distributed to the entire human race at no cost. The potential impact of this cultural belief on traditional information-distributors like newspapers and book-publishers is profound, and lively debates are already under way. But there is also an enormous potential impact on "knowledge workers" (or, as U.S. Secretary of Labor Robert Reich calls them, "symbol manipulators") who make their living by accumulating, analyzing, interpreting, and distributing information—and we haven't begun to address this impact, aside from a few thoughtful articles from people like Esther Dyson [4]. Software professionals are clearly a form of knowledge worker, and the issue of intellectual value is clearly important to us. Freeware and shareware and software piracy haven't destroyed the software-products industry, for example, but they represent a phenomenon that can't be ignored; the more proactive companies are taking advantage of the Internet by *deliberately* distributing free copies of their software prior to formal release, in order to gain mind share and market share.

During a keynote presentation at Software AG's annual user conference in San Antonio in September, 1995, Dyson summarized her views on the impact of the Internet on intellectual property and intellectual value:

- In the agricultural period of human history, land was the primary source of value; but it was people who worked and tilled and fertilized the land to make it valuable. And during the industrial age, machines and "capital assets" were the artifacts of wealth; but it was people who built those artifacts, maintained them, and helped establish and preserve that value.

- In the postindustrial age, it has been argued that knowledge, or intellectual property, has now replaced land and capital assets as the valuable artifact. But it is people who create, interpret, analyze, filter, and *process* knowledge.

- Because of technologies like the Internet, intellectual property is rapidly becoming free, but the *intellectual process* is valuable. Knowledge has no value until it's part of an intellectual process in someone's head.

- There is an oversupply of information and knowledge; and that's one of the primary reasons why the market price of most information is going down rapidly. Thus, the popular Internet paradigm that "information is free" is not about violating copyrights or contracts, but rather a recognition that if there is an oversupply of information, then in a free-market economy, the price will be driven down.

- Esther told us to write this one down: *Information consumes attention*—and there is a shortage of available attention: we're all so busy and so bombarded with information that we don't know what to pay attention to.

- Thus, one of the primary purposes of information and knowledge is to serve as a form of advertisement to gain the attention of customers, consumers, prospects, etc. Esther noted that attention can be negative, too—e.g., a product or a company that everyone consciously hates. In any case, it helps to think of attention as an asset.

- An example of a business organization that is based on this new paradigm of intellectual value: Esther is on the board of a company that sells support and service for "freeware" software. It's an interesting point: Even if software is free, it has no value if you can't figure out how to use it. The value comes from the service associated with helping people install it, customize it, debug it, use it, and so forth.

- In the future, companies will create the "illusion of attention"—e.g., by providing automated e-mail services to respond to complaints that we send (by e-mail, of course) to the customer service department. But customers will become savvy and will begin demanding "real" attention. And there will be an ongoing race to supply and demand adequate levels of attention.

- Where is value created? In people's minds. You have to *build* loyalty in the minds of customers and also employees.

- One of the big issues we're facing now involves redistribution of assets. In the agricultural age, peasants could revolt and seize the land; in the industrial age, workers could revolt and seize the factories or the buildings in order to redistribute the commonly accepted form of wealth. In today's world, the Internet provides us with a way to redistribute information and knowledge, and in so doing we redistribute the wealth currently associated with intellectual property. But even if information and knowledge become free, we don't know how to redistribute *intelligence* and the intellectual processes that know how to deal with the information.

During the question-answer session following her presentation, someone in the audience asked if the Internet represents a threat to Microsoft. Esther replied that Microsoft has become somewhat like a government and is able to take advantage of the standardization represented by the ubiquitous presence of Intel® boxes and Windows operating systems: it essentially imposes a tax on hardware manufacturers to cover the preloading of Windows into every new machine, whether they want to or not.

But the Internet doesn't value this notion of standardization in the same way; contrariwise, *diversity* is valued on the Internet. So this does indeed represent a challenge to Microsoft, which until recently might have thought it could "own" (or at least dominate) the Internet. But if Microsoft adapts to the Internet culture, it could help prevent the ossification that comes with large monopolies, and it could stay lean and agile and aggressive.

What does all of this mean? Well, it suggests that there is a new and different economic model for consultants, authors, analysts, information-providers, and knowledge workers who have enjoyed a fairly comfortable income over the past 20 to 30 years by jealously guarding the actual information content that they create; the profit has often been derived by making physical copies of the information and earning fees or royalties on each copy distributed to a consumer.

In Esther's economic model, information providers and knowledge workers will devote a considerable amount of time and effort to creating information which they consciously and deliberately distribute *for free*. A case in point: The modest, but slowly expanding, set of Web pages that I've created over the past two years (which included a complete copy of the draft version of this book) has taken a considerable amount of time and effort on my part—and so far, nobody has paid (or even offered to pay) a penny for it. So either it's a silly and time-wasting hobby or I'm making a voluntary contribution of my knowledge for the advancement of the human race—or I've already instinctively concluded that Esther's model is correct and that the eventual "intellectual value" of my work will occur in a deferred, indirect form. Naturally, I hope that Esther is right!

As for the software professionals who work in other kinds of companies: Well, to a greater or lesser extent, every company today is selling information, even if the information is packaged and combined with more tangible products. As Nicholas Negroponte argues so eloquently in *Being Digital* [10], we're going through a transformation from a society based on atoms to a society based on bits. Even though software professionals have always worked in a world of bits and have derived their value from being perceived as superior bit-twiddlers, the companies for whom they work have typically seen themselves predominately in atom-based businesses. As that changes, it's inevitable that some companies will prosper and some will falter; the jobs of everyone within those companies will change accordingly. It's not going to happen in an orderly, predictable fashion; it's going to be chaotic and haphazard, and it will occur over a period of several years. The advantage held by the U.S., I believe, is that we're embarking upon this change on a much larger scale, and at a much earlier date, than most other countries around the world.[3]

Of course, even if I'm right about all of this, there's no guarantee that the situation will persist: Things do change rather rapidly in our field. Whatever competitive advantage we may now have could vanish rather quickly, for the treasure we now hold is largely an intellectual asset, and it can flourish almost as quickly in any other part of the world. But there is more to it than that: The success of our software industry is also due to the overall social and economic culture of the North American community, as well as the success of a few key industries which do require large investments—e.g., our telecommunications infrastructure.

Will the U.S. prevail in the new world of the Internet in the long term? Who knows—anything could happen in the next 5 to 10 years. Obviously, we have no monopoly on the concepts—indeed, the Web itself was developed at the CERN research center in Switzerland before being popularized in the U.S. by the National Center for SuperComputer Applications. Like many other industries in the past, we may find ourselves losing our Internet leadership position over the next several years. But for now, I can hardly imagine a more exciting time and place for those of us who make a living in software.

---

[3] There may be exceptions, but there's a complex combination of technology and culture involved here. Singapore, for example, is arguably ahead of the United States in terms of its deployment of information-based technology to the population at large. On the other hand, Singapore has a very different attitude than the U.S. toward policing the Internet and censoring information deemed inappropriate; it remains to be seen what impact this will have on effective use of the Internet within its society. Even if Singapore does make equal or better use of the Internet, it probably won't have much of an impact because it's such a tiny island-state. It would be much more interesting to see pervasive deployment of Internet-based technology in, say, India or China—but in both of these countries, there is already evidence of government control far more stringent than what we would tolerate in the U.S. And of course, we can expect it sooner or later in countries like England, France, Germany, and other developed nations.

Conclusion: The American (COBOL) programmer is dead; long live the American (Internet) programmer!

REFERENCES

1. Angell, David, and Brent Heslop. *Mosaic for Dummies: Windows Edition.* (Foster City, CA: IDG Books, 1995).

2. Aronson, Larry. *HTML Manual of Style.* (Emeryville, CA: Ziff-Davis Press, 1995).

3. Chandler, David M., with Bill Kirkner and Jim Minatel. *Running a Perfect Web Site.* (Indianapolis, IN: Que Corporation, 1995).

4. Dyson, Esther. "Intellectual Value." *Wired*, July 1995, p. 136ff.

5. Graham, Ian S. *HTML Sourcebook: A Complete Guide to HTML.* (New York: John Wiley & Sons, 1995).

6. Kegan, Paul. "The Digerati." *New York Times Magazine,* May 21, 1995.

7. Lemay, Laura. *Teach Yourself Web Publishing with HTML in a Week.* (Indianapolis, IN: SAMS Publishing, 1995) ISBN: 0-672-30667-0.

8. Lewis, Peter H. "The New Internet Gatekeepers." *The New York Times*, November 13, 1995, p. D1.

9. Maglitta, Joseph. "Log in, Link up, Get off." (Timothy Leary interview), *Computerworld*, May 1, 1995, pp. 117–120.

10. Negroponte, Nicholas. *Being Digital.* (New York: Alfred A. Knopf, 1995).

11. Radding, Alan. "Life on the Internet." *Computerworld*, April 24, 1995, p. 127.

12. Stoll, Clifford. *Silicon Snake Oil: Second Thoughts on the Information Highway.* (New York: Doubleday, 1995).

13. Valdés, Ray. "Here's the Internet, Where's the Money?" *Dr. Dobb's Developer Update*, May 1995.

10

JAVA AND THE NEW
INTERNET PROGRAMMING
PARADIGM

One must not forget that progress in fundamental science inevitably leads in many cases to a revolution in technology and the daily life of all people. A country which in our epoch ignores this truth dooms itself sooner or later to lagging behind in science and engineering.

Leonid I. Sedov, Russian Aerospace Administrator (1971).

One of the most significant technological developments since the publication of *Decline and Fall of the American Programmer* has been the introduction of a new breed of languages and development tools for creating applications on the Internet and the World Wide Web. As I discussed in the previous chapter, the "information superhighway" is the hottest thing in the computing industry today—but when the Internet and the World Wide Web first burst upon the scene a couple years ago, it seemed completely divorced from the traditional application development community in IT organizations. Many of the frantic discussions of security and firewalls that take place even today make it evident that many IT managers would like to keep it this way.

From the perspective of IT organizations, the Internet originally meant e-mail, Usenet newsgroups, FTP file transmission mechanisms, and associated utilities such as Archie, Gopher, and WAIS. Naturally, this caused some clamoring from end users who wanted to connect their internal, corporate, LAN-based e-mail systems to the Internet, but many large IT organizations have managed to resist this. When the Web came along a little later, the typical reaction from IT organizations was, "Oh, look, a cute little publishing environment! Now maybe our users will stop pestering us about PageMaker™ and Quark™!" True, some organizations did add forms and PERL scripts and CGI gateways to access information from the corporate databases—but for the most part, the Web has been a mechanism for publishing static content for end users to browse at their leisure.

But in the spring of 1995, with Sun Microsystems' formal announcement of the Java programming language, it became apparent that this comfortable view of the Internet/Web as a phenomenon distinct from traditional application development was about to change dramatically. Internet aficionados are excited by Java's ability to bring *live content* to the user's workstation, in a manner that I'll describe later in this chapter. But for traditional programmers, there are far more profound consequences: Just when they were getting used to client-server technology and languages like PowerBuilder, Visual Basic, and Delphi, the Java phenomenon promises to change the nature of application development completely. While technical concepts like object-orientation will continue to play an important role in tomorrow's Web-based applications, just about everything else is going to change in this new world: For example, programmers are likely to spend their time building tiny *applets* rather than large, monolithic *applications*—and the marketplace could end up paying for these applets on a "per usage" basis, rather than on the licensing basis so prevalent today. If you're going to ride this new technology wave, you're going to need to change a lot of your assumptions and plans about the tools you'll be using, the development processes you'll be following, and the professional skills of the people in your organization.

In keeping with the theme of this book, I believe that Java represents an enormous opportunity for the North American software industry. As with all of the other technologies discussed in this book, there are no guarantees and no monopolies; that is particularly true of technology associated with the Internet. Java-related development *is* going on all around the world, but the concentration of activity is much higher in the U.S. than elsewhere; we may only have a head start of 2 to 3 years, but that should be enough to capture a great deal of the market share before the software industries of Western Europe, Asia, and the developing nations begin making serious efforts to catch up.

10.1 WHAT IS JAVA ALL ABOUT?

In a nutshell, Java is an object-oriented programming language based on C++ that allows small programs—or "applets"—to be embedded within an HTML document. When the user clicks on the appropriate part of the HTML page to retrieve it from a World Wide Web server, the applet is downloaded into the client workstation environment, where it begins executing.

Java's origins go back to 1991, when Sun Microsystems began looking for ways to create platform-independent code to support consumer electronic products. After some initial efforts with C++, the Sun project team abandoned it and created its own language—initially called Oak, and later renamed Java. Oak/Java was initially used to create software for a personal, hand-held remote control device; but when the project team lost a bid to develop a television set-top box for Time-Warner, attention switched to the World Wide Web. The Sun project team then built a Web browser, originally called WebRunner and then renamed HotJava^{TM}, in the Java programming language. The rest, as they say, is history: Sun Microsystems formally announced Java and HotJava at the Sun World '95 conference on May 23, 1995.

The relationship between Java programs (or "applets"), the Java-enabled browser and the Web, is illustrated in Figure 10.1. The user accesses a Web page and pulls it down to his client. In this case, though, the Web page contains an additional HTML tag called "APP," which refers to a Java applet—and that applet can be located anywhere on the World Wide Web. If the user's Web browser is Java-enabled (e.g., Sun's HotJava browser or Netscape's Navigator 2.0 product), then the applet is pulled down into the user's client computer and executed within the browser environment.

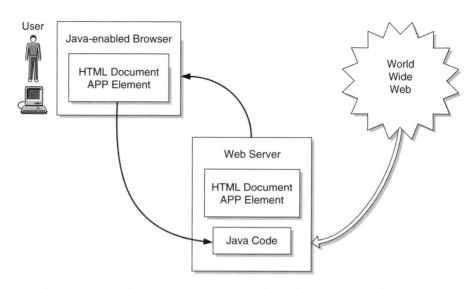

FIGURE 10.1 RELATIONSHIP BETWEEN JAVA APPLETS, JAVA-ENABLED
BROWSER, THE USER, AND THE WEB

Java is often described as a "cross-platform" programming language; it's also common to refer to Java programs as "architecture-neutral bytecodes." It has to be this way, of course, because the Web server that delivers the Java applet to the Web client doesn't know what kind of hardware/software environment it's running on. And the developer who creates the Java applet doesn't want to worry about whether it will work correctly on OS/2®, Windows, UNIX, and MacOS™.

So the key to Java is the notion of executable content, rather than static content. What capability does this provide us? Thus far, most of the demonstrations and examples have involved fairly simple graphics—e.g., a bouncing ball on a Web page. But there are some other, sexier examples you can look at (but only, of course, if you have a Java-enabled browser):

- The Rolling Stones have a Web site (http://www.stones.com/) that contains animated flags and a puzzle that allows the user to slide squares around to form the "tongue" logo.

- The NandO Times Web-based news service (http://www.nando.net/newsroom/nt/nando.html) displays a ticker tape of headlines about sports, politics, national news, and world news that scrolls continuously across its primary page. Each of the four categories of news stories is illustrated with a picture; the pictures change in synchronization with the news stories in the ticker tape, thus providing an interesting amalgamation of the best of TV and newspapers.

- ESPNET SportsZone provides an up-to-date scoreboard of football, baseball, and basketball scores.

- *HotWired* (http://hotwired.com) uses Java to animate its Web pages for the digital version of Wired magazine.

- Dimension X (http://www.dimensionx.com/) has been working on Iced Java, a 3-D rendering engine.

- VPRO (http://www.vpro.n1/), a public broadcasting organization from Hilvershum, Holland, uses Java to provide an automated, hands-off tour of its Web site.

- Sun Microsystems (http://www.sun.com/) has a number of Java examples and demos as well. This Web page links to several other important resources about Java; see the references at the end of this chapter for details.

10.2 THE JAVA ENVIRONMENT

Java is a programming language, but it's more than that: it's an *environment* in which to create and execute applications on the Web. The full environment contains the following components:

- The Java compiler, `javac`, which translates human-readable Java source code to architecture-neutral bytecodes.

- The Java interpreter, which executes Java programs on the user's PC or workstation.

- The C header and source file generator, `javah` and `java_g`. These are used to generate header files for C, as well as source files for making "methods" (roughly equivalent to procedures or subroutines in other languages) within Java.

- The Java disassembler, `javap`, which prints out information about a class file (a file containing a Java applet).

- The document generator, javadoc, which is capable of generating an HTML file from a Java source-code file.
- The profiling tool javaprof, which formats the performance data created if the programmer uses the -prof option in the Java interpreter to obtain statistics on run time and performance.

10.2.1 Simplicity and Familiarity

By basing the language on C++, Sun obviously hopes to take advantage of a large installed base of experienced C++ programmers; in so doing, they were able to take advantage of important features of object-orientation, which Microsoft will find far more difficult to do if it continues using Visual Basic as the foundation of its Internet programming technology. (Visual Basic supports the concept of encapsulation, for example, but does not support inheritance or polymorphism.)

Further, as we'll see in the more detailed discussion of the Java language below, Sun has removed several of the more esoteric and troublesome features of C++, such as multiple inheritance and pointer arithmetic. The primary reason for doing this was to ensure robust behavior—but it also has the result of creating a language that's easier to learn and understand. And in the tradition of C++ and other object-oriented languages, Java provides access to existing libraries of tested objects that provide functionality ranging from basic data types to network interfaces and GUI toolkits.

Though experienced programmers may find Java easy to learn, that doesn't mean that neophytes and end users will have the same experience. As Andrew Leonard points out in a recent issue of *Web Review*:

> A more critical question is what effect Java-esque technologies are having on the average individual's ability to use the Net/Web creatively. The online universe is becoming more complex. Is it leaving us behind? Forget about The Future of the Net. Time to switch memes. What about The End of the Net as We Know It? Once upon a time, the World Wide Web was a truly democratic medium. Learning enough HTML to put up a Web page took an afternoon. Anybody could become publisher of their own Webzine. As a petri dish for Do-It-Yourself cultures, the Web offered astonishing potential. That was then. Try learning to

write a Java applet in an afternoon. Unless you're already an accomplished programmer, the kind of person who spits out Perl scripts like sunflower seed shells or reads C++ manuals as if they were comic books, you might find yourself moving a bit slowly. And it's not just Java. Creating a 3D VRML world isn't trivial either. Just mastering all the possibilities of a new version of Netscape before the next upgrade rolls along is an exhausting challenge. And so on. The Web is stratifying. A priesthood of technonerds—a Webmaster aristocracy pulling down high salaries and wielding great power—is emerging.

The solution, I believe, will eventually involve two "levels" of Java language: the professional level and a "light" level for end users who need to create simple, one-line applets to control the behavior of their HTML pages. Netscape has already taken the initiative, with the scripting language built into Navigator 2.0. And in December 1995, Netscape and Sun announced a joint effort to continue this work in the form of a scripting language called JavaScript.

10.2.2 Security and Robust Behavior

Security and robustness are obviously important in the distributed environment represented by the Internet: If you download a Java applet from a Web server, you really don't want it to run amok on your computer and delete all the files on your hard disk. This is not as far-fetched as it might sound, because the incorporation of Java applets into Web pages means that you may be invoking computer programs written by people anywhere in the world, located any- where on the Web. Indeed, once you begin using a Java-enabled browser, you're at risk—for you don't know, at the moment you decide to retrieve a Web page (e.g., by clicking on a hyperlink within an existing page being displayed on your computer) whether it will contain embedded Java applets.

Sun has addressed this concern by imposing severe constraints on the Java programming language, as well as extensive run-time checking in the interpreter located inside the Java-enabled browser. The Java language, for example, forbids the use of address pointers and pointer arithmetic found in C and C++, which eliminates a large class of innocent errors that might otherwise plague the user of Java applets. In addition, the following steps have been taken to increase the level of security and robust behavior:

- The Java run-time interpreter verifies that bytecodes (the compiled architecture-neutral form of Java applet that gets downloaded from the Web server into the user's machine) don't violate any language constructs—which could happen if an altered Java compiler was used by a hacker. The verification logic checks to make sure that the Java applet doesn't access restricted memory, forge memory pointers, or access objects in a manner inconsistent with its definition. It also ensures that method (subroutine) calls include the correct number of arguments of the right type, and that there are no stack overflows.

- During loading of the Java applet, the run-time interpreter verifies class names (a "class" is an entire Java applet) and access restrictions.

- If a Java applet attempts to access a file for which it has no permission, a dialog box will pop up to allow the user to continue or stop the execution of the applet.

- Future releases of Java are planned to have facilities for using public key encryption to verify the source and origin of the Java source code, and its integrity after traveling through the network to reach the user's machine.

- At run time, information about the origin of the Java applet can be used to decide what the applet is allowed to do. For example, a security mechanism can be used to determine whether the compiled Java bytecodes originated from within an organization's security firewall or not. This makes it possible to set a security policy that restricts the use and execution of Java code that an organization doesn't know or trust.

This last point is crucial, for there are likely to be a number of attempts—both innocent and malicious—to circumvent the security mechanisms that Sun has built into the language. In its white paper on the Java language, Sun expresses the following optimistic statement about Java security:

> Java is designed to operate in distributed environments, which means that security is of paramount importance. With security features designed into the language and run-time system, Java

lets you construct applications that can't be invaded from outside. In the networked environment, applications written in Java are secure from intrusion by unauthorized code attempting to get behind the scenes and create viruses or invade file systems.

For the security-conscious organizations, though, the firewall protection mentioned above will be crucial—at least in the short term.

10.2.3 Portable, Architecture-Neutral Behavior

A basic objective of the Java environment is to operate within a heterogeneous networked environment; to be of practical use, it must be capable of executing on a variety of hardware platforms, in conjunction with a variety of operating system environments, and with multiple programming language interfaces.

The primary strategy for accomplishing this is the use of a compiler that generates *bytecodes* from a Java source program. The bytecodes are transferred from the Web server to a Java-enabled Web browser, where they are interpreted at run time by a Java interpreter. Obviously, the Java interpreter software has to be cognizant of the hardware/software environment in which it operates, but the Java applets do not.

To achieve a higher degree of portability, Java imposes a strict definition (based on an IEEE standard) on data types (for integers, floating-point numbers, etc.) and the behavior of its arithmetic operators. This ensures that numbers look the same and behave in the same way regardless of whether the Java applet is running on an Intel platform, a Macintosh/Motorola platform, or any one of the dozens of UNIX environments that exist around the world.

The architecture-neutral and portable language environment is collectively referred to as the *Java Virtual Machine*. What the marketplace sees is a specific implementation of the Java Virtual Machine for a specific hardware and software environment. The Java Virtual Machine is based primarily on the POSIX interface specification (which is also an open, industry-standard definition) for portable system interfaces.

In this area, Sun starts from an entirely different premise than vendors like Microsoft. Though Microsoft is certain to have a viable technology for developing applications on the Web, it's likely to be based on a proprietary language (e.g., Visual Basic) on a proprietary operating system (Microsoft Windows) with a proprietary technology for distributing objects (OLE); and all of this was created originally for a single hardware environment—i.e., the Intel platform. From a philosophical perspective, Microsoft seems to have adopted a centralized, top-down approach reminiscent of the old USSR government. Sun has adopted something closer to the grass-roots U.S. style of operation.

10.2.4 High Performance

Java was designed with the realization that performance would be important for some situations, but not all. The typical end user running a Java applet on a Pentium processor probably won't know or care if it takes a few milliseconds longer than a hand-coded C++ program would have—just as the end user who uses a Visual Basic or PowerBuilder application typically doesn't worry about performance very much. The important point here, of course, is that the Java applet does run on the user's machine rather than executing on a Web server, where the competition for hardware resources is likely to be much greater.

But efficiency and performance involve more than just CPU cycle; in particular, they involve the issue of "bandwidth." Most Java applets are relatively small (the typical demos involving graphics applets to make a ball bounce around the user's Web page are about 5 Kbytes) and will only have to be downloaded once. This is in stark contrast to the behavior that the user sees with today's Web applications, where the interaction between the user and the application invariably involves a great deal of traffic between the Web client and the Web server—since the application logic executes only on the Web server today. The network delays are typically orders of magnitude larger than any performance delay that might be noticed by an applet executing on the user's computer.

However, keep in mind that a Java applet could be written to continuously grab more Web pages and images and stuff; indeed, one or two of the popular Java demos do just that by giving the user an automated "run-through" of a sequence of pages on the server. And even if only one Web page is retrieved, it could still have a large graphic or multimedia component that could swamp the resources of the user's machine and network connection.

But if we return to the issue of Java performance on the client machine, we do have to acknowledge the possibility that a Java applet could swamp the computational resources of the user's computer. Sun has attempted to avoid as many performance problems as possible— by adopting a scheme, for example, that allows the interpreter to run at full speed without having to check the run-time environment. The Java run-time environment also contains an automatic "garbage collector," to reclaim objects and storage space no longer needed by the Java applet; by allowing it to run as a low-priority background activity, there is a high probability that memory will be available when the Java applet needs it, which leads to better performance.

To illustrate the basic performance of Java, Sun tested some simple programs on vintage-1995 high-end PCs and workstations, with the following results:

- Creating a new object takes approximately 8.4 microseconds.

- Creating a new class with several methods takes approximately 11 microseconds.

- Invoking a method on an object takes approximately 1.7 microseconds.

- Invoking a synchronized method on an object takes approximately 16.3 microseconds.

It's reasonable to assume, I think, that the performance issues for typical single-user environments will become less of a problem as the hardware technology continues to advance over the next several years and as users have more and more powerful workstations on their desks.

Sun has also provided a mechanism that allows compute-intensive sections of a Java applet to be translated on the fly (i.e., at run time) into native machine code for a specific hardware environment and then interfaced with the rest of the Java environment; this is roughly equivalent to a scheme in which a compiler's final machine code generator has been combined with the dynamic loader. Such an approach might be necessary for certain mathematical, engineering, or scientific applets, but I doubt that we'll see very much of it. The performance of bytecodes converted to machine code in this fashion is roughly the same as with native C or C++.

10.2.5 Multithreaded Behavior

It's important to note that the level of interactivity is different with Java, because user input is controlled from the client rather than the server. With current HTML interfaces, there is no response to Web input until the user clicks on an "input" button of some kind. Typically, there's only one thing going on—and while users are waiting for a response from the network, it appears to them that nothing is going on.

Java is based on the assumption that users really need and want to do several things at the same time. A user working with a Java-enabled browser, for example, can run several animations concurrently while downloading an image and scrolling the page currently displayed on his computer screen. To achieve this high degree of interactivity for the end user, it's important to have a *multithreading* capability.

Java supports multithreading at the language level with the addition of sophisticated synchronization primitives. The Java library provides a Thread class, and the run-time interpreter provides "locking" and "monitoring" operations, as I'll describe in more detail below. At the library level, Java's system libraries have been written to be "thread safe"—i.e., the functionality provided by the libraries is available without conflict to multiple concurrent threads of execution.

One last point: It's encouraging to note that Java is not a hog. Unlike many of today's bloated software packages, it doesn't fill up your entire computer; the basic Java interpreter requires about 40 Kbytes of memory, plus another 175 Kbytes for the standard class libraries and multithreading support. That will probably grow over time, as the language and environment become more sophisticated— but it's a far cry from the 2 megabytes of memory that my word processor demands as a minimum.

10.3 THE JAVA LANGUAGE

As I've noted already, Java is based on the C++ language and still looks superficially like C++. As a result, programmers who are already familiar with C, C++, Objective C, Eiffel, Ada, and various related languages should find it relatively easy to learn the language. Sun estimates the required time period to be a couple of weeks; as one textbook author put it, "the wonderful thing about Java is that it is not rocket science to use."

On the other hand, it may not be so easy for the community of business-oriented application programmers—i.e., those who are currently programming in "old" languages like COBOL or "new" languages like Visual Basic and PowerBuilder. Languages like Smalltalk and Delphi are somewhere in the middle; they have much of the object-oriented flavor of Java, but the syntax is different enough that it will take a while to digest.

And, as noted earlier, there's another community that will find Java quite difficult: end users and "casual programmers" who have learned how to create HTML Web pages but who have never learned a formal programming language. That's the primary reason for the "JavaScript" language that Sun and Netscape recently announced and that Netscape will be delivering as part of Navigator 2.0 in early 1996.

I don't have space in this chapter to provide all the details of the Java language, but it's useful to have an understanding of its main components, as well as the components of C++ that Sun deliberately removed when creating Java. I'll also discuss the object-oriented features of the language.

10.3.1 The Main Components of Java

The main features of Java show many similarities to and some differences from C and C++:

- *Primitive data types*—Java supports numeric data types (8-bit byte, 16-bit short, 32-bit int, and 64-bit long); there is no unsigned specifier for integer data types. The 8-bit byte data type replaces the old C/C++ char data type. Real numeric types are 32-bit float and 64-bit double; these types, and their arithmetic operations, are as defined by the IEEE 754 specification.
- *Character data types*—Java's char data type is different from traditional C: it defines a 16-bit *Unicode* character, which defines character codes in the range of 0 to 65,535. The Unicode charac-

ter set facilitates internationalization and localization of character codes, in keeping with the worldwide nature of the Internet.

- *Boolean data types*—Java adds a `boolean` data type, which assumes the value `true` or `false`. Unlike common programming practice in C, a Java `boolean` type cannot be converted to any numeric type.

- *Arithmetic and relational operators*—all of the familiar C and C++ arithmetic operations are available. In addition, Java adds the ">>>" operator to indicate an unsigned (logical) right shift; it uses the "+" operator for string concatenation.

- *Arrays*—Java allows the declaration and allocation of arrays of any type, and the programmer can allocate arrays of arrays to achieve multidimensional arrays. To get the length of an array, Java provides a `length()` "accessor method." Access to elements of an array can be accomplished with normal C-style indexing, but the Java run-time interpreter checks all array accesses to ensure that their indices are within the range of the array. Note that the familiar C concept of a pointer to an array of memory elements does not exist in Java; arbitrary pointer arithmetic has also disappeared, which means that programmers won't be writing code that marches right past the end of an array, trashing the contents of innocent areas of memory and causing program failures in various unpredictable ways.

- *Strings*—the `string` class is for read-only objects, and the `StringClass` class provides for string objects that the programmer wishes to modify. Note that strings are Java language objects, not pseudoarrays of characters as they are in C; however, the Java compiler understands that a string of characters enclosed within double quote is to be instantiated as a `String` object. As noted earlier, the "+" supports concatenation of strings; the `length()` accessor method can be used to obtain the number of characters in the string.

- *Multilevel breaks*—Java has no `goto` statement, but it does contain a `break` and `continue` statement, combined with the notion of labeled blocks of code, to provide the programmer with a mechanism to exit from multiple levels of nested loops. This is in contrast to C, where the `continue` statement only allows the program to escape to the immediately enclosing block of code. Java's `break` *label* and `continue` *label* statements are equivalent to the `next` *label* and `last` *label* statements in the PERL programming language used by many Internet application developers.

- *Memory management and garbage collection*—Java does not support the `malloc` and `free` commands, with which C and C++ programmers have traditionally managed the allocation of memory within the programs. Java has a `new` operator that allocates memory for objects; the run-time system then keeps track of the object's status and automatically reclaims memory when objects are no longer in use. Because Java does not support or allow memory pointers, all references within a program to allocated storage (e.g., to objects that have been created within the program) are made through symbolic references or "handles." The Java memory manager keeps track of references to existing objects, and when an object has no more references to it, then it becomes a candidate for automatic garbage collection. The Java run-time system performs background garbage collection during idle periods on the user's workstation.

- *Integrated thread synchronization*—Java provides multithreading support at the syntactic (language) level and also via support from the run-time system and thread objects.

10.3.2 Features Removed from C++

The discussion above has already illustrated some of the features that Sun removed from C and C++ when it created Java. Here's a more complete list:

- *Typedefs, defines, and preprocessors have been eliminated*—there is no `typedef`, no `#define` statement, and no preprocessor. As a result, there is no need for the header files one typically sees in C and C++. Instead, the definition of other classes and their methods are included within the Java language source files. This is more than a cosmetic trick: In order to understand the typical C/C++ program, you must first read all of the related header files, `#defines`, and `typedefs` to understand the overall context of the program.

- *Structures and unions have been eliminated*—Java achieves the same effect by allowing the programmer to declare a class with appropriate instance variables. C++ might have followed the same approach, but for obvious reasons, chose to maintain compatibility with C; the Java designers deliberately avoided committing themselves to C/C++ compatibility when they felt it was inappropriate to do so.

- *Functions have been eliminated*—anything the programmer can do with a function can be accomplished by defining a class and creating methods for the class. Thus, the Java designers have tried to eliminate the practice of creating "hybrid" mixtures of OO and procedural programming style.

- *Multiple inheritance is not supported*—only single inheritance is allowed. The desirable features of multiple inheritance are provided with *interfaces* in Java, which are conceptually similar to what's found in Objective C. An interface is a definition of a set of methods that one or more objects will implement; they contain only the declaration of methods and constants.

- *Goto statements have been eliminated*—because the most legitimate uses of the goto have typically been to exit from the innermost part of a loop, and that facility has been provided with the `break` and `continue` statements.

- *Operator overloading has been eliminated*—which means that there are no mechanisms for programmers to overload the standard arithmetic operators. Where this kind of familiar C/C++ activity needs to be carried out, it can be accomplished in a more straightforward way by declaring a class, appropriate instance variables, and appropriate methods to manipulate those variables.

- *Automatic coercions of data types have been eliminated*—on the premise that if the programmer wants to "coerce" a data element of one type into a different data type, it should be done explicitly with a "cast" operation. Thus, the fragment of code shown below:

```
int sampleInt;
double sampleFloat = 3.1415926535;
sampleInt = sampleFloat;
```

would result in a compiler error because of the possible loss of precision. To accomplish this properly would require the programmer to write the code in the following fashion:

```
int sampleInt;
double sampleFloat = 3.1415926535;
sampleInt = (int)sampleFloat;
```

- *Pointers and pointer arithmetic have been eliminated*—since they are one of the primary causes of bugs in programs (pointers in a data structure are roughly equivalent to `goto` statements in a control structure). Because structures are gone, and arrays and strings are represented as objects, the need for pointers has largely disappeared.

10.3.3 Object-Oriented Features

With the exception of primitive data types, everything in Java is an object—and even the primitive types can be encapsulated within objects if necessary. Java supports four fundamental aspects of object-oriented technology:

- *Encapsulation*—instance variables and methods for a class are packaged together, thus providing modularity and information hiding.

- *Inheritance*—new classes and behavior can be defined in terms of existing classes.

- *Polymorphism*—the same message sent to different objects results in behavior that is dependent on the nature of the object receiving the message. If you send a "move" message to an "animal" object, you don't want to be concerned with the nature of the animal you're talking to; if it's a bird, it should be smart enough to carry out the "move" by flying, whereas a snake would respond to the same message by wriggling, and a rabbit would hop, etc.

- *Dynamic binding*—as implied above, a programmer doesn't want to be required to specify, at coding time, the specific type of object to which a message is sent; the type resolution needs to be done at run time. This is especially important for Java, because objects (Java applets) can come from anywhere on the network and may have been developed by anyone.

Java follows the C++ tradition of supporting "public," "private," and "protected" variables; the default (if the programmer doesn't specify one of these three) is "friendly," and indicates that the instance variables are accessible to all objects within the same package but inaccessible to objects outside the package. Like C++, the programmer can declare *constructor* methods that perform initialization when an object is instantiated from a class. But rather than the *destructor* method that one finds in C++, Java has a *finalizer* method; this does not require (and does not allow) the programmer to explicitly free the memory associated with the object when it's no longer used.

Like many object-oriented languages, Java supports *class methods* and *class variables*—i.e., methods and variables associated with the class as a whole, rather than instances within the class. Class methods can't access instance variables, nor can they invoke instance methods. By definition, a class variable is local to the class itself, and there is only a single copy of the variable, which is shared by every object that the programmer instantiates from the class.

Also, Java supports the concept of abstract classes and abstract methods. This allows the programmer to create a "generic" class, defined in the form of a template. By definition, the programmer cannot instantiate objects from the abstract class; objects can only be instantiated from a *subclass* of the abstract class, and it's only within those (concrete) subclasses that the defined methods can actually be used.

Java comes with several libraries of utility classes and methods; these include:

- `java.lang`—a collection of language types that are always important to a compilation unit. This library contains the definition of `object` (the root of the entire class hierarchy in Java) and `Class`, plus threads, exceptions, wrappers for primitive data types, and various other fundamental classes.

- `java.io`—this is roughly equivalent to the Standard I/O library in most UNIX systems; it contains classes to access streams of data and random-access files. An associated library, `java.net`, provides supports for sockets, telnet interfaces, and URLs.

- `java.util`—contains utility classes such as `Dictionary`, `HashTable`, and `Stack`, as well as `Date` and `Time` classes.

- `java.awt`—an Abstract Windowing Toolkit provides an abstract layer enabling the programmer to port Java applications from one windowing system to another. The library contains classes for basic interface components such as events, fonts, colors, buttons, scrollbars.

10.3.4 Java Multithreading

The Java language and run-time environment support the concept of multithreading, so that Java applets can operate concurrently to play music, run animations, download a text file from a server, and allow the user to scroll down a page. Multithreading is a practical way of obtaining fast, straightforward concurrency within a single process space (i.e., taking into account that there may be programs other than Java and the Java-enabled Web browser running on the user's platform, and the user's operating system may also be attempting to coordinate background printing, spreadsheet recalculations, and various other processes).

The Java library provides a class that supports a collection of methods to start a thread, run a thread, stop a thread, and check on a thread's status. Java's approach is sometimes called "lightweight processes" or "execution contexts"; it's modeled after the Cedar/Mesa systems implemented by Xerox PARC, which in turn are based on a formal set of synchronization primitives developed by Professor C.A.R. Hoare in the mid-70s.

Java's threads are preemptive in nature, and the threads can also be time-sliced if the Java interpreter runs on a hardware/software platform that supports time-slicing. For environments that don't support time-slicing—such as the System 7.5 Macintosh operating system on the computer I used to write this book—a thread retains control of the processor once it has begun unless a higher-priority thread interrupts. This means that for compute-bound threads, it behooves the programmer to use the `yield()` method at appropriate times and places, in order to give other threads a chance to operate.

At the language level, methods within a class that are declared `synchronized` are not allowed to run concurrently; such methods run under the control of *monitors* to ensure that their instance variables remain in a consistent state. Every class and instantiated object has its own monitor that comes into play if necessary. When a synchronized method within a class is entered, it acquires a monitor on the current object; when the synchronized method returns (exits) by any means, its associated monitor is released and other synchronized methods within that object are then allowed to begin executing. Thus, if the programmer wants to ensure that the classes and methods within his Java program are "thread safe," then any methods that have the ability to change the values of instance variables should be declared synchronized; this will ensure that only one method can change the state of an object at any time.

10.3.5 Security Mechanisms in Java

Security is one of the big concerns on the Internet these days, and the designers of Java have taken it into account in their definition of the programming language, in the compiler, and in the run-time system. As we've already seen, the Java language has eliminated memory pointers—which means that programmers can't forge pointers into memory, which is one of the typical sources of security breaches. In addition, the run-time binding of object structures to physical memory addresses means that a programmer can't infer the physical memory layout of a class simply by looking at its definition.

However, it's not enough to make a more restrictive language definition and enforce it with a compiler. The problem is that a Java-enabled Web browser is importing applets from anywhere on the network—including, potentially, applets that "look" like Java, but might have been created by a bogus compiler or even hand-coded by a hacker. Thus, to ensure security, the Java run-time interpreter cannot trust the incoming code and must subject it to a verification process to ensure that:

- The incoming code doesn't forge memory pointers.
- The incoming code doesn't violate access restrictions.
- The incoming code accesses objects in the manner that they have been declared (e.g., OutputStream objects are always used as OutputStreams and never as anything else).

The complete process in the creation, compiling, loading, verification, and execution of a Java program is shown in Figure 10.2. The

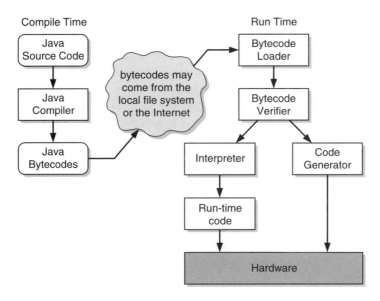

FIGURE 10.2 IMPLEMENTING SECURITY IN JAVA

key point here is that the Java bytecode loader and bytecode verifier make no assumption about the primary source of the bytecode stream that the user wishes to execute; it may have come from the user's local file system (i.e., on his own workstation), or it may have come from anywhere on the Internet.

When the bytecode verifier is finished with its examination, the run-time interpreter can be sure that there will be no operand stack overflows or underflows, that all object field accesses will be legal (i.e., appropriate usage of private, public, and protected methods and instance variables), and that the parameter-types of all bytecode instructions are correct. As a result, the interpreter does not have to check for stack overflows or for correct operand types while the Java applet is executing—and it can therefore run at full speed without compromising reliability.

While a Java applet is running, it may request that a class, or set of classes, be loaded into the user's computer—and, of course, these new classes could also come from anywhere on the Internet. The new incoming code also has to be checked by the bytecode verifier, but there's one more level of protection that needs to be explained, involving "name spaces."

Most programmers understand this concept from their previous work, but for the nonprogrammers reading this chapter, a brief analogy will help explain the concept. Suppose that you have a brother named Fred and that your spouse also has a brother named Fred. At the dinner table, your spouse casually says, "Oh, by the way, Fred called today to say hello." The question is: *Which* Fred? It depends on whether you're talking about the "name space" of your own family or that of your spouse. In the case of Java, when we refer to a class-name, we need to know which name space it's associated with.

The environment seen by a thread of execution running Java bytecodes—e.g., a typical Java applet—can be visualized as a set of classes that are partitioned into separate name spaces. There is one name space for classes that come from the user's local file system, and a separate name space for each network source of Java byte-codes. When a class is imported from across the network, it is placed in the private name space associated with its origin. Whenever a Java class refers to another class, the Java run-time interpreter first looks for the class within the name space of the local system (where the built-in classes referred to above reside), and then in the name space of the referencing class. As a result, it's impossible for an imported class to act as an "imposter" of a built-in class. And the built-in classes can never accidentally reference classes within imported name spaces—the Java interpreter requires them to reference such classes explicitly. Similarly, classes imported from different origins (e.g., attached to different Web pages) are kept separate from each other.

10.3.6 Final Comments on the Java Language

One reason for showing you all of this detail about the Java language is to impress upon you that it's obviously a serious, heavy-weight programming language. This is not something as simple as the HTML formatting syntax that someone can pick up in an hour or two; it's not intended for casual amateurs.

But by the same token, the serious programmer doesn't want a casual programming language for building industrial-strength Internet applications; to implement secure, robust, multithreaded, object-oriented, distributed applications requires something more sophisticated than the current forms of such popular languages as Visual

Basic, PowerBuilder, and Delphi. And it's interesting to see that in many ways, it doesn't require *more* than C++, but rather, *less* than C++.

Note that Java can be used to write an entire application, not just tiny applets embedded within HTML. The most obvious example is HotJava: it's written in Java. I expect that many of the tool vendors will begin using Java for their own browsers and development tools—and it's conceivable that some of the "conventional" applications could migrate to Java. I can easily imagine a scenario where my word processor and spreadsheet become Java-enabled applications.

10.4 ALTERNATIVES AND COMPETITORS

If you aren't prepared to learn Java yourself or to convert all of your existing Internet applications to Java, what are your alternatives? At the moment, there seem to be three or four, including products from Microsoft, Borland, Texas Instruments, and ParcPlace.

Of these, Microsoft is clearly the most significant. Whatever Microsoft does on the Internet will have an impact on the rest of the vendors. Hence, it's significant that Bill Gates announced in December 1995, as part of a massive Internet publicity blitz, that it had signed a letter of intent with Sun Microsystems to license Java. The company also announced it was introducing a new language called Visual Basic Script, which is upwardly compatible with Visual Basic 4.0 and which will take advantage of Microsoft's OLE as a technology for distributing objects (in a fashion similar to applets) across the Internet.

The announcement came just as this book was being finalized, and as such, it's far too early for me to assess the full significance of Microsoft's Internet strategy. But the key points to keep in mind at this early stage are these:

- Java has all the attention and the support of the media, as well as the momentum of some 30 companies that have licensed the technology—but there is little or no installed Java technology aside from the 50 to 100 sample applets that one can download from Sun's Web page. This is likely to change rapidly in 1996, and it will be interesting to see how much momentum the language is able to create in the marketplace.

- Meanwhile, Microsoft has an *enormous* Visual Basic installed base, especially in the business community—estimates have ranged as high as 3 million copies of Visual Basic in mid-1995. The business application development community has never been fond of C++ and might be more inclined to leverage its investment in Visual Basic applications than to invest in additional training and development effort to adopt the Java technology.

- While OLE is obviously a full-fledged technology and while Visual Basic 4.0 is now a fairly robust language, neither of these two cornerstones of Microsoft's Internet technology were actually designed and developed with the Web in mind. What's impressive about Java, as I've pointed out in this chapter, is the level of effort that Sun has gone to, to make it an effective tool for robust, secure applications on the Web. Visual Basic Script might compete effectively with JavaScript, and the marketplace for these lightweight scripting languages might turn out to be much larger than the marketplace for professional Java applications. But if you do want to build professional, industrial-strength applications to run on the Internet, you'd better look closely at the details of Microsoft's approach to see how it will handle security, fail-safe operations, and so on.

- While Microsoft has licensed the Java technology, it's not yet clear how much support they'll actually provide. The announcement indicates that Microsoft will be adding enhancements to Java to make it more efficient for the Windows 95 environment, but that the changes will be given back to Sun—which continues to own the technology. My guess is that Microsoft has to pay lip service to Java in order to avoid being characterized as an "outsider" and also to cover its bases if Java does end up dominating the marketplace. But I suspect that the company's primary interest will be to ensure that Java applets can somehow work compatibly with Visual Basic—and it's Visual Basic where Microsoft will continue investing its efforts.

Meanwhile, Borland will build a high performance visual rapid application development environment for creating Java applications. The product, code-named Latte, will be developed in Java and is intended to radically increase the speed of developing Java applications. Borland plans to begin rolling out stages of Latte in the first half of 1996; see the references at the end of this chapter for the Borland Java Web site, which includes a variety of Java-related information.

Also, Texas Instruments has announced a new version of its Composer development environment, which will allow Web browsers to interact with Composer-built server components, using the TI Arranger technology as the Web gateway. This doesn't change the overall paradigm of Internet applications in the fashion that Java does, because the "intelligence" of the application will still be located on the server, but it does bring higher-level analysis and design tools into the picture. See the references at the end of this chapter for TI's WWW address for more information.

Another example comes from ParcPlace-Digitalk, the vendor best known for its various Smalltalk products and tools. At the Internet Expo conference in November 1995, ParcPlace announced a new product called *VisualWave* for "live" Web applications. It consists of an application development environment, based on Smalltalk, that will automatically generate the HTML and CGI interface logic necessary to run a Web application. Again, this is more like the traditional form of Web application development than the Java approach, but it does have the advantage of providing a single, integrated graphical environment with which developers can create an application to deploy on the Web. And because VisualWave generates the Web interface automatically, it's possible to develop applications that can run both as a client and as application servers for use by Web browsers. This allows the developer to choose the appropriate deployment platform of an application without changing source code—but note that the components of the application don't move dynamically from the server to the browser during run-time execution, as would be the case with Java. For more information, see the references at the end of this chapter for ParcPlace's Web URL.

A final note on alternatives: As the manuscript for this book was being finalized, I received an e-mail message from software engineering consultant Bob Munck, who points out that Intermetrics has targeted their AdaMagic compiler to generate Java bytecodes (which is also a good illustration of the need for the SIGAda Working Group to encourage the use of Ada for Web applets and applications). The compiler is running and is very close to being validated; a beta release will be put on the Internet in early 1996.

Munck argues that Ada95 has several advantages over Java, including being an ISO standard with a large number of existing compilers and development systems, as well as a great deal of legacy code in Ada83. I'm not convinced that anyone outside the U.S. defense establishment cares very much about Ada, but it is interesting to consider that an entirely different source language—and one that has been just as carefully designed to handle secure, robust, concurrent execution of processes—might be the starting point for Internet applications. For more details, contact Munck at Munck@acm.org.

10.5 STRATEGIC IMPLICATIONS

Many articles in the trade press during the summer and fall of 1995 have been proclaiming that Java is the beginning of a "revolution" in software. Having watched "silver-bullet" revolutions like CASE technology and pen-based computing come and go during the past decade, I'm always a little wary of such euphoria. Nevertheless, it's hard *not* to get excited by all this—and there certainly are some strategic implications that you should be thinking about:

- *Java-enabled Web pages are more interesting than today's Web pages*— so if your company is planning to use the Web to attract potential customers to look at your products and services, you need to be aware that your competitors will probably be using Java to create a more tempting and interesting environment in which to participate. Judge for yourself: Take a look at some of the Java demos listed earlier in this chapter to see what kind of competitive difference they're likely to make in your world.

- *Java may replace* PERL *and* CGI *interfaces*—so if you're just now beginning to explore the idea of Web pages connected to application functionality, you should seriously consider jumping right over the current generation of tools like PERL. This will be more of a problem for the organizations that have already invested a lot of time and effort in PERL scripts. But remember, it could be worse: it's not as bad as all those tens of millions of lines of COBOL legacy code that we're trying to maintain.

- *Java facilitates a new form of client-server applications*—which may turn out to be the largest impact for many of today's conventional IT organizations. Rather than building your next application with conventional client-server tools and programming languages like Visual Basic or PowerBuilder, why not use a Java-enabled Web browser for the client, and an internal Web server as the application server, with connections to the data server on your enterprise mainframe?

- *Java could seriously decrease the interest in languages like Visual Basic and PowerBuilder*—to the extent that those languages are being used for conventional client-server development projects today. Of course, Microsoft is working to make Visual Basic a Web-oriented language, and Powersoft will presumably do the same too. But by the time they do so, it may be too late: Java may have captured the "mind share" of the leading edge of Web-oriented application developers.

- *Java may renew the interest in* C++—I've been one of the people in the computer field who has described C++ as "the assembly language of the 90s," largely because of the problems associated with language features that Java has eliminated. Maybe Java will come to be the equivalent of "safe sex" for the C++ programmers of the world.

- *Java, together with the Web, may begin to minimize the importance of specific hardware/software environments*—this is the result of the architecture-neutral approach taken by Java, together with a similar philosophy from Netscape, which owned most of the Web browser marketplace as this book was being written. Given the inertia that exists in the marketplace, I certainly don't think this will mean that Intel and Microsoft will go bankrupt tomorrow morning—but it could well take a lot of pressure off the beleaguered Macintosh owners around the world, and it could also fuel a renaissance in UNIX and UNIX-oriented hardware platforms. And even if Microsoft and Intel don't collapse entirely, the notion that those two companies might no longer "own" the desktop marketplace could be a staggering change in today's industry.

- *Applets could lead to the end of "fatware" as well as changing the distribution mechanism for software products*—which could also trigger some enormous changes in the economics of the software industry. Imagine, for example, what the world would be like if your word processor and spreadsheet program were written in Java; for starters, you wouldn't have to buy it in a shrink-wrapped box, because you could download it from the Internet, with assurances that you *always* had the latest version. And there would be a much greater chance that you could customize the features and components of the word processor in ways that you can't easily do today. If you don't like the spell-checker on your Brand-X word processor, for example, why not treat it as an applet—and replace it with a different spell-checker applet available from a third-party source? Companies like Microsoft, Novell, and Lotus who currently make a lot of money by selling us "office suites" with 80+ megabytes of software (much of which we don't need or want but are forced to buy anyway) would find it to be a radically different world.

- *Java could change the economics of paying for software*—the software industry today is based on the concept of entire applications delivered to the marketplace in shrink-wrapped boxes for a fixed one-time cost, for which the customer is given a license that allows him or her to use the software forever on a single platform. As we've already seen, Java makes it possible to market smaller, bite-sized pieces of functionality—but more importantly, Java makes it possible to sell *one-time usage* of a piece of software. This one-time usage could be defined for a single transaction, or for a single session during which the user is connected to a Web server. Software guru Brad Cox argues that a such a model will be the catalyst that spawns a thriving industry of software component-builders; see his article, "'No Silver Bullet' Reconsidered," in the November 1995 issue of *American Programmer* for an intriguing discussion of the economics associated with such a model. It's far too early to tell whether this will actually happen, though it's fairly clear that it requires a completely different business model than the one currently used by software product vendors. The companies most threatened will be the ones that sell relatively small products—e.g., software utilities and games—though those companies may be nimble enough to change their way of doing business. It will be *much* more difficult for the larger, more established software vendors to respond to this new approach.

10.6 SUMMARY AND CONCLUSIONS

As the softcover version of this book goes to press, it has been roughly 2.5 years since Java first appeared. In that relatively brief period of time, the acceptance of Java has been so enthusiastic that some computer trade magazines and market research reports are proclaiming that 25–50% of all new applications developed in the waning years of the millennium will be written in Java. Other indications of Java's popularity abound: Sun Microsystems, for example, claims that in 1996, 200,000 programmers and one-third of all organizations with more than 5,000 employees began using Java in their application development. Whether they were playing, experimenting, building pilot projects, or working on mission-critical applications is not clear; but a language that grabs the attention of such a large segment of the development community obviously has to be taken seriously. It will be another year or two before we see how Java fares against the competitive onslaught of Microsoft's ActiveX and Visual Basic 5.0; and it remains to be seen whether the 200,000 people who began using Java in 1996 were really using Java, or just dabbling with new technology.

However, the potential for Java is so enormous—in terms of its impact on the overall computing paradigm—that an organization would have to be suicidal to ignore it. Of course, *your* organization may not see it that way, especially if it has a great deal of its culture invested in current client-server technologies or in ancient technologies like mainframes and COBOL. Over the next five years, I expect to see most conventional IT organizations slowly moving into the world of Web-based application development, but they'll probably do it through extensions of existing technology—e.g., with products discussed in section 10.4, like TI's new version of Composer or ParcPlace's VisualWave. But as you make your plans for this new world, remember to make the distinction between the "Java paradigm"— where live-content applets are *dynamically* sucked down into the user's workstation for execution—and the old-fashioned paradigm of building static applications for a client-server architecture that happens to use a Web browser for a client and a Web server as a gateway into the traditional storehouse of enterprise applications and databases.

Whatever the organization decides to do about the Java paradigm, my advice to you—as a professional programmer, software engineer, or application developer—is to invest the time and effort to learn this technology. As I suggested in Chapter 2, the elimination of the "social contract" between employer and employee means that it may be necessary for you to invest your own time and money to become competent in Java. If you decide not to, you might be able to continue earning a living writing PowerBuilder programs; but you also run the risk that your organization will surprise you one day by telling you that your job has been outsourced to someplace in Guatemala or Greece, where equally competent PowerBuilder programmers work for a fraction of your salary.

There's another aspect of the Java paradigm that you need to think about, too: As I suggested above, it may be the catalyst that generates a booming cottage industry of applet builders. As a result, you may find that it's possible to create your own "cottage business" rather than working in a large organization with hundreds of other developers; indeed, it's possible that you may find it *necessary* to do so in order to maintain your current income. We can already see a small form of this with Visual Basic, which supports an industry of nearly a thousand tiny, cottage-industry companies building VBX components. In the past, one of the big obstacles to this kind of business was the cost and difficulty of marketing one's products; but the Internet, as we all know, is not only an environment for software development, but is also a wonderful mechanism for marketing one's wares via the World Wide Web.

The idea of a nation of programmers working from their individual cottages is perhaps a bit extreme; obviously, there will still be room for corporate IT development, as well as conventional software-product builders. But the scenario I've described in this chapter *does* suggest that the conventional IT organizations and Silicon-valley shrink-wrap software-product companies might not continue to be a growth industry over the next 5 to 10 years. By analogy: Mainframes haven't disappeared, but most of us don't consider it a growth industry. Similarly, COBOL hasn't disappeared, and it still forms the basis of employment for some 2 million programmers in the U.S.; but even with the recent arrival of object-oriented COBOL, it's hard to imagine it as a growth industry.[1] What I'm suggesting in this chapter is that client-server technology and all of the currently popular tools and languages for traditional client-server development may also cease to be a growth industry within the next couple of years; the Java paradigm may well replace them.

In the extreme case, this paradigm shift could put *all* of the big software companies out of business. As I said earlier in this chapter, I seriously doubt that Microsoft and Oracle and Computer Associates and the other big software companies will go out of business—but for some of them, the paradigm shift may turn out to be nearly impossible for their existing culture, just as IBM found it difficult to switch from a mainframe culture to a PC culture. But if it's hard for the American big-company culture to change, it's also hard for the big-company culture in Europe, Asia, Africa, and South America. It's easier for the culture of a small company to change, and it's even easier for a completely new culture to emerge in a startup company. There will be *many* such startup companies created by the Java paradigm, and several of them will be in places outside the U.S. But to participate in this paradigm shift requires a combination of infrastructure (e.g., easily available 28.8-Kbytes access to the Internet), technology (a Pentium-based machine in one's own cottage), and an entrepreneurial spirit. And while the U.S. doesn't have a monopoly on these items, it does have a head start. I see it as one of the best things that has happened to the software industry since the introduction of the PC and MS-DOS® in the early 1980s.

REFERENCES

Books

1. Anuff, Ed. *The Java Sourcebook.* (New York: John Wiley & Sons, 1996).

---

[1]There's a simple test that you can apply: If your children told you they were going to major in computer-related discipline in college, with the intention of getting a job in the software field after graduation, would you advise them to concentrate on COBOL? Probably not—for the same reason you would discourage them from spending much time with FORTRAN, RPG, PL/I, and assembly language. Chances are you would advise your children to learn C, C++, Smalltalk, Visual Basic, Delphi, Power-Builder—and, having read this chapter, Java. If this is the prevailing scenario in the field, then it's only a matter of time before all the existing COBOL programmers die of old age. Hopefully, the legacy COBOL code—which has been estimated at 18–200 billion lines of code—will die with them. Or, if it *must* be kept alive, maybe it will all be outsourced to some part of the world where COBOL maintenance programming is considered a pleasant alternative to growing rice or raising pigs.

2. Arnold, Ken, and James Gosling. *The Java Programming Language.* (The SunSoft Press/Addison-Wesley, 1996).

3. Au, Edith, David Makower, and Pencom WebWorks. *Java Basics.* (MIS Press, 1996).

4. Campione, Mary, and Kathy Walrath. *The Java Language Tutorial: Object-Oriented Programming for the Internet.* (Reading, MA: Addison-Wesley, 1996).

5. Chan, Patrick. *Developing Professional Java Applets.* (Sams net, 1996).

6. Coad, Peter, and Mark Mayfield. *Java by Design: Building Better Apps and Applets.* (Upper Saddle River, NJ: Yourdon Press/ Prentice Hall, 1997).

7. Coombs, Ted, Jason Coombs, and Don Brewer. *The Netscape LiveWire Sourcebook: Create & Manage a Java Based Web Site.* (New York: John Wiley & Sons, 1996).

8. Cornell, Gary, and Cay S. Horstmann. *Core Java.* (The Sunsoft Press/Prentice Hall, 1996).

9. Daconta, Mike. *Java for C/C++ Programmers.* (New York: JohnWiley & Sons, 1996).

10. December, John. *Creating Web Applets with Java.* (Sams net, 1996).

11. December, John. *Presenting Java: An Introduction to Java and Hot-Java.* (Indianapolis, IN: Sams.Net Publishing, 1995).

12. Flanagan, David. *Java in a Nutshell: A Desktop Quick Reference for Java Programmers.* (Sebastapol, CA: O'Reilly & Associates, 1996).

13. Frazier, Colin, and Jill Bond. *Java API Reference.* (Indianapolis, IN: New Riders Publishers, 1996).

14. Freeman, Adam. *Active Java: Object-Oriented Programming for the World Wide Web.* (Reading, MA: Addison-Wesley, 1996).

15. Gosling, James, and Frank Yellin. *The Java Application Programming Interface, Volume I: Core Packages.* (The SunSoft Press/ Addison-Wesley, 1996).

16. Gosling, James, Frank Yellin, and The Java Team. *The Java Application Programming Interface, Volume II: Window Toolbox and Applets.* (The SunSoft Press/Addison-Wesley, 1996).

17. Gulbransen, David, and Kenrick Rawlings. *Presenting JAVA.* (Sams net, 1995).

18. Gurewich, Nathan, and Ori Gurewich. *Java Manual of Style*. (Ziff-Davis, 1996).

19. Jackson, Jerry, and Alan L. McClellan. *Java by Example*. (The Sun-softPress/Prentice Hall, 1996).

20. Jaworski, Jamie. *Java Developer's Guide*. (Sams net, 1996).

21. Koosis, Donald J., and David S. Koosis. *JAVAProgramming for Dummies*. (IDG Books, 1996).

22. Lalani, Suleiman. *Java Programmers Library*. (Jamsa Press, 1996).

23. Manger, Jason. *Essential Java: Developing Interactive Applications for the World Wide Web*. (New York: McGraw-Hill, 1996).

24. Naughton, Patrick. *The Java Handbook*. (New York: Osborne-McGraw-Hill, 1996).

25. New Riders Publishing Staff. *Porting to Java*. (Indianapolis, IN: New Riders Publishers, 1996).

26. Norton, Peter. *Peter Norton's Guide to Java*. (Sams net, 1996).

27. Pew, John. *Instant Java*. (The SunSoft Press/Prentice Hall, 1996).

28. Ritchey, Tim. *Programming Javascript for Netscape 2.0*. (Indianapolis, IN: New Riders Publishers, 1996).

29. Sams Net Development Group. *Java Developer's Guide*. (Sams net, 1996).

30. Simkin, Steve, Neil Bartlett, and Alex Leslie. *The Java Programming Explorer*. (Coriolis Group, 1996).

31. Tittel, Ed, and Mark Gaither. *60 Minute Guide to Java*. (Foster City, CA: IDG Books Worldwide, Inc., 1995).

32. Tyna, Paul M., Gabriel. Torok, and Troy Downing. *Java Primer Plus: Supercharging Network Applications with the JavaProgramming Language*. (Waite Group Publishing, 1996).

33. Van Der Linden, Peter. *Just Java*. (The SunSoftPress/Prentice Hall, 1996).

34. Walnum, Clayton. *Java by Example*. (Que, 1996).

35. Walsh, Aaron E. *Foundations of Java Programming for the World Wide Web*. (IDG Books, 1996).

36. Walsh, Aaron E. *Java for Dummies*. (IDG Books, 1996).

World Wide Web Resources

http://java.sun.com/—the primary page at Sun's Web site about Java. Links from this site take you to a variety of places for demos, release information, documentation, etc. The anonymous FTP site for code downloading and distribution is at ftp://java.sun.com/ Subpages describe the current sites and instructions for downloading HotJava, information about the latest release of Java, current porting efforts, and up-to-date information on problems and requested features.

http://java.sun.com/1.0alpha3/overview/java/index.html—an overview of the Java language.

http://java.sun.com/1.0alpha3/doc/javaspec/javaspec_1.html—the formal specification for the alpha-3 release of Java.

http://java.sun.com/1.0alpha3/doc/appguide/index.html—a tutorial on writing and using Java applets.

http://java.sun.com/faq2.html—Frequently Asked Questions page (version 2).

http://www.sun.com/sunworldonline/swol-07-1995/swol-07-java.html—an article by Michael O'Connell on the origins and evolution of Java at Sun Microsystems, with a hyperlink to a page showing specific dates and milestones.

http://java.sun.com/mail.html—to subscribe to the Java and Hot-Java mailing list.

http://www.science.wayne.edu/~joey/java.html—a listing of information about the HotJava browser, including the latest information on ports, maintained by Joey Oravec at Wayne State University.

http://www.rpi.edu/~decemj/works/java—a book support Web page maintained by John December (see book reference above) with information about the latest released versions of Java, as well as a full bibliography of Java articles.

http://www.borland.com/Product/java/java.html—Borland's World Wide Web page for its Java plans and products.

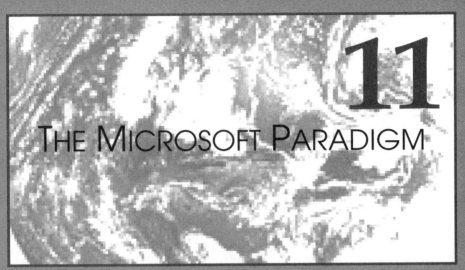

THE MICROSOFT PARADIGM

The day of small nations has long passed away.
The day of Empires has come.

Joseph Chamberlain, Speech in Birmingham, England, May 12, 1904.

August 24, 1995: It's fitting and appropriate that I finished writing the first draft of this chapter on the day that Microsoft officially released Windows 95—certainly the most publicized computing event of this decade. At the same time, I felt obliged to don my bulletproof vest before sitting down to write, for even in the remote village by the sea where I'm working this summer, the mention of "Microsoft" is enough to foment crowds into furious debates and wild accusations.

Before *you* go looking for your gun or for your Microsoft banner to wave in the air, let me set the stage for this chapter. I'm not writing the history of Microsoft or a saga of the boyhood exploits of Bill Gates.[1] I'm not an apologist for Microsoft; I don't own any of the company's stock, and until November 1996, I did all my work on a

Macintosh. I'm not going to offer any opinions on the various interactions the company has with the Justice Department, and I won't make any predictions about the viability of Microsoft Network.

Notwithstanding these caveats, hardly anyone in the software industry would dispute the assertion that we are in the midst of the "Microsoft decade." We might debate whether the 1980s were dominated more by minicomputers or mainframes; we might argue whether IBM's dominance began in the 60s or 70s, and when it really ended; but there is very little doubt that the first seven years of this decade have been dominated by the ubiquitous presence of Microsoft. Just as it was difficult in the 60s and 70s to function in the software industry without knowing what IBM was doing, so it's hard to imagine software development today without taking into account Microsoft's operating systems, languages, and tools.

And it is unrealistic to make any pronouncements about the prospects of the software industry in the United States without using Microsoft as a bellwether. Obviously, Microsoft is not the *only* software company in the U.S., and it probably doesn't have the fastest rate of growth or the highest profit ratio. But in many ways, it epitomizes the U.S. software industry; not only do thousands of young entrepreneurs want to emulate the stunning success of Bill Gates and his horde of Microserfs, but more importantly, the successes and failures have a direct, immediate impact on its partners, competitors, and suppliers around the country. To a greater or lesser extent, it's fair to say: As fares Microsoft, so fares the U.S. software industry.

That doesn't mean that every software professional wants to emulate Bill Gates, or that every software company wants to practice the strategies and tactics of Microsoft. Many software professionals will point to corporate tactics or practices they disagree with, and a few will argue that the company does *everything* wrong. Still, it's hard to deny that the company *is* successful, and that it has been successful for a number of years; it must be doing something right. My opinion is that it's doing *many* things right, and that it's getting better at some of the things software professionals have criticized for years. Microsoft *is*, in many ways, the essence of the rise and resurrection of

---

[1]In addition to dozens of books about Microsoft and Bill Gates, it's probably worth looking at the recently published *The Road Ahead*, written by Bill Gates himself. [2]

the American programmer, and we all need to take that into account when we make our career plans for the next several years.

Does this mean that we need to "be like Microsoft" (like the TV commercials that urge aspiring young basketball players to "be like Mike" as they emulate Michael Jordan) to succeed in the software business? No, but we need to use Microsoft as a benchmark for our activities; we can emulate some of its best practices, avoid its mistakes, and perhaps even leapfrog ahead of it in new areas of technology.

11.1 MICROSOFT'S APPROACH TO SOFTWARE DEVELOPMENT

During the summer of 1994, I visited India to investigate the country's software engineering industry in Bangalore, Bombay, and Delhi. I was fascinated by Motorola's SEI level-5 software operation, and impressed by the number of software organizations that are applying for ISO-9000 certification; my friend and colleague, Navyug Mohnot, predicts that within a few years, India will have more ISO-9000 software organizations than any country in the world outside the United Kingdom.

In the midst of my discussions, I asked one Indian software executive about his country's efforts to build commercial PC software products. "Surely," I asked, "someone here in India must have tried to develop a competitive word processor?"

"Of course," he said. "But we can't compete against Microsoft."

Puzzled by the comment, I asked, "But can't you take advantage of your lower labor costs? Aren't your distribution costs lower because your marketplace is right *here* in India? Can't you provide some localized features that the Indian marketplace would appreciate and that Microsoft might not think of adding to its products?"

"All of that is true," the software executive answered. "But you must realize that Microsoft—and for that matter, Borland and Lotus and all the other big American software firms—can *give away* their products for several months, in order to create a market. We can't compete with that kind of price war."

"Not only that," he continued, "but when we tried to introduce our own indigenous word processor product, we began to realize that *packaging* really matters. Our products had poorly printed manuals in three-ring binders, and they were packaged in a flimsy, cheap-looking box. Compared with the slick products from the American companies, most people felt that our products *were* inferior because they *looked* inferior."

The immediate conclusion one draws from this, of course, is that marketing, pricing, packaging, and distribution have now become key ingredients to success in the software industry. Microsoft is obviously good at all of this—it's arguably the best in the business, whatever its tactics might be for carrying it out—but to a greater or lesser extent, the same can be said for Borland, Lotus, Claris, Computer Associates, Apple, and a few dozen other smaller companies. Indeed, the only companies that seem to do a better job in this area are software game companies like Nintendo and Sega, which represent an important but relatively distinct niche within the software industry.[2]

Many software professionals are likely to shrug their shoulders and say, "Okay, so marketing and distribution are important. Fine. What's that got to with me? And for that matter, what does that have to do with my company? We're in the widget business, and my job is to write order-entry applications for our widget customers. I can understand the idea of service systems to get closer to our widget customers, but we're not building Windows 95."

One could argue that building service systems *does* put us all in a position where we have to pay more attention to marketing, packaging, and distribution—after all, if we want all of our widget customers to put our software in their machine in order to stay more closely connected to Widget Galactic Headquarters, then we have to put that software in a nice package, and we have to market it and distribute it in such a way that it will get some shelf space in the Egghead Software store, right next to the Windows 95 box.

Since marketing and distribution are not the subject of *this* book, perhaps we should all go out and scan the bookshelves for some material on software marketing. But many software professionals

---

[2]Software companies could probably learn a few things from the software game companies in the areas of testing, product research, hot-line customer support, and trade magazines, too.

would argue that they don't see themselves as being in the "business" of software marketing. My response to this argument is, "Yes, you *are* in the business of software marketing, to the extent that the cost of your software development, including your salary, has to be amortized over the number of customers who pay for your software."

For customized, in-house application development, the number of customers who pay for the software is usually *one*: the manager of the end-user department who commissioned the development of that application. For mainframe-based software product companies, the customers might number in the dozens or the hundreds; the development costs (together with the marketing costs, distribution costs, and support costs) can be amortized adequately if those customers are willing to pay $100,000 for the product. But the game changes completely, as many successful software-product companies learned brutally, when the price tag drops to $100.

Let me bring this back to the "technical" issues of software development by relating another Microsoft story. In the fall of 1994, a colleague of mine and I were involved in doing some research on the development practices and strategies of several large software firms; during that research, we conducted a number of "unofficial" conversations by phone and e-mail with several people within Microsoft. One of those conversations involved the development of the then-current version of Microsoft Word; we asked our Microsoft contact, "How many people were on the project?"

The answer was interesting: "Well, I don't really know—it went up and down."

"How many lines of code were involved?" we asked. "And what percentage of that code was 'nondeliverable'—e.g., test scripts, utility routines, etc.?"

"I could guess," came the reply, "but I don't know for sure."

"Well," we asked, becoming somewhat frustrated, "what was the productivity of the project team—in lines of code per day, or function points, or whatever metric you want to use."

"Ummm...I dunno," was the answer.

As the questions continued, our Microsoft contact was also becoming more frustrated. Finally, he blurted out, "Who *cares* how many people were involved, or how many lines of code we wrote?

Don't you guys get it? We've sold 17 million copies of Word! *It doesn't matter* how much it cost to write the code!"

Think about that for a moment. Ignore the fact that there may have been some exaggeration involved, and that perhaps our contact really *did* know the relevant numbers and simply didn't want to tell us—or that it wasn't his place to know such things and that someone else within the Microsoft Empire keeps careful track of such things. Exaggeration aside, our Microsoft contact was essentially right: It really doesn't matter whether you need 100 programmers or 200 programmers to develop a software system if you're going to sell 17 million copies.

Obviously, some of the essential characteristics of software development *do* still matter, even with numbers larger than these. For example, Microsoft has sold some 100 million copies of Windows 3.1, and market surveys predict that it will sell 200 million copies of Windows 95 by the end of this decade. So perhaps development costs can be amortized over a staggeringly large number, but that doesn't eliminate such issues as defect levels and development schedules. What would have been the impact on Microsoft if Windows 95 had been finished early enough to call it Windows 94? What would have happened in the unlikely scenario that Windows 95 was so buggy that everyone sent it back for a refund—or in the equally unlikely scenario that it has so few defects that the hot-line support staff could soon be reduced to one person, like the Maytag repair man in the television commercial?

In any case, the basic message here is that the mass-market nature of the software industry has changed the game entirely. It has changed the economics of software development, and that, in turn, has changed the strategy and tactics of the companies developing such software. Does Microsoft understand this? Listen to Nathan Myrhvold, director of Microsoft's Advanced Technology Group:

> If you write your own software, which is generally true for mainframes or supercomputers, for every dollar that you spend on software development, you get about a buck's worth of software. It's a 1 to 1 ratio. Now, if you look at minicomputers, you will find that the people in those industries typically have 1,000 to 10,000 customers. they can afford to spend considerably more on development and still maintain a decent return on investment. When you spend US$10,000 to buy a minicomputer software package, the company probably spent $100,000 to

$1 million developing it. So if you're buying from *that* market, for every dollar you spend, you get somewhere between $10 and $1,000 worth of software. Then you come to the PC industry, where for every $100 you spend, you get a piece of software that cost someone *$100 million* to develop. A dollar buys a million dollars' worth of software. [4]

This suggests two important conclusions. First, a software-product manager is likely to spend his money differently and devise entirely different development strategies if he envisions selling a million copies of his product. And second, if you want to play in the big leagues with companies like Microsoft, you may need to commit $100 million for development of highly competitive products like word processors, operating systems, and spreadsheets.

As we know, the entrepreneurial nature of the software industry is such that the next generation's Bill Gates and Steve Jobs are *not* trying to build a better word processor; they're looking for entirely new markets and applications, and they're hoping to develop a first-generation of such products on a shoestring budget. And of course, such entrepreneurs exist all over the world; two clever young programmers in India or Ireland might well develop something as creative as two programmers in Irvine, California, or Irving, Texas. But regardless of where the software is developed, the Microsoft paradigm tells us two things. First, in order to make a "presence" in the U.S. marketplace, you need a major-league marketing budget and a sophisticated marketing machine. And second, if you're going to compete against the big-league players (including Microsoft) who will quickly develop a similar (if not nearly identical) product once your first version has succeeded, then you need a major-league development budget to finance the second version. That second version has to have *lots* of bells and whistles to compete against the big-league players, and it has to sell *lots* of copies to recoup its big-league development cost.

None of this, I suspect, is of any interest to the programmers slaving away on their Visual Basic applications for the Acme Widget Manufacturing company. But by the same token, the fate of those Visual Basic programmers is of less and less interest to the programmers in Silicon Valley and Redmond, Washington—except to the extent that they are consumers (and thus endusers) of shrink-wrapped Visual Basic products. There are now essentially "two cultures" in the software field: the in-house application developers and the shrink-wrap PC software developers.[3] It remains to be seen whether the inhouse application software developers will prosper in the U.S.; the ideas suggested in Chapters 9 and 10 give me some basis for optimism, but if we continue to do little more than build in-house order-entry applications, then this portion of our software industry will indeed become a "commodity business," subject to ever more intense competition from the rest of the world.

That doesn't mean that you should go to work for Microsoft (though the company may have invited you to submit your résumé, as I'll discuss below), or Borland or Lotus or any of the other software product companies. It doesn't mean that you should start your own software-product company and attempt to recreate the stunning success of, say, Marc Andreesen at Netscape. But it *does* mean that you should be aware of where the momentum is in the software industry; you probably were already, but perhaps you hadn't thought of it in terms of your own personal career.

11.2 THE DARK SIDE OF THE FORCE

As noted earlier, I don't consider myself to be an apologist for Microsoft; but I'm not at the other end of the spectrum either, among the people who consider Microsoft to be the Evil Empire, headed by Darth Vader. Some of the Microsoft critics seem convinced that the company will take over the world if left unfettered; others are convinced that it will self-destruct and collapse within the next few years for one reason or another.[4]

I'm not worried about Microsoft taking over the world, but I do believe it will continue to be a dominant force in our industry for the remainder of this decade, if not longer. On the other hand, I've

---

[3]The phrase "two cultures" was coined by the British physicist C.P. Snow in a provocative book called *Science and Government* in the 1960s; he argued that society was polarizing into two cultures—scientists and non(anti)-scientists—who had little or no communication with one another, despite their need to coexist. In our field, perhaps we could argue that there are additional "cultures," but for the present time, I'm ignoring the culture of mainframe and minicomputer software developers, because they appear to have less and less relevance to the future of the software industry.

learned to be humble about my predictions—ten years ago, in 1985, I spent another long, hot summer writing a book entitled *Nations at Risk,* in which I cheerfully concurred with the widespread predictions that IBM would continue to dominate the computing industry for the foreseeable future:

> The new president of IBM, John Akers, expects to maintain a growth rate of 14–15 percent per year. *Business Week,* among others, predicts that IBM will achieve revenues of $100 billion by 1990, and $185 billion by 1995. [8]

In retrospect, such a prediction looks pretty foolish.[5] It's fairly safe to predict that Microsoft will have a dominant position for the next 2 to 3 years; but 5 years is a long time in this business, and 10 years puts us, literally, into another millennium. Sooner or later, I think, Microsoft will run into trouble with its efforts to dominate so many different aspects of the software business; like IBM, they'll lose their focus, so that the right hand doesn't know what the left hand is doing. And sooner or later, I suspect that the "fear and loathing" engendered by Microsoft's carnivorous appetites—which is similar to the fear and loathing associated with IBM throughout the 70s—will create a sufficiently large number of enemies that the company will spend more time defending itself than inventing great new products.

But I don't think these problems will be sufficient to bring Microsoft to its knees—just as the equivalent problems faced by IBM in the 70s and early 80s were serious, but not enough to cause mortal damage. The *real* problem, in my opinion, is that a computer company's culture, and its heart and soul, often become wrapped

---

[4]I didn't realize how much influence Microsoft had on the consciousness of our industry until someone forwarded to me a tongue-in-cheek e-mail "press release" that had been posted on one of the Internet news groups, announcing that Microsoft had purchased the Roman Catholic church, and that the Pope would stay on as a vice-president, reporting to Bill Gates. What amazed me was that the spoof had a sufficient impact that Microsoft felt it appropriate to issue a formal denial of the story.

[5]And it pales in comparison to another idiotic prediction I made ten years earlier in my 1975 book *Techniques of Program Structure and Design*: "Unless you're very rich or very eccentric, you'll never have the luxury of owning your own computer." It appears that my destiny is to say something utterly foolish at least once every ten years.

up in a single technology or paradigm; when the paradigm changes, the company finds that it cannot make the change. With IBM, the paradigm shift involved the transition from mainframes to PC's; with Microsoft, the paradigm shift will involve the transition from Windows and PC's to…well, to whatever comes next. One such possibility is the world of embedded systems, which I'll discuss in Chapter 12.

In the short run, though, there are great fortunes to be made and lost with the current paradigm. Microsoft is obviously reaping great fortunes with its products and its marketing efforts; indeed, one might ask (as the entrepreneurs in small startup companies might be asking themselves): *Why aren't they doing a better job at building and marketing their products?*

When it comes to marketing, I'm not competent to offer any substantive suggestions, though I was intrigued to learn that three days before the formal launch of Windows 95, *Computer Reseller News* announced that the company was already working on Microsoft Office 96, which was originally expected to ship at approximately the same time the hardcover edition of this book was published; as it turned out, the product was delayed and became Office 97. Similarly, what had originally been planned as Windows 97 is now looming on the horizon as Windows 98. J.D. Hildebrand [3] argues that product releases like this represent a "sync pulse" for the industry, and it reminds me of the annual announcement of new automobile models. Meanwhile, the Visual C++ group within Microsoft has announced a quarterly subscription service for new releases of its products. Whether product-release strategies like this prove successful remains to be seen, but it's clear that Microsoft is experimenting with a variety of marketing strategies—as well as spending vast sums of money on product marketing, as its $200 million expenditure on the Windows 95 launch demonstrated.

But what about product development? If you *know* that the software product you're building is going to sell 10 million copies—or, in the case of Windows 95, upwards of 100 million copies—then you would think that it would make sense to invest the money and talent to do a better job. Indeed, the bugginess of Microsoft software—and by extension, the software products from most, if not all, of the major software-product companies—has been the source of scorn and derision from "serious" software professionals. If you're building a one-of-a-kind, customized, in-house system, it's tough to justify the investment in up-front analysis and design, coupled with rigorous software processes and formal inspections, in order to generate zero-defect code. But if you're building a product that will be replicated 10 million times when it's shipped out the door, why not make this kind of investment? Is there something that we can learn from this aspect of the "Microsoft paradigm," or does this approach represent the Achilles heel in the American software industry?

A big part of the answer, I believe, is discussed in Chapter 7: *good-enough software*. Microsoft operates in a consumer industry, and the consumer marketplace dictates what's good enough—*especially* in terms of the delicate balance between functionality, delivery schedule, and defect levels. It's pretty hard to follow a "formal" software-engineering approach if the requirements for your product change every time the competition coughs and the Justice Department sneezes; and it's pretty unprofitable to ship a zero-defect product to the marketplace if someone else has beat you by six months with something that has equivalent functionality and "good-enough" defect levels. Microsoft isn't perfect at achieving this balance, but it has elevated the art of good-enough software development to an aggressive, proactive, risk-management discipline.

The other thing that we need to realize is that the cowboys at Microsoft are growing up. This makes sense, and it isn't unique to Microsoft: It's the sort of thing that happens in *any* software company whose ad-hoc, wild-and-crazy entrepreneurial development project succeeds so well that it suddenly finds that it's shipping millions of copies of its product. All of a sudden, testing and version control and configuration management and customer support and a dozen other activities unrelated to the wild-and-crazy euphoria of software development raise their ugly heads and cry out for attention.

Since companies typically improve their processes in response to *specific* problems, it's natural that problems *in the field* are the ones that get top priority. As a result, I've been intrigued to find that several of the successful software-product companies are aggressively improving their software development processes from the *end* of the process (testing, customer support, maintenance, etc.) *backwards* toward the beginning (e.g., to issues of coding, design, and ultimately to requirements analysis). Whether this is the best strategy for improving an organization's development process is open to debate, but at least it does represent progress.

As noted earlier, I'm not advocating a "be like Bill" form of emulating Microsoft. On the other hand, it's evident that the company knows something about software development (when was the last time your IT organization deployed 100 million copies of its software?), and there has been some intriguing evidence in the past few years that it's getting better at developing software. As a professional software developer, perhaps you can ignore all of the marketing aspects of the software industry, and just focus on one question: If Microsoft is succeeding with certain strategies for software development and if they're improving those strategies, is there something we can learn from them?

11.3 INTO THE BELLY OF THE BEAST

In the fall of 1994, it occurred to me that if I was going to abandon my Macintosh, buy a Windows machine and begin using more and more Microsoft software, then perhaps I should fly out to Redmond to see what the Microsofties are really like. After all, I've been to dozens of IBM locations over the years, and I've visited Apple and Digital and scores of other computer companies—but never Microsoft.

It's interesting that within our profession, we depend almost entirely on trade journals, vendor literature, and marketing representatives to explain what the major hardware and software companies are doing. We're often skeptical about the information we receive from these sources, but we rarely go to the effort of finding out for ourselves what's going on. It seems to me that one of the most valuable things you can do for yourself is list the five or six companies, products, and technologies that have the most influence—and thus pose the greatest degree of risk—on your profession and career. Though you may not be able to *control* these risks, you should *assess* them regularly and realistically; and you should look for *independent* sources of information in order to get a more realistic assessment.

As for Microsoft, the fascinating thing is that most people—including some very famous gurus in the software industry—have almost entirely negative things to say about the company's software development practices, but hardly anyone has ever visited Redmond to get a firsthand look! One very well-known OO author, for example, made the following comment in an e-mail message to me:

IMHO: Microsoft has no particular innovation in software development. They ship the same low-quality crap everybody else does. That's why they might not talk to you. I doubt that they've got anything to brag about and could only lose from talking with you.

Their innovations were to pioneer and develop new ways of enforcing their property rights and in marketing (controlling distributor channels, bundling software with silicon, etc.).

Another consultant in New Zealand put it this way:

Conventional wisdom here in New Zealand is that Microsoft produces b*&@ awful software. It is not reliable, has a high incidence of software spoilage, and they rely on their customers to test their products.... I do not believe that Microsoft uses any kind of formal or semi-formal software development method....

After visiting Microsoft and talking to a number of people there, my impression is that its reputation is based upon a "hacker" image that was largely accurate 5 or 6 years ago, but is *much* less accurate now. The popular news media still like to promote the hacker image (after all, isn't Microsoft like all of the software industry as far as *USA Today* is concerned?), and some folks within Microsoft still speak fondly of the good old days, but the reality is that the company is changing rapidly and has adopted a number of practices that are not only impressive, but worth emulating in your own company.

If your career plans in the software industry depend on the fortune or reputation of one or two key companies, make sure that your judgment of those companies is accurate. Just as technologies have a half-life of only a few years, the corporate culture in most computer companies and shrink-wrap software producers also changes rapidly. Apple, for example, is no longer the zany, small company run by Steve Jobs; it's an $8-billion empire. *Any* small computer company that grows by a factor of ten, or a hundred, or a thousand, over a period of a few years, is bound to experience major *qualitative* changes—not necessarily for the better.

This doesn't mean I think Microsoft does everything well; far from it. As I noted earlier in this book, the Macintosh version of Microsoft Word 6.0 was a bloated pig of a word processor, with substantially slower performance than the previous version; Power-Point® 4.0 had great difficulty exchanging files between Mac and PC;

and major new products like Windows 95 are frequently released *far* later than Microsoft's original schedule dates.

On the other hand, I don't think Microsoft's development practices are any worse than most other shrink-wrap software producers—and in many ways they're much better. A software company with a single, narrowly focused product aimed at a homogeneous market might well do better. But especially in the operating system area, it's fairly amazing that Microsoft has done as well as it has: After all, it's supporting some *100 million* copies of Windows 3.1, which run on hundreds of different hardware platforms, interacting with thousands of different brands of printers, video boards, and other peripherals, many of which Microsoft doesn't even know about. Its products are being used for applications, and in environments, that Microsoft never anticipated, and for which formal requirements could thus never have been developed before the products were designed and coded. I've written a lot of software in my day, and I think most of it was pretty damn good—but none of it *ever* had that kind of exposure.

All of this, of course, is subject to intense debate. The developer of one of the most successful word processing utility programs commented in a recent e-mail message to me:

> From the dealings my company had with Microsoft, and from similar tales of other small PC software shops, I tend to regard Microsoft as one of the major threats to the U.S. software industry.

But whether you like Microsoft or not, one thing is indisputable: The company is incredibly successful and has managed to maintain that success over the past 20 years. It may not be doing everything right, but it's hard to make a convincing argument that it's doing everything wrong. In any case, it's worth having a better understanding of what the company is doing, and *how* it's doing it. Thus, if a consultant or a journalist gives you an emotional sermon about the low state of development practices at Microsoft—or, for that matter, IBM, Digital, Apple, Lotus, Borland, or any other major shrink-wrap company—ask whether the consultant has actually visited the company and spoken to its development staff, or whether the opinion is based entirely on an experience with the company's product.

While at Microsoft, I met with a number of managers and directors of product development groups (C++ and Visual Basic), testing groups, and "best practices" development groups. In the discussion below, I'll focus on a few of the peopleware items and testing items that I found particularly interesting.

11.4 PEOPLEWARE AT MICROSOFT

In the July 1995 issue of *Macworld*, columnist Guy Kawasaki wrote an open letter to Judge Stanley Sporkin, arguing that Sporkin should drop his objection to the consent decree between Microsoft and the Justice Department because, among other things, "the demise of Microsoft is already inevitable, so you don't need to trouble yourself." Since Kawasaki is one of the original Macintosh evangelists and has recently been hired back into the fold as an Apple Fellow, I normally wouldn't pay much attention to this ranting and raving.

I wasn't even impressed by Kawasaki's argument that Microsoft was going downhill because of the people they're hiring, because his first example was that the new COO was hired from Procter and Gamble. But then he went on to say,

> Microsoft will go through a bozo explosion because it is now attracting the kind of people who want to work for a company that won't lay you off and looks good on your résumé.

Wait a minute! Isn't this the company that told me, when I visited it last October, it gets 10,000 unsolicited résumés a month? Surely they can't all be bozos and unemployed programmers from IBM and Digital?

But on the same day that I read Kawasaki's comments, I received an unsolicited form letter from Microsoft, extolling the virtues of writing software for the company, and inviting me to send my résumé for consideration. Why would Microsoft feel compelled to send out a form-letter mailing? I would be flattered to think the company had a specific interest in my modest talents, but the mailing wasn't personalized in any way. However, it did list an e-mail address, so I wrote back to ask what it was all about. A week later, I received the following response:

Hi Edward-

Sorry for the delay in responding to you. As a matter of fact, Microsoft receives about 2,000 resumes/week. In terms of recruiting great developers, most of these resumes (unfortunately!) aren't appropriate. Many are people interested in sales, international positions, marketing, etc....we even get resumes from nurses, accountants, pilots....you name it!

We're lucky to be as successful as we have been; the great people we have working for us has been the reason we've achieved this success. As we continue to develop new products, research new technologies and make our existing products faster, smarter, and more user friendly, we need to hire a lot more developers. We're always thinking about new ways to attract the best in the industry to us. The flyer we mailed to you is just one of the things we're doing to let people in the industry know that we are looking for top-notch technical people.

Hope this information is helpful to you.

Steve

Assuming that Microsoft's interviewing and selection process is still discriminating, there's no reason to believe that mass-mailing solicitations like this will necessarily cause an influx of bozos. Indeed, the contrast between the Microsoft peopleware culture and the culture that I see in most in-house IT departments is staggering. In one case, the organizational culture is like the Army: unmotivated, semi-literate people whose behavior is augmented with "smart" weapons and rigidly controlled with military discipline. In Microsoft's case, it's more like the Marines or the Green Berets: highly motivated, highly skilled, and highly empowered to use whatever means necessary to achieve an objective.

What I've seen at Microsoft, and most other successful Silicon Valley software-product companies, simply confirms the message that I presented in Chapter 2 of this book. Take a close look at the level of talent, and the management style, in your software organization: An organization of stupid people is going to develop stupid software, no matter how much money management spends on exotic development tools. And an organization of extremely talented people can be easily suffocated with bureaucracy. If you work in such an organization, there's no point whining about how frustrating it is—

it's not going to get any better unless there's a revolution or unless you decide to leave.

So Microsoft hires smart people—then what? One of the interesting tidbits that I picked up in my visit involved the issue of training newly hired programmers. Of course, many mediocre software organizations provide little or no initial training for their entry-level programmers, but one would expect that a successful organization like Microsoft would invest a lot in a "boot camp" for its new people, as I pointed out in Chapter 2. Some organizations, such as Motorola's level-5 software shop in Bangalore, provide as much as 42 days of initial training and 80 to 100 hours of ongoing training per year for their people.

Microsoft, though, has no boot camp; new programmers spend their first day filling out insurance forms and going through the usual orientation process, and then they're assigned to a project team and expected to start contributing right away. The reason? Because Microsoft has the luxury of hiring very bright people—many of whom have been programming since they were in high school and most of whom have done extensive software work in college—they already know a lot about software development, and they're impatient to get started with "real" work instead of classroom work.

But no matter how bright and eager they may be, virtually every new programmer needs some training. Microsoft does this by scheduling weekly education sessions; and, like IBM and other larger computer companies, it has a sophisticated training organization, since it also provides extensive educational offerings to its customers. By contrast, when I applied for my first full-time programming job, IBM told me I would have to go to school for six months. Digital Equipment Corporation, on the other hand, knew that I had been working for them as a part-time programmer; they, too, offered me a full-time job. Not only that, they expected a full day's work on the first day of my new status, and they never did offer me any training. Since all of this occurred decades ago, I should point out that IBM and Digital may have quite different practices now—but somewhere between these two extremes is what you should be looking for.

Even more interesting than the training approach is Microsoft's concept of "mentors," which I discussed in Chapter 2. Every new programmer is assigned a personal mentor; in addition to providing general advice and guidance about "the way things work around here," the mentor reads every line of code written by the new person. And new programmers read every line of code their mentors write. Can you imagine how much better a programmer you would be if someone had done this at the beginning of your career? Chances are that it would help even today, but if you've been in the field for more than a couple of years, it would be a difficult adjustment. At Microsoft, the mentoring process goes on until mentor and trainee both agree that it's no longer necessary; this takes anywhere from a month to a year. (If it goes on longer than a year, it's a pretty good indication that the employee isn't going to survive in the company.)

Here's some advice: Try to institute a mentor program in your own organization. If your management is dead set against it, contemplate what this really means: Maybe you should look for a company willing to make that kind of investment. But if you're not willing to make a radical move, see if you can implement an informal mentor program within the organization. If you're a junior programmer, look for a veteran who is willing to spend time at lunch, or after work, reviewing your work. If you're a veteran, pick a bright young kid who deserves a better opportunity than you had, and offer to play a mentor role.

As for the other peopleware practices at Microsoft: Yes, Microsoft programmers do have their own private offices, with a door that closes; yes, there are snack areas located in strategic corners of the programmer buildings, well-stocked with juice, soda, candy bars, etc. And yes, every office does have at least one current-vintage PC, and most seem to have two or three. But the most important aspects of Microsoft's peopleware practices are far less visible. One manager, for example, described to me the concept of "push-back," which I've also seen at Apple: The professional employees are encouraged to challenge the ideas, schedules, directives, and instructions from their colleagues and managers—i.e., to *push back* if there is anything about it with which they disagree. "No one tolerates bullshit around here," the manager explained, reflecting a culture that emanates from the top of the organization; after all, Bill Gates is famous for saying "That's the stupidest thing I've ever seen" to sloppily thought-out proposals.

There are some good things and bad things about this kind of organizational culture. It certainly isn't the only kind of culture that can succeed in the software business, but it does have the admirable quality that *thinking* is encouraged, and lively exchange of ideas and opinions seems to be rampant. As one Microsoft manager said to me, "All we make here is intellectual products—nothing else. The most important thing we can do is encourage and challenge our people to *think*." When was the last time you heard a manager in your organization say something like that with conviction?

Another interesting characteristic of the Microsoft peopleware culture is that the various project teams seem to have achieved a significant "buy-in" on the critical success factors. That is, because all of the issues have been thrashed out and all of the team members have been encouraged to push back, the result is a great deal of personal commitment to the schedules, deadlines, goals, and product features that are eventually developed by the team. Again, compare that with the practices in your own organization.

11.5 DEVELOPMENT PRACTICES AT MICROSOFT

Does Microsoft use CASE tools? Nope. Does the company use formal methods of analysis and design? Well, not really: As I'll explain below, there is a standard process that requires a formal specification for a new software product, but the specs are typically a combination of text, screen shots, and working prototypes rather than formal structured analysis or OO analysis models. Are good programming practices followed, including such things as code inspections? Generally speaking, yes—but the rigor and consistency tend to vary from one product group to another.

But there are some things that Microsoft *does* seem to do very well and very consistently; one of its most important practices is the "daily build." On most of the major projects, all of the components are compiled, linked, and integrated into a "shippable version" of software *every day.* This doesn't eliminate the notion of monthly milestones and various other checkpoints during a project—but it's remarkable how much discipline and rigor can be imposed on a project by the requirement of building a new version every day. As Microsoft's Visual C++ product manager, Jim McCarthy, says, it's the heartbeat of the project; it's the way the project manager knows that the project is still alive.

This approach has a more pervasive influence than one might imagine. For example, it's common for the project manager's office to be in the midst of the "build area"—so he or she is immediately aware if there are any problems. It can lead to flamboyant behavior, such as Dave Cutler's much-publicized incident of hurling a chair against a wall when the Windows NT daily build failed; but the main point is that the project managers in many software organizations have very little idea of how things are *really* going down in the trenches during the critical periods of software development.

By contrast, if you're a software manager, and your assessment of a project's status is based entirely on paper reports or the verbal assurances of one or two levels of intermediate managers between you and the real developers, chances are that you don't have an accurate picture of what's really going on. You really should consider wandering around the office at 9 o'clock at night, when the *real* work is probably being done. Stop in on Saturday afternoon to see how many people are putting in extra hours.

There's another fascinating aspect of Microsoft's development approach: the relationship between developers and testers. Word has filtered through the grapevine that Microsoft has a 1 to 1 ratio of testers to developers, and many cynics have taken this as evidence that its development approach is substandard. But heavy emphasis on testing doesn't necessarily imply bad code, nor does it necessarily imply that the testers only get involved after the code has been written. Indeed, Microsoft has a fascinating procedure in place for almost all of its projects: Development is not allowed to begin until the testing department has signed off on the specifications for the product. Why? Because the testing group develops its test cases from the specs, and if the specs are incomplete, inconsistent, or ambiguous, then the testing department can't do its job effectively.

Still, the notion of an army of testers equal in size to the army of programmers appalls some software professionals. But it doesn't work that way: *Each project* has an equal-sized group of developers and testers (plus a third category of people responsible for documentation and user training). And it goes even further than that: Each developer is typically assigned a "buddy" tester, so that a one-to-one relationship develops.

So what? Well, it comes back to the "daily build" ritual: Nobody on the project team wants to be the jerk whose newly coded module blew up the build process, which typically runs overnight while everyone is home sleeping. So developers work with their buddy testers to ensure that their code can at least pass a quick-and-dirty set of test cases before introducing it into the formal build process.

Microsoft's testing approach is a subject unto itself, and I don't have room to cover it in detail here. In addition to so-called "smoke tests" and "sniff tests," Microsoft has a variety of automated testing tools and procedures to augment the daily-build ritual. More interesting is its database of software defects, known as RAID, which has accumulated data across *all* of Microsoft's projects for the past few years.

I asked a couple of Microsoft managers where they thought the company was on the SEI process maturity model. Their answer: level 3 in most cases, with some variation in a few of the product organizations. I found this fascinating, because even though the company has not had a formal assessment by an outside organization, the relevant managers are quite familiar with the details of the SEI model; as far as they are concerned, they do have a process, and it is applied on a formal, rigorous basis.

I've also had extensive informal contacts with a number of lower-echelon Microsoft people, and it's interesting that the overwhelming majority of them (a) have never heard of the SEI, (b) have no idea where their company might be on the scale, and (c) don't care. When I asked the managers about this, they shrugged: As far as they're concerned, it's not important for their people to know that there is such a thing as a formal maturity model.

Nor is it crucial, in their opinion, to move up to level 4 or level 5. Indeed Microsoft is beginning to accumulate more and more software metrics (though typically about the "back end" of the development process), and it *is* beginning to accomplish some degree of process improvement (though its emphasis is on "best practices"), but at this point, the company sees no compelling business reason to devote large sums of money to qualify for SEI level 4 or level 5, or for ISO-9000.

A final comment on the Microsoft phenomenon: An internationally famous methodologist, whose opinion I highly respect, sent me this opinion:

> My sense, in my contacts with Microsoft developers, is that this is the quintessential heroic programmer culture, with Bill as the obvious spiritual leader.

This is indeed the popular image of Microsoft, and one that appeals to a common emotional need to criticize a company that has grown so powerful during the past several years. And while Microsoft itself may have promoted that image during the 1970s and 1980s, it's an image that's increasingly inaccurate, and it could prove to be a dangerous misperception for anyone who works with, for, or against Microsoft. The hackers are indeed growing up.

REFERENCES

1. Brand, Stewart. "The Physicist." *Wired*, September 1995, p. 154.

2. Gates, Bill, with Nathan Myhrvold and Peter Rinearson. *The Road Ahead.* (New York: Viking Press, 1995) ISBN: 0-670-77289-5.

3. Hildebrand, J. D. "Sync Pulse: Windows 95, Visual Basic 4.0, and the Software Industry Recession." *American Programmer*, February 1995.

4. McCarthy, Jim. "Managing Software Milestones at Microsoft." *American Programmer*, February 1995.

5. Mohnot, Navyug. "Quality: Made in India." *American Programmer*, October 1995.

6. Rubin, Howard A. "Twelve Lessons Learned from Microsoft-Watching: Implications for Process, Products, and Positioning." *American Programmer*, February 1995.

7. Sherman, Roger W. "Shipping the Right Products at the Right Time: A View of Development and Testing at Microsoft." *American Programmer*, February 1995.

8. Yourdon, Edward. *Nations at Risk*, Chapter 24. (Englewood Cliffs, NJ: Prentice Hall/Yourdon Press, 1986).

9. Stross, Randall E. *The Microsoft Way: The Real Story of How the Company Outsmarts Its Competition.* (Reading, MA: Addison-Wesley, 1996).

10. Cusumano, Michael A., and Richard W. Selby. *Microsoft Secrets.* (New York: Free Press, 1995).

12

EMBEDDED SYSTEMS AND BRAVE NEW WORLDS

Any attempt to predict the future in any detail will appear ludicrous within a few years. If we regard the ages that stretch ahead of us as an unmapped and unexplored territory, what I am trying to do is to survey its frontiers and to get some idea of its extent. The detailed geography of the interior must remain unknown—until we reach it.

Arthur C. Clarke, Profiles of the Future, *2nd edition, 1984.*

The theme of this last section of the book has been that "brave new worlds" are the most likely source of continued prosperity for the software industry and for a "rise and resurrection" from the increasingly fierce competition that looms before us for conventional software development. This doesn't mean that we should expect our customers will stop asking for conventional applications ranging from payroll to word processors, and it doesn't mean that we should abandon our efforts to increase the productivity and quality with which we develop those applications. On the other hand, we should assume that everyone else will be doing the same thing, and the result will be a commodity industry where profits are still available but the "cowboy" culture of the American software industry will fade away. For better of worse, much of the software industry *will* shift to a "commodity" mind-set, where millions of copies of the software system are being marketed as shrink-wrapped products; the "Microsoft paradigm," which I discussed in Chapter 11, provides some interesting lessons on how to prevail in such a world.

But for those who want a different kind of software-oriented profession, the service systems that we discussed in Chapter 8 offer a new world of opportunities for in-house IT application developers to find creative ways of using information technology to develop closer relations with the customers (and the suppliers, too) of an enterprise. It's quite likely that many of these service systems will be implemented with Internet-based technology, as the World Wide Web provides an ubiquitous, user-friendly mechanism for providing information about our company's products and services, as well as direct interactions with the customer.

But is that all there is to the software industry? Are we doomed to spend our careers working as Microsoft-style, shrink-wrapped product developers or building customer-based, service-oriented applications for big companies? Obviously not—one of the *most* intriguing things about software is its almost limitless range of possible applications. Among the possible areas that could conceivably provide all of us with exciting, well-paid jobs over the next ten years are things like:

- *Virtual reality* (VR) applications—for everything from lifelike interactive games on the World Wide Web, to movie-style entertainment, to more conventional applications such as VR "tours" of a house that you're thinking of buying, a vacation spot you're planning on visiting, or a potential new commercial site for your widget factory. Just as the transition from character-based, line-oriented user interfaces to colorful, user-friendly GUIs opened up a whole new world of applications, so we can expect VR to spawn dozens of new products, applications, and companies. We're beginning to see some intriguing, though still somewhat primitive, examples of VR applications, and my sense is that this industry is roughly where the PC industry was in 1979; it's likely to be another 5 years before the underlying technology is adequate to support a "killer app," and a few more years after that before society is ready to buy it in large quantities. But if you're recommending a software-oriented career for your high-school son or daughter, this could be it.

- *Graphics and interactive multimedia*—this is essentially a subset of VR, and it's booming all around us now. Interestingly, many software professionals tend to dismiss this area as irrelevant, because their only exposure consists of things like computer-generated special effects in the latest Hollywood movies. My advice: Take a look at the high-end CD-ROM-based educational programs and ask yourself, "What would our users think if we provided them with that kind of access to their information?" Note that I'm not talking about CD-ROM games, though offerings like *Myst* are indeed stunningly beautiful; what I have in mind is a product like Body Vision™, from Learn Technologies Interactive, which provides an interactive, multimedia, three-dimensional "atlas" of the human body; the depth and complexity of information available to the user is staggering. Another product from Learn Technologies, Case Maker, allows a student to play the role of a juror in real-world courtroom trials; one compact disk, for example, holds all of the relevant video footage of the famous Rodney King trial in Los Angeles, *plus* all of the newspaper coverage of the case, *plus* all of the transcriptions of court testimony.

- *AI, expert systems, and robotics*—yes, I know that this technology has been around for 25 years or longer. But, hey, it took 25 years for the Internet to reach critical mass and become a vital part of society. Useful expert systems and AI applications are all around us, but I don't think this technology has reached critical mass yet. I'm only a casual observer of the field, and I'm not competent to predict *when* the field might explode, but my sense is that we need at least one more order-of-magnitude increase in speed, power, sophistication, and functionality. Some of this will occur as a derivative consequence of the tenfold and hundredfold increases in hardware power that we anticipate over the next 5 to 10 years, but I believe that we still require an intellectual and/or conceptual breakthrough that will produce AI-based software that is arguably smarter than humans for an application that we care about (as opposed to chess, for example, where the 1997 triumph of IBM's Deep Blue chess program over Gary Kasparov resulted in a *Time* magazine cover story, but little more than loud yawns from most of humanity). Will this happen? Yes, almost certainly—but whether it happens tomorrow, or 5 years from now, or 25 years from now is the big question.

Indeed, from the perspective of time—that most precious of commodities we must all keep in mind when planning our career in this business—it appears that interactive multimedia is "today," practical virtual reality products and applications are still a few years off, and full-blown AI and R2D2-style personal robots are more likely 10 years off. And though interactive, CD-ROM, multimedia technology is available today, most software professionals still ignore it because, as noted earlier, they associate it primarily with "games" and "entertainment."

Leaving aside the obvious point that entertainment *is* big business, where else could we imagine investing our software talents with today's technology? What else might have some "practical" applications where we might feel that we are making a positive contribution to society, rather than just enhancing the visual and audio sensory inputs on the movie screen? The answer, I believe, is *embedded systems*—all of the systems embedded in the appliances we use, the products we buy, and the day-to-day artifacts that surround us in our work life and home life.

12.1 WHY EMBEDDED SYSTEMS?

Obviously, we already have embedded systems; there is software in your digital watch, in your VCR, in your microwave oven and dishwasher, and in your automobile. So why am I making a big deal of it? The reason is that we are on the verge of a massive transformation from early "first-generation" embedded systems to second-generation, and ultimately third-generation, systems.

12.1.1 First-Generation Embedded Systems

The salient characteristics of today's first-generation systems are these:

- They're based on relatively primitive hardware technology, with limited memory and processing power. My digital watch can store 100 phone numbers, but that's all. As a consumer, I'm not complaining: It's still amazing to me that it can store *any* data.

But the megabytes of storage capacity, as well as the high-speed computing power that we take for granted on our desktop and laptop machines is, for the most part, missing from the majority of embedded systems.

• They communicate with the outside world in a primitive fashion that would be rejected *instantly* in a conventional business application, and that often turns out to be completely unintelligible. There are apocryphal stories that 80 percent of all VCR machines still blink "12:00" even when they've been used for a year or more, because the end user can't figure out how to set the time (let alone something useful, like programming a TV show to be taped tomorrow night). Even software people typically have trouble figuring out how to program the features of their cellular phone and other sophisticated appliances, because the user interface is an order of magnitude more primitive than UNIX and MS-DOS.[1]

• The embedded systems don't talk to each other. They weren't built to do so, and they don't have the hardware or software sophistication to do so. They operate independently, in isolation from one another.

12.1.2 Second-Generation Embedded Systems

The second generation is already arriving: systems built with full-power CPUs and adequate storage. I don't expect to see 32 megabytes of RAM on my digital wristwatch in the next year or two, but it's not unreasonable to anticipate a few megabytes in the system

---

[1]In 1995, I bought a new Jeep and found that it was equipped with dozens of electronic gadgets that I couldn't figure out at all; I somehow commanded the Jeep to display all of its readouts in metric units, and it took a month to figure out how to convert it back to something I could understand. The Jeep has an optional CD player, with a storage capacity for 6 discs and with its own remote control unit. But how to turn it on? I tried everything I could think of, and finally did what I should have done at the beginning: I asked one of my children. "Oh, simple," he replied (never having done it himself but having observed a similar situation on a friend's family Jeep), "you set the radio to play on FM, and then you set the station to 88.1 megahertz. That tells the Jeep to switch over to the CD player." Say *what*? What lunatic thought of *that* user interface?

embedded in my TV, toaster oven, and dishwasher; and it's reasonable to assume *several* such systems in my automobile.

The trivial consequence of this additional power is simply additional capacity for what we're already doing. This might be marginally useful, but I doubt that we would notice it in most cases. I might complain about the ability of my digital watch to store only 100 numbers, for example, but the truth is that I've only stored 14 numbers in the watch, and I only use three of them; the ability to store 1,000 numbers would not be enough to make me run down to the nearest electronic store to buy a new watch.

The *obvious* thing that we would expect from more powerful hardware in our embedded systems is a better user interface. To some extent, this is already happening: Not only can I store 100 phone numbers in my cellular phone, I can also attach alphanumeric tags to each one, and look up by name. But the arcane commands for accomplishing all of this are still incredibly primitive compared to the user interface that I'm accustomed to on my desktop PC; and the same is true, to greater or lesser extent, for all of the embedded systems I currently use. Alphanumeric displays are better than numeric codes, but the "menus" of choices provided by many of today's "smart appliances" offer about the same level of unfriendly interface as the IBM-3270-style on-line systems that we built in the 70s.

The LCD displays on today's embedded systems offer some limited graphics capabilities, but it's a long way from what anyone would call a "GUI." And we're never going to have the kind of GUI that we accept happily on our desktop PCs, because the devices we're talking about aren't going to be equipped with a 14" display, a full-size keyboard, or a mouse. As long as the interaction between the user and the embedded system is intrinsically trivial, we can survive with one or two buttons to push—but as the interactions become more complicated, we need a more sophisticated medium in which to communicate. If it's not a keyboard and mouse, what will it be?

In some environments, the answer might be pen-based input or touch-sensitive input devices, but these devices have obvious limitations, too. The answer, it seems to me, is obvious: voice recognition. Sophisticated voice recognition technology is probably still a few years away, but we already have hand-held devices (such as the digital pocket recorder that I recently bought from Sharper Image) that can respond to a limited vocabulary of words.

12.1.3 Third-Generation Embedded Systems

Though I might complain about the limited capacity of my existing digital watch, I'm aware that I could trade it in for an equally inexpensive Timex model that will download all of my day's appointments from a calendar system on my desktop PC. Now *that's* useful. And while it might seem irrelevant to have more than 100 phone numbers stored in my cellular phone, I wouldn't mind downloading all 3,000 phone numbers from my desktop PC's personal information system (PIM), because it's the PIM that I update to ensure that I always have the most up-to-date information.

It's the ability of embedded systems to talk to one another that will really open up a brave new world of computing applications. You can probably think of a dozen examples yourself; I've listed a few possibilities in the section below. At the very least, this requires the ability of the embedded system to communicate with other devices via a cable or serial port; it's not difficult to imagine a household environment where *all* of our embedded systems are connected to one another via a LAN wired into the house. Remote communication via dial-up telephone line, coaxial, or fiber-optic cable opens up another world of application, as do infrared and various other forms of wireless communications.

Massive infrastructures of communications and networking technology are being developed and deployed, as we all know, by major telecommunication carriers, computer companies, and cable-TV operators; I expect that this will continue to be a rather chaotic field for the next 5 to 10 years, but the result will soon be an environment where everything is "wired" to everything else. On a smaller scale, the technology is more than adequate already: People thought I was nuts when I wired a local area network into my New York City apartment in 1987 to connect the Macintoshes in my office, my wife's office and my childrens' bedrooms—but it would hardly cause a raised eyebrow today.

This is an important point: At issue here is not just the technology, but society's acceptance of that technology. If Panasonic or General Electric offered a "kitchen environment" today that consisted of a refrigerator, microwave oven, coffeepot, and dishwasher all cabled together in an enclosed cabinet, I don't believe the average consumer would think it frightening that all these devices were "intelligent" and that they could communicate with one another. If the "intelligent kitchen" was able to communicate with the household TV and VCR, as well as the cellular phone, so much the better. True, the consumer might ask himself whether he really needed to replace his existing assortment of household gadgets with the new devices—but if the examples and applications discussed below sounded sufficiently practical and useful, he would probably shell out the money without worrying that he was indulging in a science fiction fantasy.

12.2 SOME POTENTIAL EXAMPLES

What are some examples of embedded systems that we might expect to see in the next few years? Here are a few.

12.2.1 Voice Control of All Common Appliances

As mentioned above, the small "footprint" of many of the devices in which we want to embed these systems makes it impractical, if not impossible, to communicate via keyboard or mouse; and the desire for more elaborate interactions with the system obviates the use of simple pushbuttons. A vocabulary of 500 words, and a simple verb-object grammar, would probably be sufficient for 90 percent of the commands we wish to give such devices for the next few years; this is well within the technology of desktop-sized computers already and should be transferable to the chip-sized devices within a very short period of time.

The relatively small number of voice-recognition systems that are currently on the market often require "personal training" in order to recognize idiosyncratic accents and vocal characteristics. This raises some interesting problems. How do we train our household appliances to recognize the voices of everyone in the family? And how do we avoid the drudgery of training each device independently? The first problem suggests either the need for identifying yourself before communicating with the device or the need for a more sophisticated voice-recognition system that isn't speaker-dependent. And the second problem suggests the need to have a common voice-recognition "engine," which consumers can install as a pluggable component in their household devices ("I'll take the Blatzco engine, please; it seems to do a good job of recognizing my Irish accent."); and it suggests the need to personalize such an engine *once* then upload the associated database of information to all embedded-system devices that need it.

12.2.2 The Automated House

We've been talking about this one for years, and a few people already have it in one form or another. The possibilities are endless: The automated house can regulate the lighting and temperature in individual rooms in a much more sophisticated fashion than we now carry out; it could shut the windows when it senses rain; it could call the police if it senses the presence of intruders, and the fire department if it senses smoke. It could turn off all of the appropriate appliances in the household automatically within a few minutes after everyone has departed, and it could turn on selected devices when the front door opens. The list goes on and on...

To make this a reality, we need three things: a household that's wired so that all the devices can communicate; a set of household devices that *can* communicate; and a marketplace that actively seeks to purchase such things. The wiring problem is the most problematic, only because it's a nuisance to accomplish with an existing house or apartment; the only reason I was able to install a LAN in my apartment in 1987 was that we were engaged in a major renovation project that required opening up all the walls to install new electrical wiring. Once the walls were plastered and painted at the end of the renovation project, I would have been risking divorce if I had suggested gouging more holes to replace my AppleTalk® network with a speedier Ethernet™ cable.

12.2.3 A Simple One: Synchronize the Clocks!

Twice a year, when daylight-saving time begins and ends, we suddenly realize that we have *dozens* of clocks in the house, because every device wants to know what time it is; my children have long since grown bored with my stories of the good old days of the 1950s, when we had only one or two clocks in the house. Have you every noticed that it's almost impossible to synchronize all these clocks so that they all tell the same time? Perhaps it's only because I'm a computer person, but it drives me nuts to wander through my apartment and see that the coffeemaker in the kitchen thinks it's three minutes earlier than the VCR in the living room, both of which are four minutes *later* than the time signal that you get by calling 976-4141 on the phone. Wouldn't it be nice if all of our household devices could coordinate and agree on a common time? The means of doing so are straightforward; I leave it as a minor exercise for the reader.

12.2.4 Meaningful Synchronization of Devices

One reason for suggesting that all of our devices should agree on the time is that it allows them to coordinate their activities in a meaningful fashion. Here's a trivial example: With today's appliances, I set the alarm on my bedside digital clock to go off at 6:30, and the coffeemaker turns on at 6:20 so that fresh coffee is waiting for me when I stagger into the kitchen. But tomorrow I have an early flight to catch, and I need to get up at 5:45 A.M.; I remember to change the alarm on my bedside clock, but I forget to reset the coffeemaker. Damn! No coffee! It puts me in a bad mood for the entire day. Obviously, what I want to do is set the coffeemaker to schedule its activities *relative* to the clock in the bedroom; when I reset the bedroom alarm, the coffeemaker (and perhaps various other devices, too) adjust automatically.

While this example is a simple one, it suggests an entire class of possibilities: pair-wise communication between intelligent devices. What if, for example, your refrigerator and your television could communicate? I could imagine the television sending a signal to the refrigerator that says, "There's a football game coming up in a couple of hours, and the family goes through a lot of liquid refreshment during the game; you'd better stock up on ice cubes. Check the inventory of beer, because the master of the house will be *really* annoyed if he runs out of suds before half-time. Also, the refrigerator door is likely to be opened and closed quite a lot during the game—you might want to lower the temperature a couple of degrees so that the lettuce stays crisp."

Similarly, what about communication between the refrigerator and the stove or microwave oven? The fundamental purpose of both devices is to regulate the temperature of the packages placed within them; maybe there are some applications that could take advantage of that. Since life in the typical household revolves around the television (or multiple televisions), we might find more marketable applications by having the TV talk to the vacuum cleaner, the hair dryer, the air conditioner, etc.

12.2.5 Television as the Home Control Center

The notion of the household TV talking to the other appliances raises an important point: It may turn out to be the primary appliance that *we* talk to for planning purposes. According to a 1994 survey, 50 percent of American families now have a home computer—but some 98 percent have a television. As a computer person, I would be more comfortable programming the day's activities for my army of household appliances from my desktop PC; but the average family might prefer to do so from the kitchen TV during a commercial break.

In any case, the television is the one device that's likely to have a large, colorful display screen. It's also one of the few devices to which we might imagine a keyboard being attached, though the average family is now so firmly attached to its hand-held remote control device that a keyboard may no longer be acceptable.

Because the television is still perceived as a relatively large, bulky device, it also makes sense to use it as the physical component for storing appropriate "household data" on a hard disk or removable SyQuest® cartridge. It's likely, of course, that most of the household devices will operate more or less autonomously, but the network of asynchronous communicating devices could also be imagined as a strange new form of client-server system. While each "client" device has its own local data, there's an obvious argument in favor of having a central server—and the television is the obvious choice for the server.[2]

---

[2] To carry the analogy further, it also makes sense to imagine a three-tier client-server network: Each room in the house has its own television, which acts as an application server for the other household appliances located in that room. Somewhere in the house is the "master television" that carries the "enterprise data" of the family and downloads information, as required, to each of the second-tier televisions. I can already imagine a Hollywood movie based on such an architecture.

12.2.6 Remote Communication with Household Appliances

How many of us have passed the grocery store, while driving home from work, and suddenly muttered to ourselves, "Omygosh! I wonder if we're out of milk at home..." Wouldn't it be nice if you could call up your refrigerator from your car phone and ask it? Communication in the other direction might be interesting, too: Can you imagine getting an e-mail message from your refrigerator saying, "Pardon me, Master, but I thought you might like to know that those teenagers of yours were grazing last night, and we've run perilously low on mint chocolate chip ice cream. The beer is safe, thank goodness, but they also wiped out the leftover chicken that you put in the casserole dish, as well as seven slices of pizza that you normally keep for emergencies. So you might want to stock up on supplies on the way home from work this evening."

Similarly, I can imagine putting a frozen dinner in the microwave oven, on the assumption that I'll be home from the office at 6 P.M. But a big meeting comes up in the afternoon, and it suddenly becomes obvious that I won't get home until 8:00; I need to call my microwave oven and tell it not to start thawing the pizza (assuming the kids haven't found it already) until 7:30. And with enough ingenuity, I could probably think of some reasonable excuses for communicating with my vacuum cleaner, my bathtub (I really need a hot bath waiting for me when I get home from a long, miserable day in the office), and several other devices that await my beck and call.

12.2.7 Disposable Embedded Systems

The refrigerator scenario described above has one difficulty: The refrigerator has to know how many quarts of milk it contains in order to respond to a query from my car phone. A moment's thought confirms the obvious: No one is going to go to the trouble to tell the refrigerator when they put an item inside—it would mean spending an entire evening reporting on the purchases at the grocery store and could lead to some frustrating interchanges. "Excuse me," says the refrigerator, "but was that low-fat milk or skim milk that you purchased? I certainly hope it wasn't that high-fat stuff—you know what the doctor has been telling you about your cholesterol."

Obviously, the inventory-control application that I've envisaged for my refrigerator only works if the inventory items *register themselves* when they are placed inside. But how can that work? Simple: Put an embedded system in the packaging, or container, associated with the food item. So the milk container, upon recognizing that it has been placed inside the refrigerator, sends a message that says, "Hi, I'm two quarts of low-fat Borden's milk. I normally expect to be maintained at 60 degrees Fahrenheit." To which the refrigerator responds, "Welcome to the club. I appreciate the temperature request, but the Master really prefers ice-cold milk, so you're going down to 50 degrees."

And this scenario raises another interesting question: What happens when the milk is used up? In today's environment, we're likely to throw the empty milk container in the trash; and if the embedded chip that it contains is cheap enough, we might continue to do so—hence the concept of "disposable" embedded systems. On the other hand, if the milk container carries a more expensive chip, a whole new form of recycling might spring up.

12.2.8 Process Control with Embedded Systems

Another moment's thought tells us that we don't need a full-scale embedded system for the milk carton to identify itself to the refrigerator; a bar-code label would suffice. But what if the embedded system played a more active role, by monitoring the contents within its package for temperature, humidity, freshness? In this case, the milk carton could announce to the refrigerator, "Sorry to bother you, but we got pretty warm while we were being brought here from the grocery store. I'd appreciate it if you could cool us down as quickly as possible so we don't spoil." And if the milk does begin spoiling, one could imagine the process control system embedded within the container doing a variety of things: beeping, flashing, changing the color of the carton to a dull black or a day-glo orange.

Interestingly, some household devices already have primitive mechanisms for signaling unhappiness with their condition. The smoke detector chirps at us when its battery is low; the VCR flashes at us (endlessly!) when its clock hasn't been set; and the bedside digital clock flashes at us to indicate that a power outage has caused it to lose time. With a little ingenuity, we could imagine another generation of intelligent devices that would complain about excessive temperature, humidity, or exposure to sunlight; and we could imagine the food-container systems monitoring acidity, bacteria level, moisture content, and various other indicators of acceptable quality.

Because of the economics, it's perhaps less likely to imagine that these packaging-oriented embedded systems would communicate to remote systems outside the household; on the other hand, if my milk container can communicate with the refrigerator, and the refrigerator can communicate with the television, and the television can communicate with the world outside, then indeed everything can communicate with everything. My milk container can report back to its manufacturer that it survived for seven days before its contents were depleted; it could report that it had been maintained at an average temperature of 70 degrees, but for a brief period it experienced a high of 85 degrees. This kind of "black-box" data recording is not just for deciphering the cause of airplane crashes; some automobiles now have such systems to facilitate periodic maintenance and perhaps even resolve warranty disputes. If a car can have such a system, why can't my milk container?

And if a milk container can talk to its manufacturer, why can't I talk to my milk container—and thus, indirectly, to the manufacturer? As it turns out, I don't have many strong feelings about the milk that I drink—but I do have some definite opinions about the cereal that I consume *with* the milk. If there were a button that could be pushed on the cereal box (voice recognition isn't helpful, because I'm tongue-tied and incoherent until well past breakfast), then I would be happy to tell Kellogg's that they need to put *more* raisins in their Raisin Bran, and that I wish they would cut down the amount of sugar and salt.

12.3 TRENDS AND IMPLICATIONS

Will any of these scenarios come to pass? Who knows? As noted above, it's not science fiction: It doesn't require supercomputers, and it doesn't require exotic artificial intelligence. What it does require is cheap, powerful chips, combined with ubiquitous networking, and supported by massive marketing. All three of these ingredients exist or are in the works. It's a truism that the technology advances more rapidly than we usually predict and that society adapts to such technological advances somewhat more slowly than we anticipate; so it could be 5 to 10 years, rather than 2 to 3 years, before we start to see a "critical mass" of the applications that I've described above. But when it does come, it will spark another wave of application development that will make the business-oriented applications of the past 20 years seem tame by comparison.

No doubt there will be some failures along the way. Someone will probably invent an intelligent toothbrush that will tell the refrigerator to hide the ice cream if it spots cavities while cleaning your teeth. Someone will invent an intelligent rug that howls in agony every time you track mud across it. And several companies will go bankrupt along the way with good ideas that turn out to be poorly executed or poorly marketed. But none of this means that the concept is invalid.

Assuming that this world of embedded systems does arrive in the next few years, here are the trends that I think software developers have to keep in mind:

- There will be a *heavy* demand for networking technology of all kinds. It's already a thriving segment of the computing industry; everything I've described in this chapter will just add to the demand for specialists in wireless computing, LAN/WAN technology, TCP/IP and Internet routers, and other aspects of communication.

- There will be heavy demand for applications involving voice recognition. As noted above, the recognition "engines" will probably be plug-replaceable components—and this will represent an important, but relatively small, component of the industry. What will be more important, I believe, is the design of applications that can deal with the ambiguity of voice input—e.g., the difficulty of distinguishing between verbal inputs of "five" and "fine." During the initial flurry of activity with pen-based applications in the early 1990s, we saw how important it was for the recognition engine (which typically has only a limited sense of the *context* of the input data) to pass back a list of *possible* values for the input, together with associated confidence levels. Thus, the voice-recognition engine might report to the application program, "I'm 90 percent confident he said 'Five,' but there's a 50 percent chance he said 'Fine.' And if he was drunk, it might have been 'Fight!' that he was muttering under his breath." It's up to the application program to make the best judgment of the likely nature of the input, based on the context at the time.

- We'll be dealing with different operating systems. Aside from the home television set, which Microsoft already covets, there won't be room for Microsoft Windows or similar memory-intensive operating systems on the intelligent appliances discussed above. For the most primitive embedded systems, there may not be any operating system at all; but once these systems have to deal with memory management, multitasking, and input/output communication with various remote devices, it's likely that we'll see a resurgence of UNIX-like operating systems, or specialized operating systems such as TSX-32, or possibly an entirely new generation of operating systems. This will provide a new career for systems programmers, but it will also create a new world for application programmers who are now building their career on a foundation of Microsoft Windows.

- While assembly language is now a relic of the past, I think that embedded systems will create a resurgence in languages like C and C++, as well as the new-age languages like Java discussed in Chapter 10 (indeed, Sun Microsystems announced a new version of Java in March 1997, specifically intended for embedded systems on small-scale computers). Obviously, there's already a strong market for these languages, but within the world of business applications, the last few years have seen a strong shift toward Visual Basic, Smalltalk, Delphi, VisualAge, and other languages that are less cryptic in nature. And since the development work for the embedded systems will surely take place on large, sophisticated desktop PCs and workstations, we'll continue to see an emphasis on visual development environments—which includes, of course, Visual C++. But the key point is that the software for the embedded applications must eventually be ported into an operational environment that will generally have an order of magnitude less power and storage capacity than the development environment; so issues of efficiency will continue to be important. Not only that, the embedded systems are likely to require more "low-level" programming for device control, communication, etc.; this, too, is likely to support a resurgence of languages like C and C++.

12.4 WHO WILL PREVAIL IN THE FIELD OF EMBEDDED SYSTEMS?

Assuming that all of this comes to pass, why should we assume that the American software industry will prevail in the development of embedded systems? Indeed, any discussion of household appliances is likely to conjure up names like Panasonic, Sony, Mitsubishi, and Matsushita, not to mention other names from Korea, Japan, Germany, France, and England. So why should we believe that this field will contribute to the rise and resurrection of the American programmer?

Common sense tells us that there will be fierce competition from companies all over the world and that there is no guarantee whatsoever the field will be dominated by the Americans or the Japanese or any other nationality. But we do have a few things going for us:

- As noted above, what makes the embedded systems field really interesting is ubiquitous networking. Of course, large computer companies and electronics firms all over the world are familiar with networking technology per se, but it's all taking place on our turf. Obviously, there's a reverse side of this argument: One might expect Siemens and Nixdorf to prevail in the German embedded systems market, for example, to the extent that it requires intimate knowledge of the current state of German telecommunications.

- Perhaps even more than the other aspects of computing, this is one that's likely to change quickly and chaotically over the next 5 to 10 years; the current state of anarchy in the increasingly deregulated American telecommunications marketplace is one indication of that. In a world of chaos, I believe that the philosophy of "good enough" computing will prevail. As suggested in Chapter 7, I believe that this style of computing is more compatible with the American "cowboy culture" than it is to the somewhat more formal and structured cultures of Europe and Asia. (But there's hope for Australia and New Zealand!)

- One could regard all of these systems as a form of the "service systems" discussed in Chapter 8. The milk company that builds an embedded system into its milk container *should* be looking at it as an opportunity to establish a closer rapport with its customers. As a consumer, I would dearly love to see (and/or hear) something besides mug shots of baseball players and lost children on the carton of milk that I stare at in the morning while munching on my cereal; but I doubt that the Japanese or German or Korean embedded systems developers have any unique talent for deciding what kind of milk-carton applications will best persuade me to buy more cartons of milk, rather than switching to bacon and eggs. Likewise, I don't give American companies much of a chance when it comes to building embedded systems for containers of Japanese or Korean food.

There's something else to keep in mind here, too: This is a sufficiently "brave new world" that the current giants in the field may be leapfrogged. It's natural to think of Japanese companies like Panasonic and Sony, and it's natural to think of American companies like General Electric and Westinghouse. But it's more likely that the future will involve some entirely new companies, based largely on software expertise; and the issues cited above are particularly relevant when it comes to new startup companies. As investment banker and technology forecaster Ted Prince says,

> We are already seeing the new players emerge...There's a Microsoft in the making for the machine world out there right now and we just have to identify it and see whether or not we can be part of it. In the short- to medium-term, being computer-nice to machines will be infinitely more profitable than being computer-nice for humans because we have just solved that problem with multimedia, and the opportunity is past us. [1]

While it's delightful to imagine another Microsoft in an industry like this, it's even more interesting to anticipate hundreds of small companies, each with its software wizards focusing on the design of intelligent toasters, coffee-makers, and refrigerators...and yes, perhaps even intelligent toothbrushes. Indeed, it's even possible to imagine that this "brave new world" will be the downfall of Microsoft, for as noted above, the *lingua franca* of embedded systems probably will *not* be Microsoft Windows or Visual Basic. But that's okay: Each new generation of computing technology causes enormous difficulty for the company that dominated the then-current paradigm, but creates a vast new opportunities for the next generation of entrepreneurs. And in this field, the important to remember is this: For every PC, there are a hundred appliances and machines that can serve as a home for an intelligent embedded system. If Microsoft has made its fortunes from a hundred million PCs around the world, think how much more money there is to be made from the vastly large number of embedded systems!

REFERENCE

1. Prince, Ted. "Nancomputing and the Future of Embedded Systems." *The Technology Fundamentalist*, June–August, 1995.

13
PAST, PRESENT, AND FUTURE

The past is of no importance. The present is of no importance. It is with the future that we have to deal. For the past is what man should not have been. The present is what man ought not to be. The future is what artists are.

Oscar Wilde, The Soul of Man Under Socialism, *in* Fortnightly Review *(London, February 1891).*

A colleague of mine, Lou Russell, remarked in a recent article[1] that the lives of computer people should be measured in "dog-years": A single year for a computer professional is equivalent to seven years in most other professions. By that measure, my career dates back to the American Revolution; indeed, anyone who has been in the computer field for five or more "normal" years looks pretty old to a Computer Science graduate just emerging from college. And it raises an interesting question: Is anything in this book relevant to today's new generation of computer professionals? Will any of it be relevant five years from now?

---

[1]Lou Russell, "Learning to Learn: Teach Yourself," *American Programmer,* January 1996.

What would *you* say to today's hot-shot young software professionals—people who think COBOL is a joke and that "1401" is a reference to a World War II bomber? What advice could you give them to help take advantage of the "brave new world" of computing that I've discussed in this book? How would you suggest they cope with the global competition that I warned about in *Decline and Fall* and that continues to be a source of concern for many older programmers?

To a large extent, it doesn't matter: Every generation assumes, in its youth, that it is immortal and omnipotent. And every generation of children ignores the advice of its parents, believing that their circumstances are so new and different that the lessons of their parents' lives simply wouldn't apply. On the surface, this seems to be true in the computer field, too: Why would today's young Java programmers believe there is anything to be learned from experiences of a mainframe COBOL programmer?

Ironically, this attitude of generational arrogance is part of the basis for my optimism for the American software industry. If today's generation of software developers followed in the footsteps of their elders and used the same kind of technology and practices, they would be subject to the same kind of crushing competitive pressures that the older generation is facing around the world. But they don't—they prefer, instead, to leapfrog over the older technologies and plunge into something new. And in most cases, the older generation encourages them to do so; even if we're trapped in our old paradigms and technologies, we have enough sense to encourage our children to try something newer.

An interesting example of this tendency occurred at the DB Expo conference in December 1995, where I participated in a panel session on the merits of IBM's newly released version of object-oriented COBOL. Though it's an elegant language, with powerful new features, it's still COBOL; consequently, I thought it would be interesting to ask the audience what advice they would offer if they had children about to graduate from college and about to enter the computer software profession. Would they recommend getting involved in OO-COBOL, or would they recommend instead something like Visual Basic, Delphi, Smalltalk, or Java? Because of the subject matter of the panel session, nearly everyone in the room was directly involved in COBOL and saw great opportunities for themselves with the new object-oriented version of the language. But they had different opinions when it came to their children: Less than 5 percent said they would recommend it as an area of professional concentration.

If COBOL and FORTRAN are obsolete, then Visual Basic and PowerBuilder have now become "mainstream" technologies; if mainframes are passé, then client-server is the order of the day. But one of the primary messages of this book is that the mainstream technologies are rapidly becoming "commodities"—they're widely available to *anyone* around the world, including programmers in India and Ireland (and a dozen other places) where the salaries are still *much* lower than in North America and where competitive ambitions often produce *much* higher levels of productivity and quality. As I've discussed in the earlier chapters of this book, there are some exciting new technologies and strategies for achieving dramatic increases in productivity and quality; and since much of it seems to originate in North America, we have an opportunity to maintain a competitive lead over other parts of the world. If we choose not to…well, sooner or later, the commodity-style application development will gravitate to whatever part of the world offers the best combination of price, functionality, productivity, and quality.

I know that if I were graduating from college today, I wouldn't care about any of this—after all, client-server technology, and all of the programming languages associated with it, has been around for some five years now. In dog-years, that's a full generation, which makes it intrinsically boring. I would be far more excited about the Internet, the World Wide Web, and associated programming languages like Java. That's the future—at least for the next couple of years.

Beyond the time frame of two or three years, we're all pretty much in the dark. On rare occasions, young computer professionals ask me about this: "You've been around for eons," they'll say, "and you've seen lots of trends come and go. What's next on the horizon? What comes after Java and the World Wide Web?" The honest answer is: *I don't know.* I can make some intelligent guesses, but many of the developments in the computer field have taken us completely by surprise during the past 30 years, and I think there are a lot of surprises left in store.

Of course, we can all safely predict that computer *hardware* technology will continue to improve for at least the next decade—CPUs and memories and other hardware components will be smaller and faster and cheaper next year than they are this year. And there's a good chance that it will advance faster than many of us anticipate, though most of us have become so blasé about such improvements that nothing much would surprise us any more. On the other hand, it's much more difficult to tell how rapidly the software technology will improve in parallel with the hardware advances; who can accurately predict, for example, when the combination of advanced hardware and advanced software will support truly sophisticated voice recognition?

More important, who can tell when the combination of improved hardware and software will create a recognizable paradigm shift in the form and nature of computing? The advent of personal computing, some 15 years ago, now appears to have been one such shift; the advent of graphical user interfaces was another. These paradigm shifts are the source of great excitement and opportunities; and to the extent that we can stay abreast of them, they help us avoid the competitive pressures associated with commodity-style technologies like programming in Visual Basic.

The Internet is arguably the newest paradigm shift, but it's important to remember that it actually began more than 25 years ago. One could argue that the steady improvement in telecommunications bandwidth, the declining cost of telecommunications, and the proliferation of PCs, contributed to the currently popularity of the 'Net; but there's little question in my mind that the explosive popularity of the World Wide Web in 1994 was the real catalyst. It's interesting to note that if circumstances had been a little different, it could have appeared a couple of years earlier—for the vintage-1992 computer technology was adequate. And if circumstances had been a little different—e.g., if Tim Berners-Lee had had other projects to worry about, or more excessive bureaucratic constraints to deal with, it could have appeared a couple of years later. Does it matter whether the Web appeared in 1992 or 1997? Remember: These are dog years we're talking about!

The point I'm trying to make is that the successful deployment of a new computing paradigm depends partly on technology issues, but even more on a complex combination of social, economic, cultural, and political issues. Those of us who work in the computer field can barely make mediocre predictions about the rate of improvement in technology; we're at a complete loss (along with everyone else!) about the rate of improvement in the other areas. Any predictions that you hear from any scientist, philosopher, guru, or politician about the future of computing should be taken with a large grain of salt.

Also, those of us who do like to ride at the very front of the tidal wave of technological change often forget that it's a *long* wave, with many people—including people in our own field—far behind us. You may be programming in Java, but the Gartner group reports that approximately half of the new application development work taking place in 1995 was still in COBOL. You may be using a Pentium-133 with Windows 95, but there are nearly 100 million copies of Windows 3.1 floating around and goodness only knows how many copies of DOS running on 640K XT-class machines. As for the Internet: A colleague observed to me a few months ago that if you express the entire Internet community as a percentage of the human race, it still rounds to zero. For that matter, half the world's population has never made a telephone call, so it may be a while before the Internet becomes *truly* pervasive.

On the other hand, there's no question that computing technology is having more and more of an impact on the world around us—not only in our business lives, but also in politics, society, and our personal lives. If you work in the computer field, you're so obviously aware of this that I needn't belabor the point, but it's just beginning to dawn on most of the other members of the human race that *they* can use computers to influence and improve their lives. My 75-year-old parents, both whom would have been dismissed a decade ago as hopelessly computer-illiterate and computer-phobic, are now both active e-mail users and Internet surfers; it's a tiny example, but one I expect to see multiplied and magnified over and over again in the coming years. Cheap, user-friendly PCs and the global Internet have made a vast amount of information available to a large segment of the population—technologically available, in any case.

But since information is power and power is associated with big business, government, and politics (among other things), it's increasingly likely that the world of computing is going to be more and more affected by legislation and public policy. The recent Congressional debates over pornography on the Internet, the right of citizens to encrypt their private communications without governmental eavesdropping, and other similar issues, are typical of what we'll see in the coming years. It's important to remember that even if the technology of computing was frozen at its current level, it would take us another 5 to 10 years to sort out the social implications of what's currently available.

No doubt you're aware of this, and you probably have some opinions about these issues. But let me put it more strongly: *The consequences of the social decisions we make with regard to existing computer technology are more important than the consequences of improved technology over the next 5 to 10 years.* Obviously, that doesn't mean that technology is going to stop advancing—But it does mean that many of us in the computing industry should consider shifting our emphasis from inventing new and sexy hardware and software gadgets to focusing instead on working together with politicians, teachers, philosophers, parents, and other thoughtful members of society to ensure that the vast computing power we have provided is indeed put to wise use.

If we don't participate in the computer-related debates, and take an active role in making the necessary decisions, they'll be made without us—but not as wisely as they would be with our participation. Should we, for example, allow pornography on the Internet, from a philosophical perspective? And if the Internet is to be censored in some fashion, what mechanisms are not only socially appropriate but technologically practical and cost-effective? Obviously, computer scientists (in the broadest sense of the term) cannot and should not make this decision on their own, but they have important and valuable insights to offer—without which, any public policy or legislation is likely to flawed and ineffective.

I believe that one of the reasons American society is so strong and vibrant today is that its economy—i.e., the productive output of its businesses—has been vastly improved by the effect of 30 years of computer technology. There is still much to do in this area, of course, but more and more of this kind of "business computing" will become, as I've suggested in this book, a commodity that all countries will enjoy. The next great wave will be *social* computing, and the question we will wrestle with will be: How can we use computers and information technology to create a stronger, more vibrant society?

And this is something we can all participate in—at the family level, the community level, and the national level. Many of us, for example, have begun taking advantage of the Internet to set up "family networks" to re-connect generations of a family that are now scattered across the country. Some of us have begun working with school, church, or community groups to set up simple Web pages or simple client-server systems that provide crucial information to people who need it. The technology involved in this is usually child's play for us, but overwhelming to the other members of the group; more important, we find ourselves playing a first-hand role in effective forms of social computing.

So, bring on the faster CPUs and dazzle me with a terabyte hard disk to replace the gigabytes I've got on my desktop today. I love the technology, and I'm as anxious as anyone to get next year's faster, cheaper, smaller machine. But let's not forget that in the end, there's only one reason for having all of this awesome power: to help people. Without people, there would be no need for *any* computing power. As the Chinese revolutionary leader, Mao Zedong, said some 50 years ago, "The people, and the people alone, are the motive force in the making of world history."[2]

Amen.

---

[2]Mao Zedong, *Selected Works*, volume 3, "On Coalition Government," April 24, 1945.

Appendix

AN UPDATED PROGRAMMER'S BOOKSHELF

A truly great book should be read in youth, again in maturity and once more in old age, as a fine building should be seen by morning light, at noon and by moonlight.

Robertson Davies, "Too Much, Too Fast," in Peterborough Examiner *(Canada, June 16, 1962; reprinted in* The Enthusiasms of Robertson Davies, *1979).*

When I wrote *Decline and Fall of the American Programmer*, I casually included a list of recommended books as an appendix. From the mail that I've received over the past few years, I have the strong impression that the so-called "programmer's bookshelf" may have been the most useful part of the book. With that in mind, I've included a new list of books here. For the most part, these are books published after the *Decline and Fall* book was released; in a few cases, the books were published earlier, but I didn't become aware of them until recently. As you skim through the list, you'll note that the selections are not exclusively concerned with computer programming; I've gotten great insight into software problems over the years from books on management, philosophy, engineering, and various other disciplines.

In today's world, lists like this become obsolete instantly; however, I'll be keeping an updated list on my World Wide Web home page, which you can find at http://www.yourdon.com As was the case with my earlier list of recommended books, I continue to feel that it's inappropriate to include my own books among all these other classics; however, for those who want to see a list of all the books I've written since 1967, that's available on my Web page, too. And for readers who complain that they don't have a decent technical book store in their neighborhood, my Web page also has a list of approximately 50 book stores across the United States; most will handle credit-card orders by phone or fax, and several have e-mail or Web capabilities of their own.

1. Andrews, Dorine, and Susan Stalick. *Business Reengineering: The Survival Guide.* (Englewood Cliffs, NJ: Prentice Hall, 1994).

2. Beizer, Boris. *Black-Box Testing: Techniques for Functional Testing of Software and Systems.* (New York: John Wiley & Sons, 1995) ISBN: 0-471-12094-4.

3. Block, Peter. *Flawless Consulting: A Guide to Getting Your Expertise Used.* (San Diego, CA: Pfeiffer & Company, 1981). (Pfeiffer & Company, 8517 Production Avenue, San Diego, CA 92121; phone: 619/578-5900, fax: 619/578-2042.)

4. Booch, Grady. *Object-Oriented Design.* (Menlo Park, CA: Benjamin-Cummings, 1994) ISBN: 0-8053-0091-0.

5. Borenstein, Nathaniel S. *Programming as if People Mattered: Friendly Programs, Software Engineering, and Other Noble Delusions.* (Princeton, NJ: Princeton University Press, 1991) ISBN: 0-691-08752-0.

6. Brooks, Frederick P., Jr. *The Mythical Man-Month.* (Reading, MA: Addison-Wesley, 1995) ISBN: 0-201-83595-9. (Note: this is a 20th-year anniversary edition of the original 1975 book, updated with four new chapters.)

7. Carrol, John M. *Scenario-Based Design: Envisioning Work and Technology in System Development.* (New York: John Wiley & Sons, Inc., 1995) ISBN: 0-471-07659-7.

8. Champy, James. *Reengineering Management: The Mandate for New Leadership.* (New York: HarperCollins, 1995) ISBN: 0-88730-698-5.

9. Coad, Peter, and Jill Nicola. *Object-Oriented Programming.* (Englewood Cliffs, NJ: Prentice Hall/Yourdon Press, 1993).

10. Coad, Peter, David North, and Mark Mayfield. *Object Models: Strategies, Patterns, & Applications.* (Englewood Cliffs, NJ: Prentice Hall/Yourdon Press, 1995) ISBN: 0-13-108614-6.

11. Coleman, Derek, Patrick Arnold, Stephanie Bodoff, Chris Dollin, Helena Gilchrist, Fiona Hayes, and Paul Jeremaes. *Object-Oriented Development: The Fusion Method.* (Englewood Cliffs, NJ: Prentice Hall, 1993).

12. Connell, John, and Linda Shafer. *Object-Oriented Rapid Prototyping.* (Englewood Cliffs, NJ: Prentice Hall, 1994).

13. Conner, Daryl R. *Managing at the Speed of Change: How Resilient Managers Succeed and Prosper Where Others Fail.* (New York: Villard Books, 1992) ISBN: 0-679-40684.

14. Coupland, Douglas. *Microserfs.* (New York: HarperCollins, 1995) ISBN: 0-06-039148-0.

15. Covey, Stephen R. A., Roger Merrill, and Rebecca R. Merrill, *First Things First.* (New York: Simon & Schuster, 1994) ISBN: 0-671-86441-6.

16. Curtis, Bill, William E. Hefley, Sally Miller, and Michael D. Konrad. *People Management Capability Maturity Model*, Draft Version 0.3. (Pittsburgh, PA: Software Engineering Institute, 1995).

17. Davenport, Thomas H. *Process Innovation: Reengineering Work through Information Technology.* (Cambridge, MA: Harvard University Press, 1993).

18. DeMarco, Tom. *Why Does Software Cost So Much? and Other Puzzles of the Information Age.* (New York: Dorset House, 1995) ISBN: 0-932633-34-X.

19. Donovan, John J. *Business Reengineering with Information Technology.* (Englewood Cliffs, NJ: Prentice Hall, 1994).

20. Garfinkel, Simson, Daniel Weise, and Steven Strassman. *The UNIX-HATERS Handbook: The Best of the UNIX-HATERS On-Line*

Mailing List Reveals Why UNIX Must Die! (San Mateo, CA: IDG Books, 1994).

21. Gilb, Tom, and Dorothy Graham. *Software Inspection.* (Reading, MA: Addison-Wesley, 1993) ISBN: 0-201-63181-4.

22. Glass, Robert L. *Software Creativity.* (Englewood Cliffs, NJ: Prentice Hall, 1995).

23. Goldberg, Adele, and Kenneth S. Rubin. *Succeeding with Objects: Decision Frameworks for Project Management.* (Reading, MA: Addison-Wesley, 1995) ISBN: 0-201-62878-3.

24. Hammer, Michael, and James Champy. *Reengineering the Corporation.* (New York: HarperCollins, 1993) ISBN: 0-88730-640-3.

25. Hammer, Michael, and Steven A. Stanton. *The Reengineering Revolution: A Handbook.* (New York: Harper Business, 1995) ISBN: 0-88730-736-1.

26. Handy, Charles. *The Age of Unreason.* (Boston: Harvard Business School Press, 1989) ISBN: 0-87584-301-8.

27. Harris, Marvin. *Cannibals and Kings.* (New York: Random House, 1991).

28. Henderson-Sellers, Brian, and Julian Edwards. *BOOKTWO: The Working Object.* (Englewood Cliffs, NJ: Prentice Hall, 1994).

29. Hitchcock, Darcy E., and Marsha L. Willard. *Why Teams Can Fail, and What To Do About It.* (Chicago: Irwin Professional Publishing, 1995) ISBN: 0-7863-0423-5.

30. Humphrey, Watts. *A Discipline for Software Engineering.* (Reading, MA: Addison-Wesley, 1995) ISBN: 0-201-54610-8.

31. Jackson, Michael. *Software Requirements & Specifications: Alexicon of Practice, Principles and Prejudices.* (Reading, MA: Addison-Wesley, 1995) ISBN: 0-201-87712-0.

32. Jacobson, Ivar, Magnus Christerson, Patrick Jonsson, and Gunnar Övergaard, *Object-Oriented Software Engineering.* (Reading, MA: Addison-Wesley, 1992) ISBN: 0-201-54435-0.

33. Kaplan, Jerry. *Startup.* (Boston, MA: Houghton Mifflin, 1994) ISBN: 0-395-71133-9.

34. Kelly, Kevin. *Out of Control: The New Biology of Machines, Social Systems, and the Economic World.* (Reading, MA: Addison-Wesley, 1994) ISBN: 0-201-48340-8.

35. Landauer, Thomas K. *The Trouble with Computers: Usefulness, Usability, and Productivity.* (Cambridge, MA: The MIT Press, 1995) ISBN: 0-262-12186-7.

36. Leveson, Nancy G. *Safeware: System Safety and Computers.* (Reading, MA: Addison-Wesley, 1995) ISBN: 0-201-11972-2.

37. Lipnack, Jessica, and Jeffrey Stamps. *The Age of Networking: Organizing Principles for the 21st Century.* (Essex Junction, VT: Oliver Wright Publications, 1994) ISBN: 0-939246-71-6.

38. Maguire, Steve. *Writing Solid Code.* (Redmond, WA: Microsoft Press, 1993) ISBN: 1-55615-551-4.

39. Maguire, Steve. *Debugging the Development Process.* (Redmond, WA: Microsoft Press, 1994) ISBN: 1-55615-650-2.

40. Marick, Brian. *The Craft of Software Testing: Subsystem Testing, Including Object-Based and Object-Oriented Testing.* (Englewood Cliffs, NJ: Prentice Hall, 1995) ISBN: 0-13-177411-5.

41. McCarthy, Jim. *Dynamics of Software Development.* (Redmond, WA: Microsoft Press, 1995) ISBN: 1-55615-823-8.

42. Meyer, Bertrand. *Object Success: A Manager's Guide to Object Orientation, Its Impact on the Corporation and Its Use for Reengineering the Software Process.* (Englewood Cliffs, NJ: Prentice Hall, 1995) ISBN: 0-13-192833-3.

43. Morrison, J. Paul. *Flow-Based Programming: A New Approach to Application Development.* (New York: Van Nostrand Reinhold, 1994).

44. Negroponte, Nicholas. *Being Digital.* (New York: Alfred A. Knopf, 1995) ISBN: 0-679-43919-6.

45. Neumann, Peter G. *Computer-Related Risks.* (Reading, MA: Addison-Wesley, 1995) ISBN: 0-201-55805-X.

46. Olson, Dave. *Exploiting Chaos: Cashing in on the Realities of Software Development.* (New York: Van Nostrand Reinhold, 1993) ISBN: 0-442-01112-1.

47. Orfali, Robert, Dan Harkey, and Jeri Edwards. *The Essential Distributed Objects Survival Guide.* (New York: John Wiley & Sons, 1996) ISBN: 0-471-12993-3 .

48. Page-Jones, Meilir. *What Every Programmer Should Know About Object-Oriented Design.* (New York: Dorset House Publishing, 1995) ISBN: 0-932633-31-5.

49. Paulk, Mark C., Charles V. Weber, Bill Curtis, and Mary Beth Chrissis. *The Capability Maturity Model: Guidelines for Improving the Software Process.* (Reading, MA: Addison-Wesley, 1995) ISBN: 0-201-54664-7.

50. Perry, William. *Effective Methods of Software Testing.* (New York: John Wiley & Sons, 1995) ISBN: 0-471-06097-6.

51. Peters, Tom. *The Pursuit of WOW!: Every Person's Guide to Topsy-Turvy Times.* (New York: Vintage Books, 1994) ISBN: 0-679-75555-1.

52. Peters, Tom. *The Tom Peters Seminar: Crazy Times Call for Crazy Organizations.* (New York: Vintage Books/Random House, 1994) ISBN: 0-679-75493-8.

53. Postman, Neil. *Technopoly: The Surrender of Culture to Technology.* (New York: Random House, 1993).

54. Robertson, James, and Suzanne. *Complete Systems Analysis* (two volumes). (New York: Dorset House Publishing, 1994) ISBN: 0-932633-25-0.

55. Rodgers, T. J., William Taylor, and Rick Foreman. *No Excuses Management: Proven Systems for Starting Fast, Growing Quickly, and Surviving Hard Times.* (New York: Doubleday, 1992) ISBN: 0-385-42604-6.

56. Ruhl, Janet. *The Computer Consultant's Workbook.* (Leverett, MA: Technion Books) ISBN: 0-9647116-0-5.

57. Rumbaugh, James, Michael Blaha, William Premerlaine, Frederick Eddy, and William Lorensen. *Object-Oriented Modeling and Design.* (Englewood Cliffs, NJ: Prentice Hall, 1991) ISBN: 0-13-629841-9.

58. Selic, Bran, Garth Gullekson, and Paul T. Ward. *Real-Time Object-Oriented Modeling.* (New York: John Wiley & Sons, 1994) ISBN: 0-471-59917-4.

59. Senge, P. M. *The Fifth Discipline: The Art and Practice of the Learning Organization.* (New York: Doubleday, 1990).

60. Senge, Peter M., Charlotte Roberts, Richard B. Ross, Bryan J. Smith, and Art Kleiner. *The Fifth Discipline Fieldbook: Strategies*

and Tools for Building a Learning Organization. (New York: Doubleday, 1994) ISBN: 0-385-47256-0.

61. Shlaer, Sally, and Steve Mellor. *Object LifeCycles: Modeling the World in States.* (Englewood Cliffs, N J: Prentice Hall, 1992) ISBN: 0-13-629940-7.

62. Skublics, Suzanne, Edward J. Klimas, and David A. Thomas. *Smalltalk with Style.* (Englewood Cliffs, NJ: Prentice Hall, 1995) ISBN: 0-13-165549-3 .

63. Stoll, Clifford. *Silicon Snake Oil: Second Thoughts on the Information Highway.* (New York: Doubleday, 1995) ISBN: 0-385-41993-1.

64. Strassmann, Paul A. *The Politics of Information Management: Policy Guidelines.* (New Canaan, CT: The Information Economics Press, 1995) ISBN: 0-9620413-4-3.

65. Taylor, David. *Business Engineering with Object Technology.* (New York, John Wiley & Sons, Inc., 1995) ISBN: 0-471-04521-7.

66. Thomsett, Rob. *Third Wave Project Management.* (Englewood Cliffs, NJ: Prentice Hall, 1993) ISBN: 0-13-915299-7.

67. Townsend, Robert. *The B2 Chronicles: How Not to Butt Heads with the Next Generation.* (San Diego, CA: Pfeiffer & Company, 1994) ISBN: 0-89384-266-4.

68. Weinberg, Gerald M. *Quality Software Management, Volume 3: Congruent Action.* (New York: Dorset House, 1994) ISBN: 0-932633-28-5.

69. Whitaker, Ken. *Managing Software Maniacs.* (New York: John Wiley & Sons, 1994) ISBN: 0-471-00997-0.

70. Whitten, Neal. *Managing Software Development Projects*, 2nd ed. (New York: John Wiley & Sons, 1995) ISBN: 0-471-07683-X.

71. Wirfs-Brock, Rebecca, B. Wilkerson, and L. Wiener. *Designing Object-Oriented Software.* (Englewood Cliffs, NJ: Prentice Hall, 1990) ISBN: 0-13-629825-7.

72. Zachary, G. Pascal. *Show-Stopper!* (New York: Free Press, 1994).

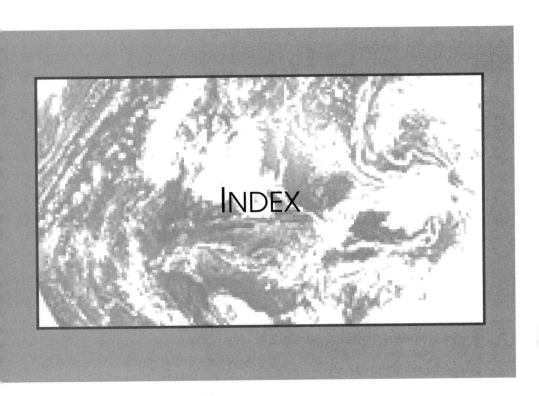

INDEX

A

Abdel-Hamid/Madnick human
    resources model, 96-102
Abdel-Hamid, Tarek, 83, 88-89
    software process model, 96-102
Accumulated knowledge, 91
AdaMagic compiler, 241
Airlie Software Council, 133-34, 136-
    37, 139-47, 153
    Principal Best Practices, 132
Alexander, Christopher, 68
American programmer, and service
    systems, 196-97
America Online, 203, 205, 207
Angell, David, 207
Animation, 66-67
Apple Computer, 127
    Newton, 201

Appraisal costs, 118
Archie, 218
Aronson, Larry, 208
Artificial intelligence (AI), 275-76
Assessment and Control of Software
    Risks (Jones), 136
Audition process, 36
    changes to, 37-38
Automated tools, 26

B

Bach, James, 113, 127, 162, 166, 170,
    175
Basalla, George, 186
Being Digital, 213
Berners-Lee, Tim, 296

309